A Community Writing Itself

Also by Sarah Rosenthal

not-chicago

sitings

How I Wrote This Story

Manhatten

A Community Writing Itself

Conversations with Vanguard Writers of the Bay Area

Edited by Sarah Rosenthal

Dalkey Archive Press
Champaign and London

First edition, 2010

Library of Congress Cataloging-in-Publication Data

A community writing itself : conversations with vanguard writers of the Bay Area / edited by Sarah Rosenthal. -- 1st ed.
p. cm.
Includes bibliographical references.
ISBN 978-1-56478-584-8 (pbk. : alk. paper)
1. Authors, American--California--San Francisco Bay Area--Interviews. 2. Authors, American--Homes and haunts--California--San Francisco Bay Area. 3. American literature--California--San Francisco Bay Area--History and criticism. 4. San Francisco Bay Area (Calif.)--Intellectual life. I. Rosenthal, Sarah.
PS285.S3C66 2010
810.9'97946--dc22
2009053582

Partially funded by the University of Illinois at Urbana-Champaign and by a grant from the Illinois Arts Council, a state agency

www.dalkeyarchive.com

Cover: design and composition by Danielle Dutton
Printed on permanent/durable acid-free paper and bound in the United States of America

In Memoriam

John W. Rosenthal
March 25, 1928–January 21, 2008

Barbara Guest
September 6, 1920–February 15, 2006

Contents

for Steve

Acknowledgements

I would like to thank the poets who allowed me to interview them for this project. In a very real sense, they made this book. I also wish to express my appreciation for the Bay Area writing community that creates this book's context. There are many dozens of vanguard writers working in the Bay Area—far too many to name—whose work deserves the close attention I gave to these twelve poets' work.

I have been blessed to participate in spirited, rigorous conversations about writing with numerous Bay Area writers over the past several years. My appreciation to the talented group of writers who attended the MFA program in Creative Writing at San Francisco State University with me. Thanks also to faculty I studied with there—Maxine Chernoff, Norma Cole, Robert Glück, Myung Mi Kim, Michael Palmer, and Aaron Shurin, as well as Wai-Leung Kwok in the English department—and to the poets who have participated with me in collaborative projects and writing groups since then, especially Stefani Barber, Nicole Brodsky, Tsering Wangmo Dhompa, Andrew Felsinger, Jennifer Firestone, Elise Ficarra, Jean Lieske, Dana Teen Lomax, Sarah Mangold, Rose Najia, Kristin Palm, Lauren Schiffman, Jono Schneider, Nicole Stefanko, and Erin Wilson. I also wish to acknowledge the students I have taught in creative writing classes at San Francisco State University and Santa Clara University and in private workshops. All of these writers have inspired me with their creative, intelligent talk about words, and I hope this book lives up to the high bar they have set.

Special thanks to the editors of the following journals where portions of this book first appeared in slightly altered form: *Jacket* no. 23 (January 2001; Leslie Scalapino's interview); *Jacket* no. 33 (July 2007; Kathleen Fraser's interview); *Rain Taxi* online edition (Fall 2003; Brenda Hillman's interview); *Rain Taxi* 9, no. 2 (Summer 2004; an excerpted version of Barbara Guest's interview); *Aufgabe* no. 4 (Spring/Summer 2004; an excerpt of Stephen Ratcliffe's interview); *Denver Quarterly* 40, no. 2 (2005; Michael Palmer's interview); *New American Writing* no. 24 (2006; Nathaniel Mackey's interview); *Xantippe* no. 3 (2005; Elizabeth Robinson's interview); *Bird Dog* no. 10 (January 2009; Juliana Spahr's interview); and *Fence* 11, no. 1 (Spring/Summer 2008; an excerpt of the introduction). I would like also to thank the entire staff at Dalkey Archive Press, in particular John O'Brien, Danielle Dutton, Jeremy Davies, Jessica Henrichs, and Martin Riker.

I am indebted to Marc Weidenbaum for urging me to create the online column that eventually led me to develop this project and to Krista Faries, Roberta Morris, Stephen Ratcliffe, and Elizabeth Robinson for providing important critique at critical junctures. My appreciation to my colleagues at the Developmental Studies Center for taking an interest in this book and for sharing my passion for learning and language. I am grateful to my mother, Patricia Rosenthal, and to my siblings for their help and encouragement. Finally, I owe an enormous debt to Jennifer Firestone, Steven Harris, Dana Teen Lomax, and Martha Sloss. No words can convey my gratitude for their unstinting support throughout.

Introduction

I. "Birds sing difficult / songs no other birds can sing."

My title here is a quote I have taped to my wall. I keep it there not because I agree with it or even understand what it means, but because it intrigues me with its strange logic, its combination of matter-of-factness and mystery. Birds—birds in general, apparently—sing difficult songs. Is that true? Certainly some birds sing exquisitely elaborate songs, but what about birds that squawk and tweet? Do the sounds they make count as difficult song? Are such birds even included in the word "birds"?

What follows says something about exclusion, privilege, hierarchy: "songs no other birds can sing." But as categorical as these words sound, they lead me only to more inquiry. The first instance of "birds," which I'd taken to mean "all birds," now seems more like "each bird." That sounds a lot more like inclusion than exclusion—unless the exclusion is of a very different sort than I might have first thought: each birdsong is inimitable, a category unto itself. I like that idea, but I'm still wondering whether the squawks and tweets count as "difficult song." They can, in the sense that each bird is hardwired to sing only its song. A squawk may sound simple, but a canary can't squawk.

Taken on its own, the quote could be an environmental statement, intended to encourage action to protect birds whose irreplaceable songs might be endangered. Yet the poem in which it appears, "The

Türler Losses" by Barbara Guest, is not an environmental call to arms, but a complex, meditative, fractured lyric about the poet's relationship to the passage of time and the losses—including the biggest loss of all, life itself—that time's passing brings.[1] Knowing that context, I'm inclined to read the lines not as a metaphor for human activity—I can still think about real birds, and the nature of bird-hood—but as a reflection of it. For the word "birds" I am free to substitute "poets," "artists," or "humans"—they all work, and superimposing them on each other seems to make the lines vibrate with possibility and suggestion. The bird/poet/artist/human being is blessed with her unique song. The lines treasure the particular, acknowledge the difficulty of pursuing that particularity, and suggest both the communal and the solitary nature of singing: we sing for each other, even as we are separated from each other by the uniqueness of our songs. (And while the line is not, I think, intended as an environmental call to arms, I am still free to read it as such, since any poem that calls out the particulars of our world may elicit the response of wanting to protect those particulars.)

I'm only describing a line and a half in a long, complex poem. The lines immediately surrounding the quoted ones are related to them obliquely at best—parataxis, or the juxtaposing of unlike elements, is a feature of much of Guest's work, and is very much on display in "The Türler Losses." If I were to go on to discuss these lines within the context in which they appear, my analysis might shift in interesting ways. But for my purposes here, I'm interested in elucidating the shimmer that the lines in isolation hold—the way in which they appear to say one thing (about exclusion), and then seem to say something else entirely, maybe opposite (about inclusion), or maybe even beyond opposition (about the way in which diametrically opposed categories such as inclusion and exclusion break down). The lines name difficulty, and at the same time enact that difficulty. And they claim that this difficulty is song—is beautiful, is art, is alive.

I offer this short, close reading because I want both to foreground an example of the experimental writing discussed in this volume, and to demonstrate at least one take on the process of reading it. And in the pages that follow I want also to place this collection within the context of the Bay Area's history as a center for experiment, and to describe some of the compelling themes and topics that emerged in the interviews.

II. Location, location, location

The Bay Area, along with New York City, is one of the two major centers of experimental writing in the United States. The Bay Area's long and vibrant history as a literary center (and one where unconventional activity is accepted and even encouraged), along with its large number of creative writing programs and its bounty of small presses and reading series, make it a magnet for experimental writers. This collection of interviews with Bay Area experimentalists allows us to have our cake and eat it too: We learn more about some of the most compelling experimental work being produced today, and we immerse ourselves in a community which is only the most recent incarnation of a history of experiment dating back a couple of centuries.

Since at least the early nineteenth century, the Bay Area has been viewed by writers as a place where risks of various sorts are not only permitted, but encouraged.[2] Writers such as Mark Twain, Ambrose Bierce, and Bret Harte, all of whom spent time in the Bay Area, saw the region as an alternative—albeit a provincial one—to the comparatively reserved atmosphere of the east. In their writing they in turn reinforced the myth of the Bay Area as a home to nonconformists. Some writers also enacted the nonconformity they identified with California and the Bay Area by inventing new personas and lifestyles for themselves. Richard Henry Dana (1815–1882) is a case in point. *Two Years Before the Mast*, arguably the first important piece of literature in English to be written about the area, chronicles the Harvard-educated Cambridgite's temporary reincarnation as a sailor aboard a ship that traveled along the California coast, including a few weeks spent in and around San Francisco a decade before the Gold Rush radically transformed the area.[3] Joaquin Miller (1837–1913), author of stilted paeans to the Northern California landscape, created for himself a flamboyant persona of the rugged frontier poet—a persona he then paraded about England to great success. (He was encouraged and assisted in this self-creation by his close friend Ina Coolbrith, first poet laureate of California and a true frontierswoman, having arrived by wagon train as a girl. Coolbrith later mentored Oakland-born Jack London.)[4] Robinson Jeffers (1887–1962) moved to Carmel in 1914 and single-handedly built a stone tower, Tor House, where he ensconced himself for the next four decades to write brooding, mythic poems that celebrated the rugged beauty of the Big Sur area.

The 1940s strengthened the Bay Area's identity as a site of renegade literary activity—a place where poets could speak out against war, assert homosexuality, or resist the burgeoning New Critical movement in poetry. Various poetry circles formed, often overlapping with each other. One of the most significant of these groups developed around poet Kenneth Rexroth.

Rexroth, who had first lived in the Bay Area in the twenties, returned in the forties to become an enormous force, through his weekly salons and later through his radio program at KPFA, the local alternative station he helped to found. Rexroth was an orphaned high-school dropout who had given himself an astonishingly rigorous and wide-ranging literary education while traveling around the country holding down an array of blue-collar jobs and marginal forms of employment (at one point owning a brothel). A committed anarchopacifist, he appreciated San Francisco not only as a haven for "rascally and anarchistic types" but also as a place where non-European (primarily, in his framing, Asian) cultures exerted a unique influence.[5] He encouraged the poets and activists who gathered around him to steep themselves in the European modernist tradition, in work by local writers such as Jeffers and Henry Miller, and in nonliterary traditions such as jazz. He performed poetry to jazz, writing that doing so "takes the poet out of the bookish, academic world and forces him to compete with 'acrobats, trained dogs, and Singer's Midgets.' "[6] The magazines that published the work of Rexroth and his group—*Circle* and *The Ark*—further extended the reach of his experimental, internationalist poetics.

Poets who attended Rexroth's salons for a time included Robert Duncan and Robin Blaser. They, with Jack Spicer, formed the triumvirate at the center of another important circle, begun in 1946 and self-named the Berkeley Renaissance.[7] The three poets had met as students at the University of California at Berkeley. Their explicit homosexuality at a time of fierce homophobia and their interest in the occult marked them as marginal, as did the passionately anarchopacifist stance which Duncan shared with Rexroth. Of the three, Duncan and Spicer made the larger impact on the local poetry scene; Blaser, who tended to keep a lower profile and moved to Vancouver in 1966, has more recently come to be recognized as an important poet in his own right. Spicer, who spent much of his adult life moving within a few blocks in San Francisco's North Beach, embraced the position of marginality with an unusual ferocity, refusing to allow distribution of his work outside of the Bay Area. He took the Berkeley Renaissance interest in the occult to a new level, developing what Robin Blaser termed a "practice of outside" in which he claimed that instead of authoring his poems, he received transmissions from Martians—a campy way of framing a serious poetics grounded in the idea that the poet must attempt to transcend the ego in order to allow into the poem ideas more various, challenging, and surprising than anything the ego can generate. Like Rexroth, Spicer distanced himself from academic verse by juxtaposing references to "high" and "low" culture and believed that poetry should entertain. On the one hand, his poems are highly intellectual and allusive—trained as a linguist, and vastly well-read, he is the quintessential "poet's poet." As he put it, "The more you know, the more languages you know . . . the more building blocks the Martians have to play with."[8] On the other hand, he peppered his poems with bits of nursery rhyme and references to baseball, and a prodigious array of figures from literature, history, mythology, and pop culture, from Ezra Pound to Christ to Billy the Kid to Buster Keaton to any number of Spicer's friends, students, and love interests. Passionate about teaching, yet frozen out of an academic career in part because of his refusal to sign the Loyalty Oath early on and in part, no doubt, because of his generally ornery, unpredictable behavior, he held a "Poetry as Magic" workshop at the San Francisco Public Library, attended by such poets as Helen Adam, Jack Gilbert, and Joanne Kyger. Applicants had to fill out an application that included questions such as "Which insect do you most resemble?"[9]

Spicer made enemies easily, and shunned wide recognition in favor of a small coterie of (mostly male) poets. Duncan too embraced the coterie model of poetic community, from his early participation in the Berkeley Renaissance to his later years lecturing younger poets in the Poetics Program he cofounded at the New College of California in San Francisco's Mission District, and at gatherings in the home he shared with his life partner, the visual artist Jess. Unlike Spicer, however, Duncan also participated actively in poetic movements beyond the Bay Area. He spent time in New York involved with bohemian authors such as Anaïs Nin and Henry Miller. He met the poet Charles Olson in 1947, and through Olson befriended Robert Creeley. Olson,

Creeley, Denise Levertov, and others formed the "Black Mountain School" of poetry, named for Black Mountain College in North Carolina where they and many other artists taught. Duncan, deeply influenced by Olson's "open field" poetics, also taught for a time at Black Mountain. In addition to extending his poetic network far beyond the Bay Area, Duncan also differed from Spicer in that he wanted to see his work reach a wider audience through publication of his books (though later in life, feeling that publishing was distracting him from his work, he took a fifteen-year hiatus from publishing). Reactions to the two men's deaths seem symbolic of their relationship to audience while alive. When Spicer, fatally ill, entered the poverty ward at San Francisco General Hospital, it took Robin Blaser three days to track him down, at which point Blaser reports that a doctor said, "What are you concerned about? This is some f___ing old common alcoholic drunk. The s______itch is going to die anyway."[10] It would be years before Spicer gained recognition beyond his small group of friends and followers. By contrast, the day after Duncan died his passing was announced on the front page of the San Francisco Chronicle.

In the fifties and sixties, the Beat writers emerged as a major force in the San Francisco poetry scene. They were promoted initially by Rexroth (he later distanced himself from the group). The Duncan-Spicer-Blaser circle developed an uneasy alliance with the Beats, sharing the umbrella term "San Francisco Renaissance." The two circles shared important common ground, including a critique of the conservative, institutionally sanctioned New Critical poetics, and of the repressive postwar American values and mores that the latter poetics seemed to align itself with. Ginsberg shared with the Duncan-Spicer-Blaser group a courageous determination to affirm homosexuality. At the same time, tensions existed between the two groups: The Berkeley Renaissance poets at times criticized the Beats as publicity-hungry and their work as undisciplined. Joanne Kyger, torn between these two stances, formed yet another circle in 1958, the Dharma Committee, which included writers such as Gary Snyder, George Stanley, and Richard Brautigan. Kyger formed the group, in her words, "in response to a need in myself to bridge the gap between our Spicer group and the world of the Beat writer, with all its attendant publicity. . . . [The group] was a flag waving attempt at attention."[11]

Central to the development of the Bay Area's alternative poetry scene was the Poetry Center at San Francisco State College (now San Francisco State University), founded in 1954 by professor Ruth Witt-Diamant. The Center, where Duncan served for a time as Assistant Director, hosted readings and talks by poets from around the country and abroad, and served as a meeting ground where a rich cross-fertilization between the various circles took place. Also central was City Lights, the bookstore and publishing company founded by Lawrence Ferlinghetti and Peter Martin in 1953, which championed San Francisco Renaissance writing including, famously, Allen Ginsberg's *Howl*.

In 1960, Donald Allen published *The New American Poetry*, a 454-page anthology providing a handy, if necessarily flawed, view of alternative poetics in the U.S to date. The book, which includes forty-four poets, is divided into sections on the Black Mountain School; the New York School; the San Francisco Renaissance; the Beats (defined by Allen as four poets of New York origin—Allen Ginsberg, Peter Orlovsky, Jack Kerouac, and Gregory Corso), and a fifth group of poets (including the likes of Amiri Baraka/Leroi Jones, Philip Whalen, and Gilbert Sorrentino), viewed by Allen as associated with no particular geographical location. Allen explained in his introduction that the poets he included shared a common ancestry in modernist poetry, a rejection of academic poetry, and an alliance with the avant-garde work being done in jazz and Abstract Expressionist painting. *The New American Poetry* went a long way toward planting experimental poetics firmly on the map of U.S. poetry, and underscored the Bay Area's importance as one of the key places where that poetics throve.

Throughout the sixties, the "New American" poets grew in stature, thanks in no small part to Allen's anthology. Many of them came together for the Berkeley Poetry Conference, a pivotal ten-day event in July 1965 held at the University of California at Berkeley as a follow-up to a similar gathering in Vancouver two years earlier. Duncan, Snyder, Olson, Creeley, Ginsberg, Spicer, and Ed Dorn all gave lectures (Spicer died just a few weeks later of alcohol-induced liver damage). The conference was attended by a number of poets who were teens or barely out of teenhood, including Anne Waldman, Lewis Warsh, Ron Silliman, and Rachel Loden. For these youngsters, the New American poets pointed the way toward a liberated poetics that mirrored the political and cultural ferment of the times, and contrasted refreshingly with the more staid poetry they were encountering in school.[12]

The "mimeo revolution" of the sixties added another dimension to the literary activity of the New American poets and the younger generation they inspired, in the Bay Area and elsewhere. Since the forties, Rexroth, the Duncan-Spicer-Blaser circle, and others had formed small presses to disseminate their own and their friends' work. The sixties witnessed an explosion of this activity, with poets using mimeograph machines, letterpress, and offset printing to create inexpensive poetry journals and books, and distributing them via independent booksellers, mailing lists, and word of mouth. These publishing activities not only disseminated new work quickly but also created opportunities to build community, as poets got together to collate, staple, and mail out the work.[13]

By the seventies, the New American poets had achieved varying degrees of recognition. The Beats were downright famous, and even a couple of the poets in the less publicity-seeking groups had attained academic posts—Duncan taught at San Francisco State College in the seventies, Olson started teaching at SUNY Buffalo in the sixties (a position later taken by Creeley), and Ted Berrigan, a New York School poet, took a teaching post at the University of Iowa in 1968.[14] This increasing institutionalization and mainstream acceptance met with criticism from a group of younger poets—most of whom lived in the Bay Area but some of whom were in New York City, Washington, D.C., and Canada—who came to be identified as the Language writers.[15] Channeling the anger and disaffection of many young people who, like them, were coming of age during the Vietnam War era, and inspired by theorists such as Barthes, Wittgenstein, Derrida, and Marx (a number of Language poets maintained active membership in Marxist political groups), these poets critiqued what they saw as the dominant ideology in service of global capitalism, which in their view was wreaking havoc at home and abroad, and which, they argued, used language to manipulate citizens into serving the system as passive consumers. They tended to distance themselves from anyone whose work they saw as pandering in any way to that ideology. They acknowledged some of the New Americans as their poetic forebears, and certainly shared many features of their poetics with the latter group. They continued the small-press revolution and the emphasis on live readings and talks begun by the New Americans; they carried forward the leftist agenda of the earlier poets; and they absorbed many of the experimental and nonlinear features of the earlier group's writing, including an appreciation of the "open-field" poetics of Duncan and Olson, and Spicer's refusal to position himself as the author of his texts. Like the New Americans, they appreciated the ground-breaking work of the modernists, though many were deeply troubled by Pound's anti-Semitic, fascist slant, and were more likely to appreciate Stein's radical re-vision of language than the "plain speak" of Williams or the contained, articulate elegance of

Moore. However, they felt that even New Americans such as Olson, Creeley, and Duncan did not have a strong enough theoretical program, and thus put themselves at risk of having their work absorbed by the mainstream. By contrast, the Language poets were ferociously articulate about their poetics.

The bull's-eye at the center of the Language poets' attack was the short, self-contained "voice" poem grounded in a coherent sense of self, of the sort written by Confessional poets such as Robert Lowell and Sylvia Plath. The Language poets viewed the coherent ego as a mental construct rather than an absolute truth. Further, they felt that this construct could serve as a kind of narcotic. By focusing the poem on personal matters of the psyche, poet and reader could collude to avoid the urgent problems of the world and their own implication in those problems. (Even outspoken critics of U.S. domestic and foreign policy, such as Adrienne Rich and Lawrence Ferlinghetti, were seen as lacking a sufficiently rigorous critique in that they still adhered to the notion of the authentic self speaking his or her truth.) The short (one page or less) length of many of the poems being published in respected magazines such as the *New Yorker* suggested a widget-producing mentality in the MFA programs then proliferating around the country. Poems were one more product being churned out by late capitalism for quick consumption—and, for that matter, poets were becoming one more version of the buttoned-down white-collar professional, strategically advancing his career through ever more prestigious publications and university appointments.

The Language poets' own work looked like the very obverse of the self-contained, easily absorbed "I" poem. It dissolved boundaries between genres—a prose piece, for example, might be considered a poem or a theoretical essay or both. It mixed pronouns and dictions, and used disjunction, collage, collaborative techniques, and chance operations to challenge the sense of a single self narrating a coherent experience with a clear beginning, middle, and end, and to defamiliarize the reader from the assumed transparency of language's operations. Language writers, rejecting the sound-and-sight-bite quality they abhorred in much of the poetry of their contemporaries, often conceived writing projects as multi-page or book-length works. Passionately, even zealously committed to their vision, the Language group hosted several active series of readings and talks and ran a number of small presses through which they produced books and magazines on both sides of the continent. Key publications that unified the movement while also helping to disseminate its ideas included *This* magazine, founded in 1971 by Robert Grenier and Barrett Watten, *L=A=N=G=U=A=G=E,* edited by New York writers Charles Bernstein and Bruce Andrews from 1978 to 1981, *The L=A=N=G=U=A=G=E Book,* a collection of pieces from the magazine published in 1984, and Ron Silliman's 1986 anthology *In the American Tree.*

It's tempting to overemphasize the influence of the Language movement in the Bay Area thanks to the group's dynamic drive to propound a coherent position. The fact is, there were other vanguard poetry scenes, schools, and individuals during the Language heyday. The local literary scene in the seventies became more culturally diversified than ever, thanks to the birth of national cultural movements such as Black Arts and local organizations such as Kearney Street Workshop and Third World Communications Collective. Notable poets and writers active in the Bay Area included Victor Hernanez Cruz, Jessica Hagedorn, Janice Mirikitani, Ishmael Reed, and Ntozake Shange. In a 1979 interview Shange asserted that California gave her as an African American poet an aesthetic freedom she didn't find in other parts of the country. She noted the existence of racism in California but explained:

> There is an enormous amount of space in the West, and you do not feel personally impinged upon every time you come out of your door, like you do in New York and in Chicago. . . . It gave us a chance to breathe, to get away from the immediacy of oppression in the East and those particular political events, which all of us experienced.[16]

Hagedorn, who counts Rexroth, Ginsberg, Baraka, Cruz, and Reed among her influences and mentors, also found release in San Francisco, not from the oppression of the East Coast but from the "overprotected colonial environment" of her girlhood in Manila.[17] All of these poets found ways to funnel the liberated, energized atmosphere of seventies Bay Area cultural life into exciting formal innovations.

In the same decade, Bolinas, a small community in Marin County, served as home or way station to dozens of poets and writers—many of those represented in Donald Allen's anthology and many not affiliated with any particular school or movement.[18] Writers as various as Richard Brautigan, Jim Carroll, Joanne Kyger, Robert Creeley, and Bill Berkson all formed part of the Bolinas community, finding common ground in a love of the land, a countercultural stance, and a determination to create community across differences. (Kyger, Grenier, Berkson, John Thorpe, Stephen Ratcliffe, and others still make their home there.) Further afield, centers of poetic activity such as the Poetry Project at St. Mark's Church in Manhattan's Greenwich Village and the Jack Kerouac School of Disembodied Poetics at Naropa University in Boulder, Colorado have for decades served as loci of cross-fertilization among vanguardists claiming a wide variety of aesthetic lineages.

Notwithstanding the great diversity of the Bay Area poetry scene, the debate provoked by the Language writers in the seventies and eighties was a salient feature of the community at the time. The group raised the hackles of others from English department scholars to poets who honored various identifications such as ethnicity, feminism, and queerness. Academics reacted negatively to the notion of non-academics propounding literary theory. Some poets who shared the Language writers' marginalized status and critique of mainstream culture were uneasy about a group comprised mostly of white, straight males from relatively privileged backgrounds (with notable exceptions such as Lyn Hejinian, Rae Armantrout, Carla Harryman, and the less involved but highly sympathetic Leslie Scalapino), and felt excluded by writing and public events that they saw as inaccessible and exclusionary. Attacks flew back and forth in what came to be called the "poetry wars," playing out in a particularly vicious way in exchanges published in the Bay Area journal *Poetry Flash.* A relatively small group in terms of numbers, the Language group's forceful presence impelled many other writers to examine and articulate their own positions.

Certain Bay Area groups especially benefited from dialogue with the Language group. One such group was what came to be called the New Narrative school inaugurated by Bruce Boone and Robert Glück. Boone, Glück, and the writers who attended Glück's workshops at Small Press Traffic (including Michael Amnasan, Dodie Bellamy, Kevin Killian, and Camille Roy) admired the Language writers' commitment to theory. As queer and/or working-class writers committed to telling their community's story, however, they did not feel they could discard narrative to the extent that Language writers had. Rather, they chose to embrace narrative while complicating it through use of many of Language writing's techniques such as disjunction and collage.[19]

Feminist experimentalists in the Bay Area such as Kathleen Fraser, Beverly Dahlen, Frances Jaffer, Patricia Dienstfrey, and Rena Rosenwasser also identified with some but not all approaches of the

Language group. Like the New Narrative group, these writers shared Language writers' interest in theory and study and their desire to fold rigorous thinking into writing. They also shared the Language group's respect for Stein. Yet they wanted to resuscitate other, forgotten female modernists such as Dorothy Richardson, Mina Loy, and Objectivist poet Lorine Niedecker; showcase work by emerging experimental women writers; and apply experimental techniques to traditionally female issues not addressed by many in the Language group—issues such as mothering, intimacy, and domesticity. For many of these writers, an interaction with visual art was also an important dimension of their writing and publishing. In 1974, Dienstfrey and Rosenwasser formed Kelsey Street Press, publishing books by innovators such as Barbara Guest and Mei-mei Berssenbrugge; many of Kelsey Street's books, including works by the latter two poets, involve collaboration with visual artists. In 1984, Fraser, Dahlen, and Jaffer founded the journal How(ever), with the mission of publishing scholarship on overlooked female avant-gardists from the early and mid century, alongside new experimental writing by women.

Several Bay Area experimental poets developed their poetics without aligning themselves clearly with any particular school or movement. This is the case with Michael Palmer and Nathaniel Mackey, for example, who maintained close friendships with Robert Duncan, one of the New Americans whom Language poets critiqued as having become too enamored of mainstream success. Both poets share Duncan's interest in the lyric and in history and myth; in addition, Mackey resonates with Duncan's mysticism, and Palmer with his renewal of Romantic poetry. Yet Palmer and Mackey were and are friendly with Language poets, attended and participated in readings and talks hosted by Language poets in the seventies and eighties, and share many aspects of their poetics. Similarly, Aaron Shurin and Norma Cole blended Duncan's influence with elements of Language poetry. Stephen Ratcliffe, whose work enacts many Language procedures such as collage, chance, and multivalence, writes poetry that is less explicitly political than that of many Language writers. Bob Grenier, one of the originators of the Language movement, has over time developed a unique hybrid of writing and drawing that, while clearly influenced by Language poetry, exists somewhere beyond those tenets and indeed beyond language itself. Gloria Frym, Laura Moriarty, and Stephen Vincent are further examples, among many, of poets whose work has long engaged with aspects of Language writing while forging unique paths.

Locally, by the mid-eighties the Language heyday was over as the poets involved increasingly turned their energies to raising families and holding down jobs.[20] Elizabeth Robinson recalls arriving in the Bay Area in the early nineties, "on the heels of a period in which the community seemed in one sense more defined and cohesive, but also very feisty in a way that had left some people shell-shocked."[21]

The Language movement continues to exert influence on Bay Area and American poetics. Yet even as many younger poets incorporate some of the Language poets' principles and make use of some of the group's tools, they have by and large rejected the binary oppositions and programmatic injunctions that animated Language poetics, as several of the poets interviewed in this volume note. Glück says:

> Now, younger poets backtrack in order to recover some territory. Representation may be a lie, but that does not make it less a part of life, or less interesting, especially as it intersects with emotion. It can no longer be simple: us against them, narrative against "non-narrative." Or even, if you like, commodified against non-commodified. And certainly not stances of political purity against the world. With the pressure off, the use of fragmentation is no longer heroic, but merely one end of a spectrum, many parts of which may be

> used to suit the needs of a particular work. This ease characterizes the writing of younger poets. It's ambivalent writing—both theory-based and disbelieving in systems.[22]

Scalapino observes:

> There are shifts in poetry syntax and view that are cumulative and that create a range, finally a broad spectrum where current writing contains the past as well as the changes. One of the ideas put forth by many poets in the public talks and readings of the early eighties, for example, was that paratactic sentence structure in paragraphs rather than line breaks should be used by everyone, even uniformly. That is, the word "mechanistic" was used as a favorable designation to mean absence of individual self, a communal, social-political purpose. This is not an approach that is spoken of now. Yet in works like Renee Gladman's book *The Activist,* there's a subtle sense of a kind of new, "simple" as if one-dimensional, confessional/autobiographical tone that is used to get at a group sensibility and communal action, undercut in the sense of questioned by a kind of light humor that's as if all of the characters' thoughts at once.[23]

Fraser comments:

> I've been reading through a small library of books and pamphlets by a new hybrid generation of young poets. . . . This work shares the quality of being highly researched and valuing an extraordinary range of imaginative and historical intervention. It has given me back my love of reading poetry and seems to embrace a huge range of what's possible in a language unearthed from deepest necessity.[24]

Juliana Spahr, who did her graduate work at SUNY Buffalo while Bernstein chaired the program there, speaks in her interview of the impact on her writing of anticolonial poetry in Hawai'i, which pragmatically uses all formal strategies, Language or no, to fight for the rights of native Hawaiians. Truong Tran, whose work has been lauded by Hejinian and Silliman, does not consider himself a Language poet or even an experimental poet, and places Lucille Clifton alongside Myung Mi Kim as an important influence.

Whether we focus on the differences or the similarities between experimental poetries then and now, it's clear that the current Bay Area poetry scene is thriving. New reading series and small presses sprout up regularly, and the Internet has strengthened a sense of communion among experimental writers that transcends geographical boundaries. The hefty anthology *Bay Poetics* includes 110 experimental writers, and its editor, Stephanie Young, points out in her introduction that the collection provides only a partial view of the local avant-garde scene.[25]

As with any community, artistic or otherwise, the Bay Area experimental poetry world has its share of dysfunctions. But on the whole, poets tend to thrive on the support and stimulus they find in the local scene. Barbara Guest, the renowned New York School poet, moved to Berkeley in her seventies and continued to produce important work. Brenda Hillman—whose work has become markedly more formally adventurous in the past decade—observes:

> The Bay Area is . . . a very exciting place to be a poet right now because there is a growing collaborative spirit. I know a lot of people have to make their living from teaching, and that means you have to compete for certain things, and it's hard to get published. But there's a real acceptance of a lot of different kinds of poetry.[26]

And Camille Roy describes her deep, ongoing relationship to the Bay Area scene in this way:

> I feel embedded in and attached to a community of writers that accepts me. Every experimental tool that I've ever learned from others—all the ones I haven't developed myself—I've learned here.[27]

III. What we talked about

Sitting down and talking for a few hours with a serious artist after months of immersion in his or her work isn't just a privilege—it's a peak experience. When the process is working at its best, all the preparation and study sets the stage for conversation as a collaborative improvisation, not unlike those that take place in jazz and dance. There is the procreative mixing of two world views, two sets of preoccupations, with a particular body of work to move around in together and a strong, shared desire to make something of value.

The writers included here represent a range of formal strategies, focusing on everything from lineated poems to prose poetry to fiction to works that seem to burst all genre definitions asunder. Each has his or her own "family tree" of poetic influences, including poets and schools from across the centuries and around the globe. And each brings to bear on the work unique extra poetic passions, from fairy tales to Gnosticism to flamenco.

As different as each writer in this volume is, though, it's fair to say that all are well versed in contemporary theories about language and philosophy; all reclaim the terrain of hard thinking from the province of academia, making it an integral part of their art-making; and all are interested in both critically examining and reinventing language. As a result, the interviews provide an intellectually stimulating opportunity for the reader to engage with pressing issues related to areas such as politics, language, poetry and other arts, spirituality, the nature of self and community, and the writing process.

I'd like to introduce here some of the issues that crop up across the conversations. A few caveats: Interviews are a unique form requiring preparation on the one hand and spontaneous collaboration on the other. These interviews were born of in-the-moment interchanges. On another day, or in another form of communication, the interviewees might have talked about these topics in different ways, or addressed other topics altogether. Second, the following categories are highly artificial—much of what we discussed could be grouped under "politics," or "language" for that matter, and often in the interviews several of these themes are woven together.

A) *Political Issues*

Spahr, describing her motivation for writing her book *The Transformation,* says,

> I felt that I needed to think hard about issues around living with one's political convictions, about trying to figure out one's political life in the U.S. right now. What does one do with one's identity—all facets of it? What does one do with one's sexuality, race, class; what does one do with one's unavoidable consumption of unprecedented amounts of resources?[28]

Several interviewees in the collection address sexual politics. Glück talks about the profound impact being gay has had on his trajectory as a writer—from guiding his reading choices early on, to informing his New Narrative poetics—while Tran discusses the pressure he feels, as a gay man of color, to favor representation and narrative over abstraction—"to tell the story and convey the experience."[29] Roy describes her view of her women characters, many of whom have suffered various forms of abuse and discrimination, as veterans of combat, and Fraser talks about supporting her female students at San Francisco State University in the seventies as they struggled to gain access to literature by women.

Race also emerges as an important theme. Spahr argues for the importance of clarity in writing so as to support unambiguously anticolonial movements by people of color. Mackey describes his ongoing investigation of the lore and traditions of African cultures, Ancient Egypt, the Caribbean, and Brazil, and the musical forms of jazz and flamenco, as well as the connection between his poetry and various forms of African-American cultural production that respond to oppression. Tran speaks of the stereotyping he experiences in the academic world, both as a teacher and an author, and the self-doubt that such stereotyping inevitably engenders:

> I am constantly examining my role in academia—how I fit in and what I represent. . . . I am also constantly aware of how my writing can be perceived as fitting nicely into an identity-based curriculum in an ethnic studies department, rather than being received in a more complex way. For example, if Asian-American Studies professors teach my work, they almost exclusively teach *placing the accents,* because it's accessible. So then I have to ask myself, am I being rewarded for being a rigorous artist, or am I just the immigrant who fills the niche?[30]

"The first casualty of war is truth," Hiram Johnson famously observed, and several writers in the collection discuss how their work examines the twisting of language and failures of communication evident in war and global politics, especially post-9/11. Palmer discusses his recent interest in figures of speech taken from ordinary language, particularly in light of, as he puts it, "the strange language of hypocrisy and prevarication" that we have faced during the Bush era,[31] while Robinson reveals the thinking behind "Topple," a poem based on the "Chicken Little" story:

> [The poem is about] a sense of impotence combined with the vast control the United States is exercising over the rest of the globe. I remember Bush saying that the people who attacked the World Trade Center and the Pentagon were cowards. It seemed odd to use that kind of language, because I don't consider him particularly courageous. So I was thinking (somewhat ironically) about the way the United States has behaved in the world in recent years.[32]

Glück, speaking shortly after 9/11, speaks of the "dishonest fictions" our culture uses to shield itself from harsh truths:

> The United States has just been attacked and the whole country is amazed. Can we ever be more than credulous children? Our culture frantically expresses its own inability to communicate or touch its own realities—our labor takes place in conditions of raw capitalism across the world, our old age is locked up in institutions, our wars don't make it to the news, our homeless don't make it to Federal politics. No wonder we are slightly crazed.[33]

B) *The Self and the Collective*

The nature of self and various notions about collectivity come up again and again in these conversations. Scalapino, for example, explores the complex interaction between an individual's interior life and the world outside the individual, which produces what we think of as the self. She examines our definition of self as part of a larger investigation of the frames we construct around experience, and describes her interest in stripping away that definition in order to discover the true nature of self. By contrast, Glück describes the challenge that faced him in the seventies and eighties as he sought to form a poetics that reconciled his view of self as a construct with his need to create representations of self in his writing, in order to communicate his experience as a gay man:

> I did not think there was an "I"—a self—that existed apart from representations—texts of one kind or another—but I was urgent to "tell my story," a completely different kind of truth, the strange story of the marginalized experience of a sexual minority whose existence was rather experimental itself, and had yet to appear in our literary forum. For about ten minutes anyway, a community without norms. Could a writer simply step out of the power discrepancies by becoming a community talking to itself?[34]

Glück describes strategies he has developed to enact the notion of a community talking to itself: using literary types (characters who represent entire groups of people), and adopting the persona of the local gossip who mirrors back to the community its own news. Mackey and Spahr also investigate notions of collectivity, but with a different slant, describing the way they inhabit plural pronouns in order to examine the troubling nature of identification with groups.

Mackey describes his ambivalence toward the pronoun "we": "I've been working with the pronoun 'we' in recent years. . . . [O]ne is of more than one mind in this desire to be a part of a 'we,' whether it's a couple, a nation, or some other collectivity."[35] He describes a wariness of "the harmonies and the symmetries of conventional, bonded ways of public belonging."[36] Spahr describes inhabiting the word "they" in places where the reader might expect her to write "I" or "we," as in part a way to see herself from the vantage point of people of color so as to explore how as a white person she is implicated in colonial oppression.

C) *The Self and the Lyric*

Lyric poetry, traditionally understood as a single voice expressing thoughts and feelings, often in a mellifluous way ("lyric" comes from "lyre") poses an interesting challenge for contemporary experimental writers who, as I've said, tend to see the self as a construct, and resist the idea of poetry as a soothing retreat from the world. Thus it's perhaps no surprise that the lyric emerges as a pressing topic for several of the poets included here. All of the poets who discuss the lyric take into account, implicitly or explicitly, the Language poets' position—which tended to dismiss the lyric as a bourgeois tool. At the same time, they explain how their own work attempts, to a greater or lesser extent, to reclaim and revitalize the lyric—which, they argue, was a more political and complex form in the hands of earlier poets such as Sappho, Dante, and the Romantics than it has become in recent times. Palmer describes his poetry's "increasing focus on the strange mechanism of interiority mixing with a kind of antilyricism and bringing the congeries of unpolished material of the world itself into the midst of it,"[37] while Hillman describes her interest in writing a "lyric that is also social," and speaks of her interest in the "much more stretchy sense of 'I' " employed by many contemporary experimental writers—"one that doesn't lose the depth and feeling tones."[38] Fraser describes her origins as a lyric poet, her determined effort over many years to break the hold of lyric poetry on her writing, and her return in the late eighties to the rich musicality of the lyric:

> I started understanding that in fact I really loved highly compressed musical textures but I needed to find my own peculiar "condensations"—to use a Niedecker reference. Instead of pushing them away as a threat, I knew that I would work to foreground that pleasure.[39]

Robinson too associates the lyric with pleasure. She speaks of the resistance to lyric poetry among experimental poets early in her writing life as a repressive force that she has had to resist:

> I came of age as a poet in an experimental writing milieu where certain things, such as confessional work, or even traditional syntax, were impermissible. Using first-person pronouns was a no-no. Even now, some taboos are in place. Yet I have always had a strong affiliation with lyric. I was at a conference where Jennifer Moxley said, "I write lyric poetry, but it's not fashionable to say that." I'm in the same boat. Lyric gives me pleasure, and pleasure is a really important part of writing.[40]

D) *Language: Capacities and Limits*

All of the writers in this volume take risks with language and think deeply about the capacities and limits of language's ability to represent experience. Some of the interviewees addressed these problems directly. Ratcliffe explains how, for him, the fissure between word and world, instead of being cause for alarm, is an opportunity to explore what words *can* do:

> I think my work does appear to be description, but it's trying to test the boundary of what description could be. There is always a gap between writing something down as words, and the world that's out there being described. The world out there can't ever be exactly reenacted. But through working in these repeating forms over a long period of time, I'm exploring how the things of the world can be enacted in language.[41]

Ratcliffe is referring here to how, in the spirit of Stein, he uses repetition and variation in a way that undercuts words' referential function while at the same time underscoring their own object-hood, and the very alive, human, moment-to-moment experience of mouthing, hearing, thinking about, and creatively assembling them.[42] Robinson echoes Ratcliffe's focus on words' physicality, while holding out for a kind of meaning-making in poetry that Ratcliffe's work distances from:

> Language comes from the body: We feel it in our mouths and we perceive it in our ears and we see it on the page. But it also conveys meaning and the way meaning gets lofted on time as we say the words we say on breath and air, and this can take a writer or a reader through experience that is not completely limited to the way the tongue hits the palate.[43]
>
> I enjoy reading some of the more transgressive work being written. Some of the material is interesting formally. But then beyond the shock effect or the figuring-out-the-device,

> I admit that I ask myself why I should continue to read. I don't at all think that meaning is docile or stable or eternal, but still I embrace the possibility that through all the shifts and uprootings of daily life, meaning is shape-shifting along with us.[44]

Palmer's discussion reveals agreement with Ratcliffe about the gap between language and the world, while pointing out the necessity of language for communication:

> One lives the truth of skepticism, but one also makes a path to language to allow it to occur. That's what we do, we make an agreement, since it's the only one that's going to work. It's a social agreement, a negotiation, maybe. But at the same time, as poets, in any case, and maybe in everyday language too, we come up against the limits of expression and the limits of reference: The fact that words are *not* things, they're not the same as things. It's a problem that philosophers have forever wondered about, not just poststructuralists.[45]

He describes how his poetry examines ordinary figures of speech—an investigation which seems to combine both his interest in language as a vehicle for communication and an awareness of the limits of reference:

> I have an ironic relationship to figures of speech as they are in the world, and a fascination with the mystery that occurs as we reframe them. We let them pass as everyday-life words, and yet if we pull back just a step, they acquire a kind of poetic estrangement.[46]

Hillman, too, celebrates the defamiliarizing quality of language:

> Our very greatest human thing—which is language to me—musicians would say it's music, but I think it's language—our very greatest human thing is wild. Uncontrollable. It is impossible to put boundaries on your words, even if you make a poem. Each word is a maze. So you are full of desire to make a memorable thing and have the form be very dictated by some way that it has to be. But the poem itself is going to undo that intention. It's almost like you're knitting a sweater and something is unraveling it on the other end.[47]

E) *Writing and Spirituality*

Given that many experimental writers would disavow the concept of a soul, it is interesting that discussions of spirituality are laced through several of these interviews. The poets' views range from that of Scalapino—who argues that hypothesizing the existence of a soul limits the investigation of self by setting up a given framework through which experience is seen—to those of Guest, Hillman, Mackey, and Robinson, who freely use words like "soul" and "spirit." Hillman speaks of a continuum between language and spirit:

> There's an essay by Walter Benjamin . . . called "On Language as Such and on the Language of Man." It's about how we can't get away from meaning and yet we don't know what it is, but there's something about language and the way language relates to the primal that precedes experience and precedes words but is only purely enacted by them. So the language of God is much bigger than words. That made me really think about the connection between

> spirit and language. In one sense, I don't believe in pure spirit outside of culture, but I do think there are mysteries that we don't know through culture, and in that way it is not all about being human.[48]

While Hillman describes language as a link to the spiritual realm, Mackey explains his view of music as a form that combines the immanent (the physiological experience of producing music, and the sense that our response to music comes from inside ourselves) and the transcendent (the experience of music as something arriving on the airwaves, from outside the self). He also speaks about duende and "the spiritual supplement"—the idea that there's a realm beyond death that gives life the quality of a test or a rite of passage, suffusing it with a sense of urgency. Robinson, who holds a Master of Divinity, does not discuss the idea of life beyond death, yet she seems to converge with Mackey in her view of humanity as existing in a state of extremity. She uses the words "precarious" and "contingent" to describe our spiritual and physical state, and asserts that poetry can serve as a wedge against that constant sense of endangerment. Robinson also discusses the charged nature of her relationship to Protestantism, the tradition in which she was raised, and the ways in which she both retains and disrupts elements of that tradition in her writing. Tran too ponders the effect of religious tradition on his writing, describing for example his attempt to create forms that enact the combination of structure and chaos that he associates with the Catholic household in which he grew up. Guest, while not spelling out her own spiritual or religious beliefs, acknowledges the use of New Testament language in her book *Rocks on a Platter* to convey a quality of miracle, transformation, and elevation, and argues that this quality is necessary in poetry.

F) *Other Art Forms*

Mackey is not the only writer in the collection to describe a relationship between his writing and other art forms. Almost every writer here names other art forms, from visual art to music to drama to dance. What is the impetus behind this involvement with other media? No doubt there are several, including a desire to view their own medium—words on the page—through the lens of another—action on the stage, paint on the canvas, notes on the score, etc.—and thereby to gain fresh ideas about how to innovate. Another may have to do with the value many experimental writers place on collaboration, in part as a way to explode what is seen as a myth of single authorship. Whatever the reason, it's invigorating to hear about the range of involvements these writers pursue. Ratcliffe—who has an interest in both Renaissance and contemporary experimental music as well as in contemporary art—explains the centrality of both the sound and the visual appearance of the poem to his work. Fraser, whose work has reflected an active conversation with painting over many years, describes a number of poetic works in which she attempts to enact formal elements of painting by artists ranging from the Etruscans to Joan Mitchell. Guest, who mentored Fraser early on and is well known for her decades-long involvement with the art world, describes one of countless experiences of responding in language to a painting:

> "Blurred Edge" [a poem in the collection *Miniatures*] came about because I was writing a review of a painting by the artist Leatrice Rose, who is a niece of Clement Greenberg. As I was working on the review, I began to see her painting not as painting but as words. The painter had given the painting her own words. This doesn't make rational sense. I found that what I was doing in my review was copying the shape of [what I was seeing as] her words. So I began to

> write about the shape of the words. It was hard for me to find the right words to go with the shape of her words. This poem didn't have a voice for a long time. It was a curious experience; a strange transformation.[49]

G) *The Writing Process*

Many of the interviewees talk about writing in response to painful experience. Mackey, for example, describes working on a book at a time both of dark developments on the political horizon and the passing of several close family members. Others speak about the heavy emotional toll that writing itself can take: from stripping away boundaries between self and subject matter to the point of extreme pain and confusion, to losing faith in one's writing to the point of nervous breakdown.

Many also discuss the process of developing and inhabiting forms for their writing. From the elaborate and highly disciplined daily process Ratcliffe developed to write a series of book-length works, to the happy accidents and moments of discovery that have aided Fraser in the writing of many poems and books; from the boxes Tran constructed around his apartment and then wrote in, in order to shake up his idea of poetic form, to the "tool kits" of experimental strategies that Roy has developed in order to deal with various narrative challenges, we hear a plethora of ways that these writers generate their work and continually challenge themselves.

I took up this project after four and a half years of writing a monthly, online column that featured more than fifty Bay Area poets. Increasingly frustrated by the format, which required me to boil down lengthy interviews and a great deal of study into 1,000-word articles,

I sought a project that would better communicate my enthusiasm for much of the writing I was presenting. Eventually I landed on the idea of a book of twelve interviews—twelve in part because in an utterly naïve way I imagined that the project would take me a year (an interview per month!)—but twelve, too, because I felt that number would allow me to include a range of poetics within the Bay Area experimental community. Nine years later, as I bring this project to completion, I find myself unable even to begin to fathom the gifts it has given me. Amidst the highway-racing, channel-surfing, let's-do-lunch, skim-the-anthology tenor of these times, I have had the chance to slow down and dwell in the rich terrain of a handful of poets' work. I have had the chance, by visiting other artists' worlds, to view my own poetics with fresh perspective. And I have had the chance to enact some of my own ideals about the importance of deep attention. We all hunger to be read, to be heard, to be answered. We all bear urgent news. Let's speak. And let's listen.

KATHLEEN FRASER

Placing Silence

Sarah Rosenthal: Silence has been a central trope in your writing since early on. It carries a range of meanings, from erasure to grief and loss to the spaciousness of an open field. Perhaps we could trace some of the ways in which silence has come up in your work over time.

Kathleen Fraser: That sounds like a good way to go.

SR: Silence is central to "Something (even human voices) in the foreground, a lake," which appeared in a book of the same name in 1984.

KF: It's true that when I wrote that poem, I was very much in the witness position. It was maybe my third summer in Italy, after several weeks spent with a group of non-English-speaking Roman friends who had welcomed my husband and me into their lives even though we couldn't yet speak Italian very well. They would gather every Sunday afternoon, in the country outside Rome, at the lakeside home of friends. After lunch, the men would sit at a long outdoor table talking politics, money, and sports while the women sunned themselves on a vast green lawn that stretched down to the water, exchanging information about where they'd had their hair done, remedies for children's illnesses, pasta recipes, and their fascination with American TV soaps . . . the day's endlessly fascinating banalities. Very culturally imposed divisions there. Given my limited Italian I could barely enter into the women's conversation, especially because it was composed of the intimate chitchat of people who'd known each other for years. The Romans talk rapidly and continuously. Silence is barely admitted. It's not exactly that they're nervous about it, but it's such a habit to be talking. Their swift ease underlined my shyness since I had few words or apt phrases at my command.

The women understood that I was a writer, and they were probably somewhat interested in that and yet threatened by it too, at least those who hadn't pursued an education. As it turned out, our hostess was a big reader and later on had a book of my poems translated—the same book we're talking about, in fact. Eventually she became my close friend. But in the early years spent with these friends, I'd sit there at the edge of the group, smiling but feeling painfully outside of the exchange. What kept me company was my journal. Since I couldn't say much, I took notes on what I noticed and thought I was hearing: In every direction I looked, there was an incredible visual treat of food, bodies, trees, birds, and water.

I wrote shorthand "newsreels" starring my new Italian friends. They were always in their bikinis and continuously comparing their tans—so into their bodies and surfaces of presentation—what they call *la bella figura*—"looking good." So that's how I dealt with the particular awkwardness of a self-imposed silence—really the silence of being unlanguaged in their mother tongue. The benevolent but isolate situation thrust me into the witness position and it shaped the disjunct quality of the serial poem that I began to write out of—down to the very placing of the phrases. Being in the deficit position vis-à-vis words also gave me an entirely new and visually privileged subject matter.

SR: The writing is also tonally disjunct. I had the sense of the witness operating very close up physically yet very far away emotionally. That makes sense given the fact that the interpersonal situation was isolating, thus thrusting you into a heightened state of sensory awareness. The disjunct tone helps to enact that sharp contrast between the ways in which you could and could not connect. The last sentence in the poem reads, "It is believed that she understands partially but cannot speak except haltingly and about nothing in particular."[1] I read that as a fear of not being seen as having anything to contribute.

KF: That's not how I felt at all. It was more like being in neutral—unable to move forward or backward, realizing that most of them had no idea what kind of person was sitting with them or where my mind was. I sensed that most of them needed to identify me in a familiar, even simple way that they could deal with. It seemed reasonable on their part.

SR: There are other moments in your writing where again you articulate the experience of entering the difficulty of silence and making something out of it. In *Each Next* you write, "Walking up to a new edge, I discovered in myself an old mute, but I stayed, allowing my curiosity to teethe on the silence."[2] The silence is seen as dangerous or problematic but the speaker, instead of trying to escape, chooses to stay and investigate.

KF: I wrote that at a time when I was attempting to take big risks with my writing. I was searching for ways to chart the difficulty of human relationship, or my version of it, yet do it in a way that wasn't mawkish and me-centered. I wanted to map it as truthfully as possible, but obliquely and ironically. For a long time in the late seventies and the eighties I was struggling to get off of that "I" place that was so prominent for those of us who came into poetry in the sixties. Being in New York City, I encountered a number of other kinds of poetries that gave me alternatives. But living with Plath, Lowell, and Sexton in my ear, I had to work to uncover another poetics focused on syntax and unease. I wanted to speak from the unidentified witness perspective instead of positioning the private ego's needs at the center of all writing.

I was often "speechless" in groups. I felt ashamed that my thoughts were not sufficiently coherent to share in public. What ultimately pushed me into becoming articulate was the situation of erasure—the classroom and publishing politics that I eventually saw my students facing too.

SR: Had you been aware of the problem of erasure before you began to teach?

KF: Well, sure. It was a felt experience for many years before it was consciously named. I don't think one becomes so passionate about a phenomenon as I did, unless you've felt the impact of it upon your own development and that of your peers. As a child I was often required by my parents' vocation in the community to wear a social personality, and I felt increasing resistance to that. I was very aware of not being read correctly, or perhaps of being read too simply in a way that satisfied others' needs. That early misreading *is* a kind of perceived erasure for anyone who feels it—it is almost like acquiescing to a profound lie. I suppose that as I attempted to maintain an inner sense of balance—and imbalance—the process of growing up required a kind of masking; that is, concealing my uneasy thoughts and observations in order to avoid what I sensed as an ever-hovering critical judgment from a community of values I had not formed for myself.

When you are publicly contextualized in this way—that is, usefully misread within a social network—you tend to develop a strong resistance to being categorized. Within the family it was OK, we were encouraged to share anything that came to mind—and fortunately, this purposefulness was interrupted by my father's whacky English humor. He was very keen on our memorizing silly poems and very turned on by each of us bringing our experiences to the dinner-table conversation, regardless of our age. But outside of home life, we older kids were aware of a kind of scrutiny that felt intrusive and that encouraged silence or deflection as a sort of protection or refusal to submit. In this context, silence became a bit like the blind a naturalist kneels behind to observe the behavior of birds.

When I went away to school, there was an immense sense of relief—getting away from all this personalized sensitivity and parental need for appropriate social behavior. In New York City, at the end of college, I was just one of hundreds of "struggling young writers" trying to educate myself and get a fix on the contemporary art world. This included a vast potluck of poetry readings one had little taste of in school. It was an entirely different immersion that required an appetite for the new and strange—the brilliantly performative as well as the difficult, more private investigations. I did a lot of listening and reading and sorting through of the writing—and the ideas about writing—that seemed compelling to me—everything from letters between Robert Creeley and Charles Olson to Levertov's Welsh-inflected lyrics, Duncan's open-field song, Spicer, Neruda, and Bishop. All of it seemed immense, rich, and inconclusive.

To listen to how one wanted to write. It was the compelling thing to be doing. Coffeehouse open mikes were where one listened and often got bored. There weren't any writing programs. You hovered at the edges of conversations among the older writers and learned who to read. There were so many tones and shapes evolving within the house of "the poem." While I was intrigued to read the Black Mountain poets, I discovered that there was a lot of humor and celebration going on in the New York School atmosphere. I needed it and thrived—in particular on O'Hara, Schuyler, Guest, Edwin Denby, Kenward Elmslie, and the second-generation writer, Joseph Ceravolo.

Then Oppen came into my life in 1966 and a few years later, in California, I stumbled upon Niedecker in a "women poets anthology" called *Rising Tides*. These two relocated me in silence and the regardfulness for each word's pitch and placement, the space of quiet between lines that allowed this to happen. But I would have had no room to hear that discretionary music without first knowing the wild ride of poetry in Frank O'Hara's hybrid of high culture and camp invention or the surreal mystery of Barbara Guest's hidden language. They were the beginning, for me, of a true freedom and linguistic exploration.

SR: I want to make sure I understand the connection between the evolution of your own writing and involvement in the writing community, and your wish to support the emerging writers you were later meeting as a teacher. Because you had struggled with feeling silenced, and because you had come to recognize your own need to make contact with that silence, respect it, and find ways to put it on the page, you were particularly sensitive to what you saw your students experiencing, and you wanted to help create a safe environment for them to do that exploration too.

KF: It was a two-part urgency, really, once I began to teach in the late sixties—first, to create a classroom environment in which private and often "inarticulate" writers could learn to trust their imperfect, partially formed thoughts aloud—because *that* risk was necessary in order *not* to be spoken for. The other strategy was to introduce nontraditional readings from many sources and to invent assignments with sufficient permission built into them so as to invite intense listening—that act of attention to what was being inadvertently refused or censored as poetic material—and to find ways of getting its barely-there quality onto the page.

When I first started teaching at San Francisco State I was conscious of this. The previous year, at Reed College, I'd assembled an unofficial reading group with a handful of my students to read a small selection of the erased modernist women writers, including Gertrude Stein, Mina Loy, and Dorothy Richardson, with a feeling of adventuring into unmapped territory. I arrived at San Francisco State the next year primed to teach the works of these mostly unknown, untaught writers. But I soon got into trouble because I noted in meetings that there were seldom any women authors being taught or included on required reading lists in English or creative writing courses. As far as the modernists went, they were represented by Joyce and Eliot and sometimes William Carlos Williams. Virginia Woolf certainly wasn't on the "Twentieth-Century Novel" list at San Francisco State. The evidence was adding up to a warning I couldn't avoid.

SR: How were the women students in the program reacting to this state of affairs?

KF: Since I'd been hired to direct the Poetry Center as part of my job, women students began coming into my office to complain that they weren't being allowed to study women authors for their "Major Authors" exams. There was a committee that traditionally decided whether a graduate student's selection of three major authors was "appropriate." These committees were composed only of men since there were no women teaching in our department when I was hired, except for Kay Boyle, who was retiring. The reasoning went that hardly any women writers could be considered as sufficiently "major" because not enough critical scholarly work had been done on them. But since students weren't encouraged to read, do research, or write papers on these writers, it was a catch-22. This was the norm in universities across the country.

Things clearly had to change. I thought that our faculty might listen to the students, so I suggested that if they really wanted to make an impact, they would need to organize. I'd heard word of a women students' union starting at U.C. Berkeley, so I suggested our grad students put together a group and let the faculty know in a respectful way what they wanted to study and why they thought it was important. Within about three days they'd organized the SFSU Women Writers Union. The poet Karen Brodine was one of its first leaders. Soon they were doing presentations on campus and in the community—giving papers on modernist women writers and readings of their own work.

SR: You've been describing silence both as something one seeks out and as something that is foisted on one.

KF: Exactly. We worked to claim the necessary silence needed by us as writers to listen and sort through our thoughts, and to pay attention to self-censoring. But the "being silenced" took just as much work to become conscious of.

SR: It seems to me that both problems are political, in that the woman artist's need for silence in order to tune into her creativity has often been thwarted. Her tuning-in capacity has been exploited to meet others' needs rather than to create her own art.

KF: I agree.

SR: Your poem "Electric railway, 1922, two women" addresses this need to protect one's tuning-in capacity: "When you listen, everybody's talking. They want you for your attention."[3]

KF: That poem was suggested by the painting on the cover of the first edition of *Herself Defined,* Barbara Guest's biography of H.D. Guest chose the painting because it suggested H.D. and Bryher in a secure relation to traveling through unknown territory—in a beautifully upholstered train compartment, looking out at the world passing by. I was thinking about that movement between, on the one hand, interiority, preserving or protecting, traveling safely in known terrain, and on the other hand, curiosity toward "the new" that impels the traveler and the writer into uncharted territory. That movement between interior and exterior happened in the work and life of both H.D. and Barbara Guest.

As the poem "Electric Railway" developed, my thought moved from H.D. and Bryher to a woman friend of mine who was, at that moment, traveling alone in Europe, not buffered by a partner or luxurious arrangements. There's a fine balance between protecting your inner life so that you can work—a continuous struggle for most women, who are so often "being wanted for something"—and opening up to the excitement and risk of independent experience that continues to deliver new information in unpredictable ways. I think that if you don't attend somewhat jealously to that balance, the artist self is thrown off kilter—and usually the writing suffers.

SR: While "Electric railway" addresses the need to protect silence in order to write, "La La at the Cirque Fernando, Paris" is about a girl breaking out of silence into speech.[4]

KF: That's one of the first poems in which I began consciously working with the suggestion of partial or error-prone language. The poem came out of a visit to Mont-Saint-Michel—the island promontory and its cathedral, adjacent to the west coast of France. A statue of Saint Michael is mounted atop the cathedral's southernmost spire, raising his sword to protect France. We'd stopped there on our way down to Italy one wintry February day on a kind of pilgrimage to visit cathedrals that embodied both the Romanesque and the Gothic, and had walked through the Mont-Saint-Michel cathedral as well as viewing it from below and from a distance. When I arrived in Rome some days later, still with that wintry landscape inside me, I came across a postcard sent to me two years earlier, of Degas' painting *La La at the Cirque Fernando, Paris.* I suddenly imagined a life for this young girl La La, living with her mother in the mud flats at the base of the Mont-Saint-Michel cathedral, spending her days collecting shellfish to sell in the nearby town market. Saint Michael's presence is iconic and absolutely reliable but without the human lure that an actual living man might breathe into an encounter. Then a living person wanders into the market one day and offers to put La La in his circus. Fernando is an itinerant "carny" man who sees the young body of La La as a moneymaker. He is opportunistic and she has been looking for a way out of her small-town life.

It took me a couple months to discover this sequence, but its unfolding was one of those magical gifts. Although I began with a familiar lyric description, the syntax begins to disintegrate midway through the poem until finally blurting into bits of code.

In the early stages of the writing, while rereading a draft, I discovered that I'd inadvertently typed a capital *D* in the word "FernanDo." I thought that the typo looked interesting and that instead of correcting it I should intentionally look for other words in the sequence that broke naturally into their own hidden parts. I very quickly found a series of multisyllabic words with other single-syllable words inside them. Without stopping to think about what these meant, I capitalized the inside words. When I assembled these "little" words they formed a revelatory, coded message.

SR: The last section in the poem is a coda about breaking the code, but it also reads like a code itself. Code has come up elsewhere in your poems. What draws you to it?

KF: One thing that comes to mind is that it's a way of protecting oneself from being too vulnerable to an oversimplified reading. One of my earliest books, *In Defiance of the Rains,* while not written in code—not "this equals that"—was definitely written slantwise, under the wire. I was getting uncomfortably close to dangerous material that I was only half-prepared to shed clear light on, so those poems were written almost as hidden messages to myself. There's still a lot of reference to "I," but it's already more encoded or displaced.

SR: It sounds as if encountering the work of poets such as Oppen, Niedecker, Spicer, and the women modernists helped you break away from that insistent "I" and bring more silence as well as more innovation to the page. What else helped you make that shift?

KF: Starting to spend part of each year in Rome began to deeply affect my work. In 1981 I spent six months in Europe on a writing fellowship, entirely away from teaching—much of that time in Italy. By the late eighties I was living in Rome regularly for the entire spring semester. I had time to take in the history around me—the architecture and the crumbling ruins and the layers of buildings pushed on top of each other through centuries. Living there opened me up and lifted me out of my personal and narrowly American situation into a much larger sense of history and community. It created a temporal and spatial shift in my work—through the very dailiness of a larger, older world flagging my attention. I began to let the visuality of history enter the compositional field and claim space.

In *when new time folds up*, the four poem sequences focus on Italian history from Etruscan times up to the continuous reconstruction and repair of present-day Rome—and visualize, sometimes playfully, elements of alphabet, notation, and erasure. To give one example, in the poem "Etruscan Pages" I got involved in the look of Etruscan writing and alphabet and incorporated little visuals as part of the text. This graphic notation had cropped up in earlier work, but in this sequence its presence demanded more space. I'd visited a number of largely untraveled Etruscan ruins and was quite taken by the beautiful Etruscan alphabet carved into tombstones recovered in several museums. I wanted to presence the letters I saw there, originally scratched into tuffa (volcanic rock used for burial stones) with red berry juice, as well as those letters pressed into a very thin gold tablet or "page" that now hangs in the Villa Giulia, the Etruscan museum in Rome. These are some of the only linguistic artifacts that remain to instruct us, because the Romans, who conquered the Etruscans, erased all their sources of writing by burning their wooden tablets of carved writing and melting down the metal tablets of writing to make ammunition. There had existed this life-celebrating culture, with its dancers and beautiful pottery and erotic presence vividly alive on the painted tomb walls, and the Romans just wiped it all out.

My interest in typography was reawakened—an interest going back to high-school days working in the composing room of the local print shop with the guys who used the old linotype machines to set the text. Scrolls of hot metal were always littering the floor. You had to hand-compose the type for headlines and lock the words and letters into a wooden frame. I loved the smell of ink and working with those craftsmen—real life, in the isolated context of public high school. That's where I began to understand how words were put together. "Etruscan Pages" returned me to that interest. I drew some of the Etruscan letters by hand, inside sections of the poem. I wanted that hands-on feeling.

SR: Both the notion of erasure and a playful approach to language and the page are also manifest in "AD notebooks," which appears in *Discrete Categories Forced into Coupling*. You wrote that poem in response to the fact that both your mother and one of your favorite painters, the Abstract Expressionist Willem DeKooning, got Alzheimer's disease within the same period of time.

KF: My mother had suffered from Alzheimer's for about five years by the time I wrote "AD notebooks." She was, at that point, unable to recognize me. The last time she could travel to San Francisco for a visit, I showed her the artist's book *boundayr*, a letterpress book that I'd collaborated on with Sam Francis. She'd always loved art and had been intrigued by my poems early on. She turned to me and said, "Oh, wouldn't it be wonderful to do something like this? Do you know the person who wrote these?" I said, "Mama, it was me, your daughter. See, here's my name." "You're my daughter?" she said. It was alarming, but at the same time it was just part of the process, the beginning of this absence, this taking away of the person I could most count on in the world. A lot of the descriptions in "AD notebooks" are about the place where she was cared for in Southern California.

There were two specific events that propelled me into that poem. One was a show at the San Francisco MOMA of late work by DeKooning, who was still living at that time. There'd been a lot of argument among critics about this exhibit. Some were saying that he didn't know what he was doing; that his assistants were mixing the colors for him. But several of these assistants had made videos of him working on the paintings and argued that the work was DeKooning's. It was clear to me that he still had access to the part of his brain responsible for movement and spatial distinction. It was the memory function that was shattered and confused. I saw in the work something that often happens with older artists: They begin to simplify.

DeKooning was famous for the women he'd painted in the fifties—pictures filled with slashing brushwork and intensely conflicting colors. Now he'd finally reached a very clear and peaceful place on the canvas. The colors were calm—extraordinary rich whites, yellows, and pinks. In one picture, he'd painted over earlier layers but there was a little area—a small aperture—that revealed a fragment of an early work, like a piece of one of his paintings from the fifties. I was amazed to see that.

The other event that engendered the "AD notebooks" poem came just before I saw the show. I'd gone down to Pasadena to see my mother. The medical staff had needed to put her on a calming drug because she'd taken out her upper bridgework and had thrown it across her room. This had been replaced at great cost, and then she'd thrown it away again. She clearly didn't feel good with something "foreign" in her mouth. This was very aggressive behavior, of course. When I saw her confused and angry face, it so reminded me of DeKooning's enraged women. I could imagine her that way, because she sometimes had outbursts of temper when I was a child. It wasn't present most of the time, but when she got mad, you knew you'd better pay attention.

"AD notebooks" is a fiction. I placed DeKooning and my mother in her health-care facility as fellow patients, passing each other and making slight contact, and him painting her. But it's full of real, observed details, such as facial expressions, eating behavior, and the continuous movement and attempts to escape the building so characteristic of Alzheimer's patients. Also, there are real descriptions of his paintings in this piece. I included quotes from some of the critics in one section.

SR: "AD notebooks" explores a vanishing point that, as an artist, one tries to get to—a place where the ego is quieted. The characters in the poem are approaching that vanishing point. They're experiencing the disintegration of the self, the entry into silence. They're leaving behind language and memory, both of which are fundamental to the construction of identity. You've talked about how you'd been working for years to break the grip of the "I." Now you were confronted with two people whose physiology was doing it for them. It was a very high-stakes situation because one of the people was your mom—

KF: —and the other was one of my favorite painters—

SR: —who was still serving as inspiration even as he was in the process of disappearing. So the investigation of presence and absence takes on a whole new layer of meaning. There's a palpable sense, in the poem, of the little fragments of language bubbling in and out of the silence. It's almost scary how deeply you entered into the experience of your mother and DeKooning. Witnessing and creating seem to become one and the same. I wonder if writing this poem took a toll on you.

KF: It did really affect me. I worked on it for two years. I didn't want to put it out there until I had it right. I did place one early version in a journal, but I never should have done that. It wasn't ready yet, and I was always sorry afterward.

SR: There's a wonderful quote by DeKooning in the poem: "*because when I'm falling, I'm doing alright . . . when I'm slipping, I say / hey I'm really slipping most of the time, into that glimpse.*"[5] It's such a liberated image. The permission to fall, the act of falling—falling into artistic vision, or into some sort of state of grace, perhaps—seems especially significant because elsewhere in your work, rising is clearly the desirable action, for example in the image of La La being raised up high in the circus tent.

KF: With the audience on edge, waiting for her to fall. As you get older, you realize that there's some horrible part of human nature that wants that to happen—that anticipates a violent ripping of the fabric.

SR: Tell me about the section called "making more white."

KF: In that section, I was trying to physically enact how DeKooning was working. I took an earlier section in the poem, "radiant inklings," and I erased words from it. For the most part the words in "making more white" are in the same position on the page as in "radiant inklings." I did add the phrase "THING SIFTS THROUGH."[6]

SR: This poem prepares us for all the white space in *hi dde violeth i dde violet*, a poem published as a chapbook by Nomados Press. That poem also deals in a very intense way with the dance of presence and absence, manifesting it aurally, visually, and thematically.

KF: I wrote that poem for Norma Cole, who had suffered a stroke just before I left for Italy that year. She was still in the hospital doing rehabilitation and couldn't yet speak, and there wasn't going to be any way to be in contact. But I wanted to communicate with her. I wrote the poem to share with her some of the experience of being in Rome over Easter—*Pasqua* as it's called—and little Easter, *Pasquetta,* the day after Easter when everyone goes out to the country and has a picnic.

We were staying with our friends Wanda and Oliviero at the lake. Everything that was going on was so Roman—sweet, bourgeois, and nutty. I started the poem by simply writing through a lot of notes I'd taken, again and again trying to make a coherent poem of the foreign cinema I felt inside of. Finally I just got sick of the coherence of "the poem." It seemed too good, too well made. It wasn't acknowledging enough of the theft of speech, the linguistic derailment that Norma had encountered. Nor did it sufficiently address my feelings of loss throughout that spring, due to the death of four other friends in that same interval. In truth, I was filled with a sense of *in*coherence and of everything cracking apart.

During this time some friends in Rome, visual artists, were putting up a show. They wanted me to give a reading for it, but I wanted to make something with my hands. One morning I woke up and reconfigured my poem text to the largest typeface I could find, and printed it out and then began cutting into it, not paying attention to meanings. I cut straight up through the pages vertically and then horizontally, cutting through words and letters. I made one rule for myself: to use every word and letter in the original text. Then I spread everything out on the floor of my workroom and started collaging the words, gluing them in different arrangements onto sheets of Fabriano paper. It was so absorbing. When I finished, I hung them all up on my wall and made a little show. I invited two guests: my husband, Arthur, and my scholar friend Marina Camboni, who had translated a lot of my work into Italian. Then I felt satisfied.

Soon after that, my friend Peter Quartermain wrote that he and his wife Meredith were doing a new series of small books, and asked if I could give them something. I thought that I had nothing, but after a few days I wondered if I could reformat the wall hangings into pages. I proposed this to the Quartermains, knowing it was not what they had in mind, but they decided to do it.

SR: *hi dde violeth i dde violet* and "AD notebooks" are both visually inventive in terms of form. For me, though, the dominant feeling of "AD notebooks" is awe in the face of silence, whereas reading *hi dde violeth i dde violet*, my dominant sensation is joy—tremendous joy against a backdrop of grief and loss. In addition, *hi dde violeth i dde violet* takes the stutter, the error, the disintegration of language much further than "AD notebooks"—here the language breaks down into not just words and phrases but phonemes and letters. James McCorkle wrote something about "Etruscan Pages" that I think applies even more acutely to *hi dde violeth i dde violet*: "To be in error, to mistranslate, or to invite accident becomes a means to re-present and re-iterate the possibilities of process."[7] This poem foregrounds the process of language coming into being and going away—the constant vibration between presence and absence—and invites me to reinvent and re-imagine language. I encounter new words that yield rich associations: for example, "(&ndles" looks like "(endless"—the eternity of Heaven, or of time, made to seem even more eternal because of the lack of a closing parenthesis—and "candles," which are used in church rituals. Another invented word, "skwywr d," suggests Christ rising skyward, and "sky words"—the transcendent dimension of poetry, perhaps.[8] The comical swirl of sounds in my mouth when I try to pronounce the word reveals an irreverence toward received language.

KF: I was feeling very irreverent.

SR: The irreverence comes through in the content, too. You've got woofing dogs and mozzarella—

KF: Yes, Wanda feeding the dogs the leftover mozzarella from the traditional Easter feast—such a casually luxurious and horribly unconscious thing to do, given the hunger in the world. But she grew up in Italy during World War II and was used to having no food at all. So for her to have so much food that she can just throw stuff to the dogs is the ultimate gesture of freedom. There's a great Italian word, *butta*, that she often uses with joyous definiteness in reference to leftover food. It means "toss it."

Part of the poem's irreverence is informed by the ironic relationship that Wanda's family has to Easter. We've been sharing their Easter celebrations for twenty years and it's fascinating to watch all the funny rituals that these completely nonreligious people participate in. For example, one of the aunts sits in the middle of the living room watching a broadcast of the pope and the long Easter Mass celebrated at the Vatican, with the TV turned up fairly loud, while everyone else is cooking or hiding eggs and completely ignoring her. My own irreverence comes into the poem in the "Christ arose" section where I layered words from the song we sang at Easter when I was a child—"Christ arose, Christ arose"—with Gertrude Stein's "a rose is a rose is a rose" and *arroz*, the Spanish word for rice.[9]

SR: The poem uses the whole page as a field. You do that in other poems, though often you make a clear distinction between what constitutes the poem and what constitutes the marginalia.

KF: Yes, like the sonnets in the poem sequence "when new time folds up."[10]

SR: I'm also thinking of "Champs (fields) and between" in *Discrete Categories Forced into Coupling*, where both the "field" part and the "between" part are represented on each page, conversing with each other across white space.

KF: That project was written in response to the painter Joan Mitchell's work. I was fortunate to see her *Champs* and *between* series displayed together in Paris in the eighties at Le Jeu de Paume museum. The *Champs* series stunned me with its complicated overlays of paint and motion. In contrast, the *between* series looked as if she'd taken little moments out of the larger works—just a few lines, a few colors—and framed them as a response, a zoom lens moving in on a detail, the two sides of a conversation speaking across the room to each other. I wrote notes to myself for years about trying to attempt such a movement between two sets of language.

SR: In *hi dde violeth i dde violet*, that distinction between "field" and "between" is gone. The whole poem is simultaneously "field" and "between," center and margin. I was also struck that while each page works as a solo canvas, there's very much a sense of continuity, of a book-length composition.

KF: Since I'd done them as pictures to hang on a wall, I didn't initially compose them with any order in mind. When I decided to do the book, ordering the pages took another kind of focus. I went through a lot of versions to find what felt right, so that each page would converse in some way with the next.

SR: After the language has been fractured so radically and exuberantly throughout the text, the last page is surprisingly coherent and quiet.

KF: I meant it to work as a kind of blessing. "[L]ight opens over trees' abundant suspend" is as close as I can probably get to whatever sense I have of a mystical presence or the event of new beginnings, new growth—a periodic possibility for hope.[11]

SR: What you're saying reminds me of something you wrote in the poem "Horologic," which appears in your chapbook *20th Century*: "Said he wasn't spiritual / but could feel the awe—that little Yes material."[12]

KF: That's an interesting connection. *Orologio* is the Italian word for "wristwatch."

SR: "Horologic" echoes both *hi dde violeth i dde violet* and "when new time folds up." It evokes the latter not only because the concept of time appears in both titles, but because the music and the forms of the two poems—the time-keeping devices—echo each other. Both poems have a spilling-forward sound, but "Horologic" is loaded with hard stops that bring it up short, make it stutter, show the sutures. Both poems use a highly formal container: "when new time folds up" is a series of sonnets with the last half-line sprinkled down the right-hand margin of the page, while "Horologic" comprises twelve long-line stanzas with one dangling line at the end. "Horologic" reminds me of *hi dde violeth i dde violet* in its rich, chewy sound: "rose geranium whistle-stop nape of neck thistle"; "lawd low Atlantis shallow."[13]

KF: "Horologic" represents an important shift in my thinking about sound. As I mentioned earlier, I began as a lyric poet but when I moved to New York I connected with the poetry of Black Mountain and the New York School and also started paying close attention to the improvised phrasing of jazz and Abstract Expressionist painting. All of these movements re-grounded my poetry in the modernist idiom. I didn't know yet about Pound, H.D., Louis Zukofsky, or Basil Bunting, but I did know from that point forward that I wanted to escape into the American idiom. One of the means I developed to get away from the internalized values of "good" English prosody still making its unconscious demands on my ear was to go back and forth between writing poetry with line breaks and writing long sentences and paragraphs to stretch out the sound so it wouldn't be so tightly wound and musically compressed by the old ear habits. In the late eighties and early nineties, after exploring a number of visual and sound devices in the long sequence poems published in *when new time folds up*, I started understanding that in fact I really loved highly compressed musical textures but I needed to find my own peculiar "condensations"—to use a Niedecker reference. Instead of pushing them away as a threat, I knew that I would work to foreground that pleasure. "Horologic" is what came out of that.

SR: *hi dde violeth i dde violet* seems to come out of that too. It's such a piece of music.

KF: Yes, it's the purest formal experiment so far, in my work. In fact, I turned to writing prose after I finished *hi dde violeth i dde violet* because I couldn't imagine where my poetry might go after that.

SR: You said in a talk called "The Secret Life of a Convicted Lyric Poet" that you're vigilant about making sure you don't get into habits of composition—that every few years you attempt to shake up your writing practice. That seems to be where you are now, asking where you can go next. As a writer you seem to take the word "experimental" very literally, as in, going into the laboratory, entering the unknown, mixing things around, and seeing what you find.

KF: I've come to prefer the word "investigative" to the generic and often blurred term "experimental." One investigates the nature of language as one constructs it, and privileges the moment of work rather than any prefigured idea of what one thought one wanted the writing to look like before one started.

SR: I want to ask about your relationship to the Bay Area writing community. I'm assuming that for you that means the Bay Area innovative writing community?

KF: In the context of my own writing practice, I've always been attracted by the nontraditional in art and by contemporary work that finds meaning—even necessity—in testing the established, pre-approved limits of its medium. My first thrills in poetry, as a teenager, were Walt Whitman, Gerard Manley Hopkins, and e.e. cummings. They were each breaking against the status quo in their particular historic moment. This was way before San Francisco or New York City.

SR: How has your relationship to the Bay Area writing community evolved over the time you've been here?

KF: In May of 1972, Mark Linenthal called me at Reed College and invited me to replace him as director of the Poetry Center at San Francisco State, a job that included teaching two courses for the creative writing program.

I arrived in the fall of '72 just as identity politics and student protests were hitting full tilt at university campuses nationwide. San Francisco State had recently been torn apart by a two-pronged strike asserting faculty rights to unionize and African American students' demands for relevant ethnic studies courses. President S.I. Hayakawa's response was to fire strikers and cut back all supporting funds for the Poetry Center as punishment for its unanimous support of the strike. When I arrived, the only resource we had was a small office with three desks, a funky old couch, some bookshelves, and a few filing cabinets, with the electricity and local phone service thrown in, probably because he couldn't separate it from the entire Humanities building in which it was housed. There was literally no budget for the Poetry Center reading program I'd been hired to "direct." Then Donald Allen made us a gift of a thousand dollars for that year's reading program, with the proviso that we lead off with a reading by Gerard Malanga. There it was in a nutshell, conflicting aesthetic and community interests entangled with economic bait.

Radical measures were needed and that's precisely why and when the American Poetry Archive got invented—to pay the bills, as well as to document, via the new video technology, the complex range of American poetries being written. Because our only funding issued from a new National Endowment grant and because I had *not* grown up inside locally formed tastes, I saw the first year's program in somewhat more national—and "democratic"—terms. Every invited poet was offered fifty dollars, whether they were a "star" or had just published a first chapbook. People coming into town anyway were, for the most part, happy to read. Robert Duncan read for free. Alan Ginsberg, on the other hand, demanded that his father appear as a paid poet on the program with him—with meditation cushions, flowers, and special tea onstage—and that they be put up in the Hyatt downtown for two nights.

I was intent upon making space for a newly evolving consciousness around gender and ethnic awareness and a range of innovative poetries in the programming. This did not sit well with leaders of various poetry communities vying for reading space. I became an instant magnet for critique and projection.

That was one early difficulty. The second hurdle was arriving at San Francisco State as the only woman faculty member in a department of some twenty men, as a replacement for the glamorous token woman, Kay Boyle, whose famous activist politics did not include gender consciousness. By that point my feminism had become internally acute, but was not yet aligned with the ability to publicly articulate my students' grievances to a very skeptical, all-male department of colleagues. In these first years, my learning curve was ferocious and I had little community support except for the friendship and encouragement of Mark Linenthal and his wife, Frances Jaffer, and George and Mary Oppen—all of them loyal companions who helped me to sort through the political issues and the poetics of the several closed communities that viewed me warily as an outsider.

Thanks to a small but fierce writing circle organized by Frances, who invited Beverly Dahlen and me to join her, my off-campus writing life began to flourish. Regular discussions and reading of our new, often improvised work changed my relationship to literature and to the local writing community. We read feminist theory together and discussed it as a deep part of our writing practice, including works by Luce Irigaray (translated by Carolyn Burke) and Julia Kristeva, as well as formative essays by Rachel Blau DuPlessis and young feminist scholars beginning to speculate on questions of erasure, power relations in publishing, and whether there was such a thing as "female language."

We also studied the writings of Lorine Niedecker, H.D., Mina Loy, Djuna Barnes, Dorothy Richardson, Zora Neale Hurston, and other modernist and contemporary women writers who had not been included in our university reading lists, and were subsequently able to enlarge each other's awareness of how things worked. Reading and reevaluating the texts we'd been left without gave us strength to reclaim them. The journal *HOW(ever)* emerged from these discussions. Editing *HOW(ever)* gave us a chance to assert some choices and to engage with the new scholars who were bringing support and curiosity to twentieth-century women writers and providing the missing links. Empowering ourselves replaced the feeling of needing to play by others' rules or not play at all.

From that period on, my relationship to the writing community was more fluid and often a great source of stimulation and nourishment to my own writing. I've continued to be intrigued by the invention of particular writers, and skeptical of group rule and privilege.

SR: What are you reading these days?

KF: One highly compelling nonfiction work I read recently was *The Mind of the Raven,* by Bernd Heinrich—curiously, it was very near to my beginning the book that large black crows—or ravens—began appearing every morning on the telephone lines outside our bedroom window and on the railing of our deck. Over the last few months I've been reading through a small library of books and pamphlets by a new hybrid generation of young poets—David Larsen, Catherine Wagner, Jeanne Heuving, Sara M. Larsen, Martin Corless-Smith, Stephanie Young, Elise Ficarra, Cedar Sigo, Melissa Benham, Brandon Brown, Lauren Shufran, and Brent Cunningham, to name just a few. This work shares the quality of being highly researched and valuing an extraordinary range of imaginative and historical intervention. It has given me back my love of reading poetry and seems to embrace a huge range of what's possible in a language unearthed from deepest necessity.

ROBERT GLÜCK

A Community Writing Itself

Sarah Rosenthal: I want to start with your sense of responsibility for telling the truth to your reader. I was looking at something you wrote in your essay "My Community" in 1983: "New form, new content demand a new way of being, a new way of seeing your own life, just as new vocabulary calls forth its meanings in your life. It is at this starting point that an art movement or a political movement has moral life. The appearance of a gay self in fiction can rarely be naïve, even now. It will be tested and taken as a demand as much as a description. A dishonest picture is a traitor, the enemy of the common good."[1] Elsewhere, in an essay called "Truth's Mirror Is No Mirror," you write, "I follow the dictates of my plot, but not beyond the reader's credence."[2] How do you decide what that credence consists of?

Robert Glück: To answer the last question first, that statement should alert the reader that I am putting in question his faith in narration itself, using that belief and disbelief as a stage for my writing. But more specifically, I was talking about gossip and its relation to the collective truth a community tells itself. I wanted my writing to tap into that living source of storytelling. I guess I was imagining that the face of my little readership would draw back skeptically, an eyebrow raised. I was thinking about how a gossip might tailor the events in a story in order to evoke or avoid that expression. So a gossip is telling the truth by telling a community its own truth—perhaps the only place a truth can exist.

In the late seventies and early eighties we were asking ourselves, How do you write without oppressing your subject matter and your reader? The question assumed that representation itself is oppressive, creating a power imbalance between writer and reader that plays out some of the power imbalances between society and reader. And that naming itself is a form of execution. The awareness that fiction is a lie, that representation itself is inevitably a distortion, was very pressing. But where to take that lie? I could not afford to abandon representation, for a good reason. I did not think there was an "I"—a self—that existed apart from representations—texts of one kind or another—but I was urgent to "tell my story," a completely different kind of truth, the strange story of the marginalized experience of a sexual minority whose existence was rather experimental itself, and had yet to appear in our literary forum. For about ten minutes anyway, a community without norms. Could a writer simply step out of the power discrepancies by becoming a community talking to itself?

It was not that simple. There were so few depictions of gay people that the existing ones exerted too much power. In fact, they enacted the kind of power imbalance that I just described. Any fiction does—a mirror ordering you to become the self that it chooses to reflect. So there were two literary politics that did not jibe: one that wanted to dismantle representation, and one that needed a different kind of representation to work its magic. The next question was, if fiction—especially the kind of fiction purveyed by the mainstream—was a lie that didn't know itself, then what would a lie that *did* know itself look like? For example, in order to create a literary object that isn't a lie, I might have tried to found my aesthetic on disjunctions so extreme that all you could see was language happening, forcing awareness of the ways language makes meaning.

SR: Yet you chose a different track. Did you find a lack of sensuality in Language poetry that alienated you from that form?

RG: Well, we all know that there was a Puritan strain in Language poetry. Was that intrinsic? As though disjunction that described itself with technical vocabulary had to eliminate the body, or as though formal purity had to eliminate sex along with other kinds of content? Yet there are plenty of "subject matters" in their work from that time. Was it the Marxist politics? I used to wonder about their prudery with Kathy Acker and Bruce Boone. Bruce was my teacher. Now there are plenty of younger poets like Stacy Doris, whose writing is very juicy, as is, say, the poetry of Laura Moriarty. And some of the Language poets have taken a sensual turn.

My need for a sensory life in writing—in fact, my need for need—has been terribly important to me in my adulthood as a kind of tonic note. In my next book, *Denny Smith,* I keep coming back to the idea that feeling pleasure makes strange experiences normal. In fact, when I put the book together, I saw that an alarming number of stories end with an orgasm, as though a real conclusion only happens when feeling and event come together. I've tried to space them out, so that the orgasms are equidistant, like molecules obeying the gas laws.

Remember, when I was a kid homosexuality took only two forms: an insult and a disease. First I experienced my body as a distant planet orbiting light years away. Then I felt as though my very flesh were sick, dense with sick desire. Surely being gay was less a problem for some people, people with less fear, people with less amour propre. I didn't feel secure, but I inherited from my family a towering indignation.

So you could say I come to the senses as a surprising discovery, and sex for me will always be something of a shock. That I could hold someone naked against my body and have access to his body seems like the most improbable miracle. That I knew how to fall in love—even knew how to have a broken heart—where did such knowledge come from? I was glad to be at least that much a member of the human club.

If I entered a sexuality that was exotic from the point of view of the larger culture, for me it possessed great inner necessity, as it well may have, since it had to be mighty enough to overcome so much shame and prohibition. And sex itself was not just release, or even just contact—it carried the force of the destruction of an identity and the establishment of some new, untried way of being. Sex made me incredibly light-hearted—think of how much psychic drudgery went into keeping my body at a distance, keeping desires unexpressed, and maintaining an identity whose goal was to make a disguise out of rags.

The resistance of language to describing sensation has preoccupied me during my entire writing life. Describing sensation is another way of staying at one limit of what language can do. It is a way out of the box of psychology. At the extremes of intimacy I find a strange anonymity—taking a sip of water when you are thirsty, the feeling of thirst, would it matter who feels that? It is thirst that speaks. Also, I am not very handy with plot, and sensory exploration can substitute for plot expectation. And of course it's easy to believe in the senses; an intimacy is assumed. You could say intimacy is my subject. The splendor of everyday life always exists in a state of humility. I love domesticity, the wonder of objects that touch me every day, my cup, my spoon . . .

Still, in recounting sex, or anything else that tests the bounds of intimacy, what is true may be the assertion that the truth of such a confession is to be found in its performance rather than its validity as a record. And that in itself suggests a community that may recognize itself in the performance of certain kinds of nakedness.

Let's just say that in the early gay days, we had the sense that new experience was leading to new representation every bit as pressing as anything else being written. Shifts in the meaning of public and private experience, for instance. Or the absurdist theater of heterosexual norms which could be visible only to an outsider. Of course, we were fucked up and suffering and living horrid toy versions of our parents' relationships, just like all young people. But look how promiscuity was a new way of relating—physical intimacy first and conversation later, perhaps. You might cross race and class boundaries—in fact, without knowing it!

SR: In the dark . . .

RG: The lights go on . . . wow! So, suddenly there is a great fluidity. In the larger society most community life is turning to garbage before our eyes, and here's a gay community that's thriving. In fact, it's thriving within exactly the same milieu that causes the other communities to break down, that is, inside urban life and the commodity. Yet I suppose it was an outgrowth of hippie culture.

SR: In terms of access to altered states?

RG: In the belief in the power of a good heart to make something happen. We hadn't examined power relationships yet; our Marxism was rather fanciful, us against them. Power relations in our actual lives had to wait for feminism to reach us later in the seventies. I couldn't buy hippie life entirely, but it created a free zone in which I could hide out and try to piece together a life that included some of the things I needed. For a moment the need for contact and self-expression and flat-out love and tenderness took precedence over the "work ethic." A society based on something other than disgust. Remember the term "sublimation"? It was big in the fifties and early sixties—last gasp of the morality of restraint fostered by all expanding empires. Those of us who were hippies in the sixties and seventies entered professional life much later and with a great deal of skepticism.

SR: You believed the hippie message.

RG: Yeah, I believed it. Anti-professional. Hippie culture was my gateway to all the other bohemias, demimondes, countercultures, and avant-gardes past and present. I thought the way to be a writer was to be known by a few who thought your work helped them understand the world, and I still think that. Somebody like Jack Spicer, a little-known poet with a small, ardent following—he was, for me, the image of a writer. I saw most contemporary literature as entertainment for a conversant audience, not evil, but not applicable. It had weird, overblown claims to greatness, and generally it was better than TV, but worse than the movies.

SR: But you were reading a lot of gay male writers who were well known as intellects and creators, people whose writing helped your coming-out process in multiple ways. You had a whole string in addition to Jack Spicer and Frank O'Hara, right?

RG: Burroughs, Proust, Genet, Cavafy, Pessoa—oh, plenty of others. Homosexuality sent me to world lit.

SR: But your model was really Spicer, that was your image for yourself.

RG: Perhaps for myself as a writer in the world. O'Hara's poetry was equally important to me. Well, none of them had much recognition. In 1972 I did my master's orals partly on O'Hara, and they couldn't find anybody at school who knew his work. A man on my committee pressed me to talk about the short stories and I kept saying, "Oh, the stories . . ." Later I realized he meant *John* O'Hara. Same with Burroughs. It's hard to think back to a time when Burroughs wasn't an international culture figure, but in the sixties and early seventies, he was still a cult writer.

SR: I'd like to thread this back to the quote I read, "A dishonest picture is a traitor, an enemy of the common good." Just to be provocative, this sounds like some oppressive and limiting political doctrine. Same with "I follow the dictates of my plot, but not beyond my reader's credence." You have a huge sense of responsibility toward this common good or this reader, and I want to know what that stems from.

RG: I was being provocative, waving a word like "dishonest" in the face of postmodernism. I meant that we should discover in our writing the prevailing conditions. We almost never—perhaps never—experience the world except through the scrim of representations that already exist, that we have unknowingly agreed to. The politics of representation is to bring that agreement to light, or revise that agreement toward a more exact or inclusive experience of the world. So, rejecting the vile mainstream versions of who we were, but also rejecting those sugar-coated versions delivered to ourselves by ourselves. I would say that an honest fiction is one that is mindful of its own power relations. When you enter a reader's psychic life, that's power, and you either own that or you don't. You can figure out how you want to enter the reader's psychic life; you can make those dynamics apparent; you can manipulate them in order to give the reader choices; you can even try to bring the reader into the process of constructing the meanings that are being generated. You can top the willing reader, producing spasms of genre pleasure. But you can't will away power. I had the idea that there is such a thing as a common good in the first place. Who knows? Maybe it comes from the Orthodox Jewish tribe I grew up in. First I embraced all these identities with relief. Now they seem to pass by me and I feel even more relief.

SR: OK, so the idealism you are talking about: the idea that there is goodness . . . and that it is common. [*laughter*] Is that a utopian fantasy on your part?

RG: Yes, and on your part too. The common good: Is boiling water, steeping tea, and pouring it into a friend's cup a utopian fantasy? Is meeting a lover for Japanese noodles and then going to the movies a utopian fantasy? Having a job that is not completely alienating? A lover who's kind, or a body that doesn't sicken and die, or a government that doesn't kill people in my name? A school system that teaches all of us to read all kinds of literature? When I write, am I a community—several—speaking to itself, ourselves? Certainly, in some instances, the common good equals the annihilation of the self. I wish there were another word for "community," one not so worn out, degraded. Using it, I feel the attrition of twenty-five years of non-profit grant proposals. I did want to concentrate on the local, almost like being a court writer—the gay community would be my court as the court of Louis XIV was La Fontaine's. Or, say, as the Upper West Side Jewish community was I.B. Singer's.

We are speaking of the gay community, but of course there is also the small, heated writing scene that has been just as important to me, a few men and many women, and I suppose I import notions and expectations from one group to the other. It would be interesting to dissect these different identities that sometimes feel so separate in me—and yet they are not. In fact, what have I done if not to make a group and a writing practice in which my disparate selves do not rule each other out, in which some part of myself is not always already a freak?

Sexuality comes first? But before sexuality, the life of an artist! I studied ballet and visual art during most of my childhood—I was hoping ballet would lead me to the vague, beautiful life of my vague, beautiful dreams. I loved the movie *The Red Shoes*, where Moira Shearer has to choose between art and life. A choice I had already made. Much later I assumed rightly that art would lead me to other homosexuals and even offer us some protection. I studied visual art in different ways—summer painting scholarships, art school in Scotland. I studied with Peter Voulkos at Cal. I even had my own kiln.

By "community" and "the common good," I mean an occasion of shared gestures and recognitions that can be an ephemeral cobweb or the thunderous formation of identity. How we know ourselves—one side of the collaborative project that is the self. How we recognize what lies inside or outside acceptable behavior. In general, how we make meaning. By "community," I don't mean a fantasia of lederhosen, where we are all singing "The Future Belongs to Me" and clanking our beer steins, but simply a place where people shape their being, for better and often for worse.

Perhaps another take on "the common good" goes back to Georges Bataille, who wrote about sundering the bonds of self in order to experience nothingness. To enact this "unknowing," an individual needs to die, or needs the help of a group or at least a sex partner. Certainly I was mute before I entered these communities; they gave me a language to express a sense of loss and futility central to my being. I believe that the attainment of nothingness is a community activity. My books are generally about failed romances and loss of self. This terrain is built on contradictions. For instance, to be desired, I need to assemble an identity that is stable enough to be recognized. So desire—which supposedly destabilizes the self—does just the opposite. Too bad I can't found my identity on the moment of orgasm.

SR: Do you think that by believing in the common good you help create it? That in a sense your belief is a gift to your reader?

RG: I think that the way art operates is that the reader experiences the belief of the writer. So whatever the writer is believing, whether it is the form of the work, or the depth of engagement with language, or the existence of the world, whatever it is the writer demonstrates faith in, that is the heart of the reader's experience. That's why people say art is consoling. I mean, what is the consolation? You are witnessing someone's faith in the world, in some aspect of the world. And even if the reader can't match that depth of faith, just experiencing it conveys the feeling that life has value and meaning.

SR: That's an approach that could take the pressure off of people who feel unsure about how to connect with a piece of art unless it is already familiar to them.

I am also thinking about your essay "Fame," where you write, "I propose self-community-story as a tonic for the loss of human scale. By naming self-community-story I participate in their disintegration, their progress from invisibility to something to be named and manipulated—to be reintegrated later in a new context, in a third term that history must provide."[3] So you are trying to address the problem of lack of community—yet the irony is that you're simultaneously participating in the disintegration of community. It's like the Romantics writing about nature: Once you say "nature," nature is over.

RG: Right, name it and we lose it. Then imagine a third term, in which a reintegration takes place. It would have to include some knowledge of what constitutes a community, knowledge that had been invisible because "natural." So the natural would be located in some other, unnamable arena.

SR: When I read that passage I thought about how as a 22-year-old I moved into the Fillmore District, the classic young white urban "pioneer" who moves into the low-income neighborhood, making it safe for an influx of upwardly mobile whites who ultimately displace the original residents—unwittingly participating in the destruction of a solid community.

RG: To be replaced by a different kind of neighborhood, more affluent, where integration is taken for granted. And a different kind of city in which poor people are shunted like scum to the outskirts. You are responsible for both. Say you are a white person from a white suburb—now you become an intimate of an African-American family, a tremendously enriching experience. And you are part of the historical process that is homogenizing the world. One thing does not cancel another. And that solid community was not really so solid. It had a serious drug problem, for example. I worked as a ghost writer for an illiterate in the Redevelopment Agency during the seventies. He was supposed to help congregations of storefront churches construct actual church buildings. The program was a flop because none of these churches had a nickel to accomplish such a task. When people *did* make money, they fled to the suburbs. There were gospel songs about that—someone gets affluent, goodbye neighborhood, goodbye church.

I do not mean that history gives us happy endings, only that the action of history becomes apparent. I think about my trip to Guatemala, where we were just bumbling into Native American villages with the idea that our good hearts should give us entrée. When I said that an understanding of power relations was missing in the early hippie days, I wasn't just whistling Dixie. On the other hand, Mayan Indians have traded goods with outsiders for the last 1,500 years, and I'll bet they were glad to have our money.

SR: So in terms of literature, what is the third term, the reintegration you're proposing?

RG: Well, the third term—and not necessarily a good one—history (not Bob) must provide. The strange thing about our condition is that oppression (we are used, lied to, disregarded, robbed, and murdered) does not seem to rule out complicity (we inflict terror and poverty on each other and the world). Both exist at a pitch that we don't seem to be able to name. We are kept from that self-knowledge. So perhaps the third term exists in that particular ignorance. Really, we are talking about the ability to articulate the contradictions that make up one's life. Insofar as writing knows these contradictions and makes them known, that is the degree that the writing knows itself as writing. And the degree the self knows itself, because self is a bundle of the exact same contradictions. Good politics start with the one-and-only life that belongs to one person, but we can't issue ourselves exemptions from inequality. Where would we stop? We citizens of the Roman Empire, we homo sapiens, we sentient organisms?

SR: That bounces off something else in your essay "My Community": "So it would be sloppy to say I moved away, came out, and became free, because one can only measure this brand of freedom, which is the freedom of language to make representations, by contrasting it with a state of captivity, the dishonest fiction which the present is for anyone."[4]

RG: What is the present but something unspoken, something that has yet to be put into words?

SR: So you see honesty not in any particular moment, but as a process.

RG: You could say it's an effort to recognize what is radical. The United States has just been attacked and the whole country is amazed. Can we ever be more than credulous children?[5] Our culture frantically expresses its own inability to communicate or touch its own realities—our labor takes place in conditions of raw capitalism across the world, our old age is locked up in institutions, our wars don't make it to the news, our homeless don't make it to Federal politics. No wonder we are slightly crazed. The nineteenth century felt remorse; what should we feel now? Distraction? But people live with radical truths because circumstances force them to.

But there are lies that are just as pressing, and there are the compulsions and obsessions and psychological eddies that are just as true—and it would be a mistake to leave them out of the mix of literature. There is our frantic, unrequited love for the world. Daydreams, night dreams—to make up a truth you need all of these, not just a stance toward Afghanistan. And opposites are true together; they don't cancel each other out.

I think my books are spherical: They make a sphere out of a lot of disparate matter. It's my desire to put all of these things in a book to make a true resemblance. That means endless reframing, sometimes with every sentence the use of a different lens: long shots, close-ups. I suppose the awareness of living inside different valences is my version of the truth, and writing about them is my loyalty to experience.

I'm also interested in working with different versions of time. There's linear time and there's circular time, there's the time of reading and the time of writing. The Gnostics conceived of time not as a straight line but as a broken line. I was working with that concept in *Margery Kempe*. And each of those versions of time has the truth of experience. A poem whose lines are no longer than five words is not just a poem, it's a version of time. It's saying, Here is the unit, here is the measure of time for me, when I look at the world, that's the measure I experience, that's the beat. Here's one unit of time, now here's another, and here's another. By the same token, if someone's allegiance is to chapters, or scenes, or sentences, he is saying, here is a unit of time for me.

SR: Do you feel you have developed a unit of time, or do you feel you are always investigating that and trying to come up with what's right for a particular piece of writing?

RG: I think this big hodgepodge of a world can be divided up in a trillion ways and they are all accurate. I would want to use more than one in any given work, to acknowledge that important fact. I experience one version of time while chopping onions, another while having sex, another while looking at a tree blown by the wind, another while being chased by a man down the street at night, and another while watching the World Trade Center collapse over and over in my mind. People often assume an extremely disjunct narrative is subversive. But actually, it can only subvert a longer or shorter section of narrative. So, what is it subverting once the expectation of the reader has been established? The subversive thing, perhaps, is to include a variety of temporal units, so that no single measure can dominate. For example, what if I sometimes make the sentence or the fragment my unit of composition, rather than the paragraph? What if I use sounds or repeat certain words throughout a long work, that makes one unit of the whole book?

SR: I'd like to ask you about your use of types in your writing and the relation of that practice to your ideas about community and psychology. In your essay "Caricature" you write, "[B]oth the audience and the writer are responsible to their community. The responsibility is not moral blackmail; it aids the writer. It releases him from the burden of psychology and gives him access to history."[6] This is an essay about the value of using types in fiction. In your story collection *Denny Smith*, the characters Darryl and Trent start out as types: In "The Purple Men," they're very simplified, abstracted. But in "Purple Men 2000," they begin to accrue a depth of personality.

RG: Yeah, who doesn't? Daryl and Trent were meant to be exactly the community's self-description to be found, say, in the gay press. But they are assembling interior lives throughout the eighties in their first story—in fact that's the plot—and of course they are lovable morons, so the stories are not uncritical. They are based on myself and amalgamated boyfriends.

SR: Yet given the way the characters start to spill out of their types, is it really possible to sustain this idea of literary types?

RG: I'm playing with such notions. I'm not finished with Daryl and Trent. They are my dear puppets. It was my pleasure to give them some of the world's gravity—their second story is a retelling of *Mrs. Dalloway*. The Day, shopping, the crazy guy, the party. As Camille Roy says, a character can be anything—a climate, a landscape, some assortment of contradictions, a deity. At any rate, Daryl gains interior life because of HIV. Trent does not change much. He continues to have a radical existence, almost inhuman in the clarity of his drives, like Blake's Orc: "The fiery limbs, the flaming hair."[7] But their second story is told from the middle distance, the point of view of a coherent self, so Trent seems deeper.

I had planned for Daryl and Trent to stay young forever, along with myself. Their relation to their community becomes more complicated as they age. I mean, you need a community when you're younger, because there's an urgency to see yourself reflected back. When I was young, I could meet somebody for coffee and talk for three hours nonstop and feel as though I'd delivered myself. I went away feeling exalted and empty, as though I'd given that person the substance of who I was. As I get older, I find that I sit with old friends and sometimes we don't say too much. Or if we do, we're talking about details and perhaps about entertaining things, but I don't come away with the feeling that I've delivered myself whole cloth, because that would be impossible. As I age, my problems become simpler—does my character become more complex?

In the essay you cited, "Caricature," I was thinking about Georg Lukács's *Theory of the Novel*. His idea of an integrated work of art is one that contains its audience; the story is like the community writing itself. So, how to make that happen? In the seventies and eighties, you can't even imagine how few examples there were of fiction writing that wasn't located inside of psychology and the self. I was proposing one solution: Locate community types and so gain a vigorous relation to a very lively community. And at the same time I wanted to dovetail the characters' individual fortunes, and the fortunes of the writer, with the fate of a community. Earlier in the seventies, I felt trapped inside of "Bob"—but I didn't want to lose "Bob," I just wanted to open Bob up, make Bob more porous. My use of caricature was one of many experiments.

SR: You were looking for more balance, because literature had become so grounded in interior life that the awareness that self is a construction was completely lost. Yet as a writer you're also very interested in the psyche.

RG: Certainly, why would I deprive writing of the biggest summer blockbuster on Earth? But I have my ways of opening up interior life, whether by using appropriation, or long shots of historical matter, or close-ups of sensory life shared by everyone. In *Margery Kempe* I solicited nuggets of experience—people relating to their bodies—and distributed the insights to dress my fifteenth-century characters, like the miller's wife. It's not that I think there is no such thing as inner life, but that our inner lives protect themselves by not letting us know how porous they really are.

SR: Such methods of opening up interior life are no doubt familiar to many fiction writers.

RG: Perhaps. I do it with signposts. I announced in the preface of my book, "Here's what I'm doing." Any alert reader would know that a certain incident involving pepper and anal intercourse was more likely to belong to Tom Gunn than to a cleric in the fourteenth century.[8]

SR: In *Jack the Modernist*, Bob is frustrated that Jack lacks interior life. Jack's personality is so hard to grasp, so empty. He's always circling wisdom passages in books—a parody of appropriation.

RG: I was making fun of his idea of self-improvement. Basically, I was trying to discover a place for human beings to live, as opposed to modernism's "family of man" one-size-fits-all idealism. One version of postmodernism is an examination of human scale. That includes the many fundamentalisms, from Tammy Faye to Islam to restoring a building to its exact nineteenth-century condition. What is human scale in a world that is always more fragmented and more global? In *Jack the Modernist*, Bob maintains differences even inside himself—he's a teacher, a gay lefty, a Jewish son, a piece of meat at the baths. Language changes accordingly.

SR: You write, in your fiction and essays, about jerking off to porn.

RG: Yes, though interest in that hobby comes in spurts, so to speak. Perhaps I wrote about it because pornography seems to lead into language, even visual pornography. Presently I am distracted by a website called guystats.com where men from all over the world display naked photos of themselves—if you like what you see you can contact them. The ways they choose to display themselves fascinate me. For instance, one guy presents only one photo, his boner with gallons of sperm flowing down the shaft, and his note reads: I'm looking for a long-term monogamous relationship, holding hands on the beach, sunsets, fine dining, moonlight, Italy . . .

SR: As an idea, pornography seems to slide two ways: toward community and toward alienation. It's an experience of sublimity through reading; you're "reading" or gazing at these images to reach orgasm and momentarily lose yourself. It's alienating in the sense that one usually does it alone, but it participates in a common act within the larger community, and the images are available to everyone, so there's something leveling about it. In your story "Hidden in the Open" in *Denny Smith*, you're trying to produce sperm for a baby: You're isolated in a clinic room but people are walking by, interrupting your train of thought or adding to it or some of both.

RG: Yeah, with even more people strolling around in my mind—even Judy Grahn is in there with me.

SR: And the reason that you're doing it is to create life and participate in a family.

RG: In that story I wanted to take a solitary sex act and show how layered such a simple act could be—after all, as Earl Jackson pointed out, sex is just an involuntary muscle spasm; all the rest is cultural elaboration. I wanted to demonstrate that there is nothing simple about any kind of sex; that each gesture carries a tremendous amount of history, and gets complicated in more ways than we have words for. That story should have continued for a thousand pages.

Also, the jack-off stories tie into an overall theme in my work of trying to bring together feeling and event. I am thinking of the story "Three from Thirteen" in *Denny Smith*, where an act of masturbation means that I can no longer avoid knowing that I am attracted to men, that I am gay. In that act I had to acknowledge a strange future—a future that was in no way a part of my plan. Or, say, at the end of *Jack the Modernist* there is a moment when all sorts of knotty plot twists get unraveled suddenly and I know I've lost Jack—that moment is happy, because I suddenly understand that the alienation I was feeling was not a mistake.

SR: That's similar to your title story in *Denny Smith,* where you're being dumped. Along with the feeling of total rejection, there's a hysterical ecstasy, because you're being released into what you already in a sense knew, but couldn't admit: that the relationship had gone flat.

RG: Right. I've recently come to realize that from the very beginning I've worked on this problem: Feelings and events are not stitched together very well. My stories often attempt to find a relation or acknowledge the distance between them. Sometimes I do it by borrowing a plot. My own story does not seem to match my feelings so I borrow a plot that is commensurate with my feelings. "Night Flight" in *Elements of a Coffee Service*, for example, or *Margery Kempe.*

SR: Margery seems to pick up where Bob in *Jack the Modernist* left off, in terms of her ability to be in touch with her intense desires. She's not any less miserable than Bob is at the end of *Jack the Modernist*, but she has a lot more access to her feelings than he did for much of that first novel. There is something very lovable about her, a loveableness due perhaps not only to the way she wears her heart on her sleeve, but to the fact that even as we're moved by her vulnerability, we never forget that she's a creation. In part she's her own creation: She modeled her autobiography (which you draw from) on the stories of other medieval women. And in part she's your creation. This awareness that she is a creation somehow heightens our awareness of her fragility.

RG: Of course, we are all fictions, and that should make us feel tenderness for each other rather than contempt. Her vulnerability is also based on the fact that she couldn't really know what her experience meant. She was medieval in her goals but middle-class in her ways and means. That mix-up of scales of interpretation could not be known by her, but they can by us. And then we can wonder about our failure to understand our own experience.

SR: She seems to carry the weight of Bob's emotional life.

RG: People have often asked me, Why isn't there more Bob? There wouldn't have been a reason for Margery to exist in the book if there had been more Bob. I could only come in as a frame.

SR: You're the metatext in that book.

RG: Yes, I suppose. I don't seem to use that term any longer, though surely I have assimilated the idea in my writing. Now perhaps I'd say a continual reframing. I wanted to reveal the way I was projecting my life onto Margery and make that part of the book. When Jesus says, "I'm horny," a reader should get that I am crudely transferring events in my life to Margery's life, and should follow that assumption into less obvious areas of her story.[9]

SR: We could also say that she is the metatext—or, if you prefer, a continual reframing—for you. The use of this reframing device in *Margery Kempe* feels much more seamless and less deliberately dazzling than in *Jack the Modernist.* It comes in as humor, often, as in the passage where you describe an angel who looks like he's a maitre d' uncorking a bottle of fine wine. By comically slamming together these two radically different worlds in one image, you create a situation where each sheds light on the other.

RG: That image is from a painting by Manet. Jesus is lying down; you see him foreshortened, and there is a ministering angel on either side. And the scene itself is based on a photograph by Larry Clark from his book *Tulsa.*[10] It shows a pair of naked teenagers. The girl is shooting up and the boy is getting a hard-on, not from watching her, but from watching the needle. I wanted Jesus to have that excitement about Margery's tears; they are his drug.

SR: How deliberate is your use of humor in your fiction? It seems to be something you think about; I remember a passage in your story "Violence" in *Elements of a Coffee Service* where you write about your dad's deliberated method of telling jokes, which are really stories.

RG: Oh yes, I absorbed humor at home, from my dad and his jokes, and through that Jewish humor to the dark farce of Central European writers, and from Proust (because his book is a comedy, isn't it?), from Burroughs, from Frank O'Hara. I was reading transcripts of Lenny Bruce when I was beginning to write stories—wonderfully lyrical in their condensation. There's so much to say about humor—where could we stop? Humor adjusts and alters the relation to audience. It can make a place for the unacceptable; it can operate critically; it can indicate community tenets, as gossip does. If a joke is founded in the realm of the incommensurate, then too many jokes can make us feel the incommensurate without the solace of reconciliation.

I also believe in tears. I cry in my books; there's always a chapter on tears. That was one attraction to Margery, she's always crying. She allows me to weep in so many ways—thank you, Jesus!

SR: Before I get too weepy, I'd like to loop back into our discussion of community, and ask about your impressions of the Bay Area writing community in particular. In your essay "Long Note on New Narrative," you write about coming of age as a writer and making all these discoveries in the context of a Bay Area writing scene. You describe how you encountered some elements of the scene that were compatible with your own investigations, and other elements that you needed to reject. To what extent do you think there is something called a Bay Area writing community?

RG: A community is basically just an environment where people share gestures. It's pretty basic; it's where meaning happens and where you can recognize yourself. Different communities engage me at different levels. The "campus community," as San Francisco State calls itself, does not equal the writing community for me (not enough sublimity, plenty of abjection), though perhaps for some it's the whole of life.

SR: So your notion of community is that it's temporal and provisional. It can occur anywhere under lots of different circumstances; it might take place when you're buying a soda in a 7-11 in Milwaukee.

RG: That's right. After all, it's not as though I ever recognized myself in all parts of the gay community, and now, like the rest of the culture, it has dumbed down and become mainstream and uh, that's not me. [*laughter*] Or it is more than I care to admit. A gay publication like *Fag Rag* in the early seventies might have a scholarly article along with some bad art and some lovely Joe Brainard drawings and some bad poetry along with some poems by Frank O'Hara. I confess I am nostalgic for the amateur position which characterizes the beginning of anything really new. Like modernism itself—a bunch of amateurs—Isadora, Pound—carrying on while the professionals were minding the store. In the early seventies, anything that had to do with being gay was relevant subject matter. Gay intellectual life didn't take place primarily at universities; it didn't take place at universities at all. Now, gay life is fragmented like everything else, for good and ill. Intellectual life is professionalized and comes, like all professions, with its permitting and excluding vocabularies.

SR: In your experience, class divisions were crossed more readily in the gay community?

RG: I entered adulthood with no real expectations of the kind of life I would lead. Being gay but not out, being a writer but divorced from myself, seemed to cancel any of the futures prepared for me without replacing them with another plan. There was not a place for me in the world. I became very poor.

Later, I crossed boundaries readily, yes, in my literary and sexual bohemianisms. In fact, my real life seemed to begin when I entered a sexual minority. Maybe coming-out stories are just a different version of being "born again." There was a metaphor of constructing a new family in the gay community, and then AIDS made that a necessity. All that can be said with certainty is that our horizon of pleasure was generally wider than most other groups enjoyed, that before AIDS we seemed to be the caretakers of the nation's libido. We have enough "issues" to mount a vast alternate parade of Gay Shame. Alcoholism, drug abuse, racism . . . I remember picketing gay clubs that turned away my lover, Ed Aulerich-Sugai, because he was Japanese. I could picket a bar, but it took some time for me to understand how class and race were operating in my own little union with my working-class Asian-American lover—the difference in the way we used language, for example. I used it to satisfy an unconscious, relentless goal orientation—learn, learn, learn, defend an idea, generate an opinion, solve a problem. Even politeness meant asking questions. Ed used it more as a kind of verbal caressing, to make agreeable contact, keep the moment alive, while the content was not so important.

Now I think my life also may have started when my relatives were kicked out of Spain in 1493, or when some great-great grandfather left a muddy village in the Transylvanian Alps to find a job in an unknown city. I have his red beard, his love of learning, his sense of humor, his temper. Boy, would he be mad at me—I haven't even gone to temple to say Kaddish for my dead father. What can I do to appease that ghost? Instead, I have made it restless by writing stories about my father that are untrue and unfair.

But back to your question about my current sense of community: I know I live in a writing community because I love and hate its members and how they act and what they write and do and say. And sometimes the writing community says hello to me.

While I see this heated little Bay Area writing scene as my community, or one of them, I rarely feel the pitch of urgency to recognize myself in it as I did when I was younger. As my generation ages, our schools break down and individuals cobble together lives with friends they've culled from different places. One thing I liked about the flaky West Coast was that an aesthetic was experienced as a kind of religion, a belief system. That created a sort of "city on a hill" for each aesthetic program. In New York, I'd go to a dinner party and find a gathering of people at the same stage of professional life with a variety of aesthetic positions, whereas in San Francisco, I'd go to a dinner party and there would be one aesthetic position, perhaps distributed across the mediums. The seventies and eighties were a time in the Bay Area when writers were defining themselves against each other, certainly. There was anger, vituperation. I recall I spoke with a few others on a panel to a full house at Intersection. The subject was "Who Speaks for Us"—simply, who gets to talk! That issue came out of the talk series the Language poets were running at 80 Langton. In fact, the essay "Caricature" that you cited was part of that series. I was the first non-Language poet to speak in it—when?—in 1983. To give you a taste of the times: After my talk we went to the Hotel Utah. One poet was so furious that I had compared John Cage to Ozzie Nelson that he was red in the face and pointing at my chest with his finger—I was afraid he was going to take a punch at me! No one seemed upset that I compared Frank O'Hara to Lucille Ball. I could name this poet but instead I will add this to the story. I was attracted to his passion and his work. I felt a kinship with him, and I still do.

I suppose the goal I set for Small Press Traffic was to get these different writing scenes to speak to each other, since I somehow contained many of their positions. Our Left/Write conference in 1981 was emblematic of that effort. We brought together writers who were famous in their own scene and hardly known beyond it—like Judy Grahn and Ron Silliman speaking on the same panel. Of course in this way I helped to end the interesting development of writing scenes working in relative isolation—getting back to our earlier theme: How was Language poetry a Guatemalan village?

SR: Do you think the lines have crossed more in recent years?

RG: Oh yes, I know they have. The scene is a lot softer now, and more porous. That can partly be explained by the Language poetry diaspora: Bob Perelman, Tom Mandel, Barrett Watten, Ron Silliman—what would the local scene be like if they were still here? In any case, there is already a local tradition of innovation that's a couple of generations old, the way generations work now. There's less to fight against and less to measure oneself against. What is innovative writing that comes out of a tradition; whose practice is taught at universities; that does not automatically take an embattled stance?

SR: I think today one does have more ability to roam across boundaries than when you were coming of age, and that this greater freedom of movement can enrich the writing.

RG: That is a great thing that's been gained: Writers include narrative and fragmentation in a single work. Also, and related to that, many more women and people of color are prominent in this community of innovative writers. The experience of gender, race, class, and sexuality seems to have jumped over the barrier between content and form.

In a moment of glory, Language poets developed a poetics based on the isolation of a word from the world and the observation that meaning is generated by placing one word next to another, so words stand in dazzled isolation. As writing projects in the seventies became more conceptual, they tended to swallow their progeny. You could say that the battle was won, but the victory is different from what might have been imagined. Now, younger poets backtrack in order to recover some territory. Representation may be a lie, but that does not make it less a part of life, or less interesting, especially as it intersects with emotion. It can no longer be simple: us against them, narrative against "non-narrative." Or even, if you like, commodified against non-commodified. And certainly not stances of political purity against the world. With the pressure off, the use of fragmentation is no longer heroic, but merely one end of a spectrum, many parts of which may be used to suit the needs of a particular work. This ease characterizes the writing of younger poets. It's ambivalent writing—both theory-based and disbelieving in systems. There's more contingency inside the poem, more hurt, more existence outside the poem, a dreamy, bemused intellection that can become a kind of vertigo, a kind of nausea about creation itself, and an anxiety—played out formally—about how words attach to each other and to the world. There's more awareness of self as performance, performative syntax, and there's the assumption that a tiny fragment can be a narrative.

I suppose my contributions to this scene are the ideas around New Narrative writing—especially mixing narrative modes—and my encouraging a zillion generations of students to enlarge their reading and writing practices. I never wanted power outside my own writing—I fled from it when it came my way. When New Narrative was gaining momentum, and we saw people imitating us, we abandoned the project in self-horror. Now our Narrativity website seems more like making a certain kind of information available.

SR: I would think that over the years, your affinity group would start to be more national and international.

RG: You know, I have a funny career. On one hand, I've never published a book with a trade press—they don't want me. But on the other hand, my biggest fiction publications have been in gay mainstream anthologies, most of whose readers are not interested in experimental writing. But yes, more and more I have the pleasure of friendship with writers and academics from all over, even writers whose work is part of my psychic life, like Juan Goytisolo in Marrakech and Marcel Cohen in Paris. And the Narrativity site has given me a few new friendships. And I have the pleasure of getting to know young writers who are coming into the scene and whose work I've been reading. Am I an avuncular presence? You tell me.

SR: No, I don't think of you as an uncle. But you do write a lot about aging. Your interest in the process of aging ties back into the ideas in your essay "Truth's Mirror Is No Mirror," which discusses the Lacanian mirror stage at six months of age. Previous to the experience with the mirror, the baby is an undifferentiated body. Then it sees itself in the mirror, and that's the birth of the self, of the image.

RG: Right, it's outside of you.

SR: In the essay you go on to say that one way we re-experience the undifferentiated pre-mirror stage is to be aware of our mortality.

RG: The body as matter.

SR: The determination to investigate death as a way to be yanked back into the reality of the body is an essential through line in your writing, so it makes sense that you would track the process of aging. But I would think too that there must be some anxiety about it, especially given the focus in gay male culture on physique. So I appreciate that in spite of that anxiety, you choose to face this issue.

RG: Thank you. I've been no slouch at charting my anxieties. I even do a column on aging in the *Bay Area Reporter* because there's so little space devoted to midlife in the gay media. I wrote my own piece and then wheedled and strong-armed friends into writing pieces for me. A few said, "No, no, I'm not middle-aged," and they would be, you know, pushing sixty! I've always been my age, never precocious, a little slow in fact. Now at 55, dying is the only thing left for me to do if I want to be ahead of schedule.

BARBARA GUEST

Clearing the Ordinary from the Room

Sarah Rosenthal: One of the themes that stood out for me in your book of essays, *Forces of Imagination,* was the notion of a ghostly presence in poetry. You write about not putting everything in the poem, not being concerned only with subject matter, because there are ghosts behind the poem, and they need to remain ghosts to add a kind of excitement. In your essay "Wounded Joy," you write, "Do you ever notice as you write that no matter what there is on the written page, something appears to be in back of everything that is said, a little ghost. I judge that this ghost is there to remind us there is always more, an elsewhere, a hiddenness, a secondary form of speech, an eye blink. Not on the print before us. And yet the secret is that this secondary form of writing is what backs up the primary one. It is the obscure essence that lies within the poem, that is not necessary to put into language, but that the poem must hint at, must say, 'This is not all I can tell you. There is something more I do not say.' Leave this little echo to haunt the poem. Do not give it form, but let it assume its own ghostlike shape. It has the shape of your own soul as you write."[1] In your later books, this concept is manifested more visually, where the language is more sparse and there's more white space on the page where the ghosts can hide. Earlier it was present too, but your early poems often had more words in them.

Barbara Guest: Yes, I think that the words began to fall away.

SR: Do you identify with that director in *The Confetti Trees*? "No WORDS."[2]

BG: I hadn't thought of that! Yes! And there is also the cutter—the film cutter. That's the most important of all the roles in the film industry.

SR: *The Confetti Trees* has a lot of words.

BG: It has too many words.

SR: The prose form makes it deceptively simple to read. I glide along, like watching a movie. It could be a difficult, contemporary movie, but I have the illusion of it going down easy. Then I get to the end of a poem and realize that so much has transpired, I have to go back and read it again. *Miniatures* has some prosey ones that work in a similar way; "Photographs," for example.

BG: Yes, and "Coal" is prose. I think "Coal" is my favorite in the first section of that book.

SR: "Coal" makes huge leaps from sentence to sentence, constantly shifting the focus: from nature, to house, to memory, to fantasy, to almost a spiritual vision. Yet like the poems in *The Confetti Trees*, its surface appears simple and storylike.

BG: I'll tell you something about *Miniatures*. That book cost me a great deal of pain. I had a sort of nervous breakdown as I was writing it. I felt I couldn't finish it. And it was [my daughter] Hadley who helped me. She said, These are very good poems. I had no belief in them. None at all.

SR: Is that unusual for you?

BG: Yes. You have to have belief in what you write. I'd lost it all. Now, I'm terribly amused by that woman who goes down the street in the poem "Petticoat." I love that poem! It's so funny. But you see, I didn't see any humor in it when I was first writing it. Hadley was wonderful about that. She gave me faith.

SR: Do you think that because you've published so many books, it's hard to follow your own act sometimes?

BG: No, I wish I could say that! I think what bothered me in writing *Miniatures* was I felt I couldn't make it move. It was just coming out as stories. I wrote that book while reading a biography of Chekhov, which I quote in the front: "I, too, am an Ardent Defender of Miniature Pieces."[3] You'd think with him to hang onto I'd have been in better shape. The story of Chekhov's demise is typically European. He was extremely ill. He went with his wife to Germany. A doctor came to see him, and said, You're really sick; I can't offer you much hope. One day later on, Chekhov knew that something was going drastically wrong, and that he was probably going to die. He called the doctor, and the doctor came, and looked at him, and said, "Have some champagne." What a way to introduce the idea of death.

SR: I'd like to ask you about white space as it ties into the theme of the ghostly other. In some of your later work, the white space adds to that sense of the unsaid. I'm thinking for example of the minimalism of "Blurred Edge" in *Miniatures*. Interestingly, that poem is placed right after "Pathos." In "Pathos," the whole poem is infused with a female persona who is one and many: the girl skater, the woman poet, and perhaps the poem itself. She reminded me of the comparison you make between the poet and the dancer or acrobat in your essay "Forces of Imagination"—you talk about how both the poet and these movement artists take risks.[4] In "Pathos," we are constantly aware of this skater—her motions and emotions. In contrast, "Blurred Edge" is much more quiet. One of its lines reads, "Candor, // where candor approaches the cube,"[5] and that's a good description of this poem, which seems to be a work of subtraction. Instead of directing the attention, as "Pathos" does, "Blurred Edge" kind of opens a door and then says, "Walk through it. How do you look through this space? How do you assemble what you find here? Where does your eye travel?"

BG: That's true. "Pathos" is a story. "Blurred Edge" is an abstraction.

SR: "[B]are bones of the iron seat."[6] Here again, the poem seems to be pointing to its own minimalism.

BG: That's from the painting I was writing about. "Blurred Edge" came about because I was writing a review of a painting by the artist Leatrice Rose, who is a niece of Clement Greenberg. As I was working on the review, I began to see her painting not as painting but as words. The painter had given the painting her own words. This doesn't make rational sense. I found that what I was doing in my review was copying the shape of [what I was seeing as] her words. So I began to write about the shape of the words. It was hard for me to find the right words to go with the shape of her words. This poem didn't have a voice for a long time. It was a curious experience, a strange transformation—I don't want to do it again. That was what became "Blurred Edge." I have her painting here on my wall.

SR: We're looking at an interior.

BG: Yes, it's her interior. She lives on the water, in New York. This is her kitchen. You see, you can feel that iron seat. It's her dumb little kitchen, but it's a good painting.

SR: It's interesting how the figuration emerges out of the white undefined space around the edges.

BG: Yes. She doesn't always do what you expect her to do.

SR: That blue rectangle—

BG: It's a blue shade.

SR: It seems to push out of being a shade into being an abstract blue rectangle.

BG: Yes. That's "Blurred Edge." The shape of the painting inspired the poem.

SR: Like "Blurred Edge," *Rocks on a Platter* is filled with white space. And in that book, ghostliness becomes an articulated theme. For example, you write, "In a room // 'not alone' // enters // midday // appears // massive."[7] Syntactically there are a lot of ways to work with that, but one reading is a sense of the deep solitude of creative practice, and within that, a conversation with something that is beyond one. That otherliness seems personified in the "he" on page 27: "[H]e told me // he is a king himself entering life on a whim, // *language* attached, gerunds. // In the loneliest hours to share a flamboyance, // an attraction to distance and disappearance." I don't want to lock this down in a simplistic way, but I felt that this presence, who had come into the room as a kind of visitation, was now talking with the artist. This is loneliness, and yet it is conversation, a sharing. On page 28 you write, "Cannot dream except in 'two's' or be alone, is hollowed out." So there's the solitude of the creative act but also a need for connective dyads. Perhaps at times the other is not a human being at all; it could be imagination itself.

BG: There is the ghostly other in this poem, as you say. There's no question about it.

SR: The word "phantom" also appears, followed by two phantoms: Schoenberg, evoked by the twelve tones, and Helen in Egypt.[8] I think not only of the figure of Helen herself, but of all those years you spent writing your biography of H.D., immersed in a kind of conversation with a ghost.

BG: Very much so.

SR: In the final section of *Rocks on a Platter*, that conversation with something or somebody beyond gets taken to a more spiritual level, where the other becomes a figure no longer human. Ultimately it's a dolphin that slides into view.

BG: I need that dolphin. I'm very fond of him. He comes into other work, and is not kept. Yeats wrote about the dolphin also.

SR: There's such joy and nobility in this godlike dolphin. "*Grandeur* oversteps, / artificial and strange." Earlier in the book there were "loaves and fishes" and "transubstantiation"—the sense of transformation but with an elevated, miraculous quality.[9]

BG: That's true. And I think that that is so necessary to a poem. But not every poem is strong enough to take it. Some poems back away from it.

SR: The poems in the first section of *Miniatures* didn't have grandeur; they were after a different aesthetic. But there too I noticed a lot of words like "heaven" and "lift" and "goddess."[10] So I got a similar feeling of a glorious, joyous, winged elevation. Did you feel that?

BG: Yes. I felt that throughout the poems. That's a very important word, "elevation." I'm going to think about that more. Take it along in my portmanteau.

SR: I know you said *Miniatures* took quite a toll on you. What was your subjective experience of writing *Rocks on a Platter*?

BG: Oh, I loved it. It's so seldom that one has a vehicle that one can ride like that.

SR: The vehicle being the poetics essay that evolved into a poem enacting your poetics?

BG: Yes.

SR: Turning to *The Red Gaze,* was there anything in particular that instigated this volume?

BG: The Museum of Modern Art asked me to write a poem about De Chirico's painting *Nostalgia of the Infinite*. For the first time, I wrote a Surrealist poem. And then I found I couldn't stop. So I just kept on going.

SR: Once again, the accidental played a key role in your creative process.

BG: I think that's the case with many poets. The accidental plays a part. You have to expose the poem.

SR: One of the striking features about Surrealism as a historical movement is that it was so political, similar to the way in which Abstract Expressionism is thought of as having a political dimension: anger at the mainstream culture's repression of imagination. The European Surrealists were worried about fascism and the devastation of war. And according to David Lehman's book *The Last of the Avant-Garde*, the New York School was responding to the repressive society of the McCarthy era.

BG: Well, we lived through that. Of course it was awful. But it didn't affect my writing. I discovered Surrealism very late. I was resistant to using it, because the French believe they own it, and to a degree that is true. But when I came across certain passages in De Chirico's writing, I was just thrilled. It was a fairy-tale land. But I deliberately did not read the Surrealist literature or study the history of the movement, because I wanted to be sure to have my own Surrealism.

SR: Tell me about the title.

BG: The red gaze is that strange red that arrives with dawn on a fair day. It's beautiful.

SR: How do you see narrative in this work? For me, narrative was always present but always porous—always being acknowledged but always being let go.

BG: Well, there is narrative, certainly—more than usual. I traveled in it.

SR: Did you revise much?

BG: I got picky. I'd pick out a word or something that I'd change. I changed things constantly.

SR: Is that a usual pattern for you?

BG: No. But I loved the experimental feeling that continued. There's nothing like it.

SR: That's what the work is about in some sense: a constant reaching for the new and the unknown. That was also the focus of Hans Hoffman's life work, and Hoffman has a strong presence in this book. It's what the Adorno quote you included is about ("In each genuine art work something appears that did not exist before"),[11] and it's what the Surrealists embraced. Is that part of what you mean by Surrealist—this radical imagination inhabiting unknown vistas? The absolute freedom of the imagination?

BG: That's a very good way of putting it. Because in writing these poems, I was released. And then I would get caught. And then I had to work for my release.

SR: Nietzsche makes an appearance early, in the first poem, "Nostalgia." I think of him as pointing to the artist as the ultimate version of the human being; the one most committed to individual expression and creation.

BG: What you're saying is true.

SR: There are several appearances by royalty and nobles in the volume. "Who is protecting us, / we who were noticed by the Emperor / cruising in his vessel?" "Lo, Royalty had placed a hand on your head. // Now nobles twist rings in corridors, / worried about painting's future."[12] There are also references to old Europe and the great cities of Italy. I imagine you could relate to the past as a treasured lineage of art and culture, but also see it as a potential repressor of the new.

BG: I guess I include those references because since childhood I've been fond of the "olden times." Tennyson often introduces "olden times."

SR: So there's a childlike delight in thinking about the past, as it's filtered through literature, perhaps? A "once upon a time"?

BG: Yes, exactly. I'm interested in that "once upon a time," and in magic. I think that I was under a spell when I wrote these poems. Surrealism has a certain effect.

SR: It's great to hear that you were under a spell, because I felt the same way reading them. I felt I was in a place of vision—

BG: Up on the mountain.

SR: Yes. There's so much about climbing, and mountains. "[W]e are climbing. The urge enters to see more." "[O]ur imaginary route, / it leads through the mountain." "Pierrot of the mountain. / In the Alps of your being there is trust." "Maple red now splashes the mountain."[13]

BG: I was thinking of a trip I made to the Alps. We took a car up to the top, which is a marvelous thing to do, and then we rode down and took a train into Venice.

SR: There are also a lot of references to stairs: "I saw the stair mount upward and could not stop / its climb until the heavens opened blinking."[14] This seems like an impulse toward expansion, toward the new, and it carried a majestic feeling. That ties into the images of navigators going off into distant lands, which seem to represent the place of imagination. Do you feel that?

BG: Yes.

SR: And it gets tied into magic. You speak of the dreamer at one point: "On his feet are shoes of magic, they will carry him hither and yon. / He has dipped his pen into magic ink and cleared / the ordinary from the room."[15] So it's all tied together there. Magic, the new, travel, writing—it's all one thing.

BG: Yes, absolutely.

SR: "Distribute these newly sought wings of artifice, / for each raid on the moon."[16]

BG: Well, you know, I see it as, down here [reaches down from chair toward floor] is the water, and then we're up in the mountain. That was how I saw it when I first started writing, and I kept to that. I always get to the mountain, somehow or other. And then there's a Western mountain, in the poem called "The Trickster," which is about the figure of Coyote in Navajo culture. We were watching a film called *Coyote Waits* on PBS, based on a story by the mystery writer Tony

Hillerman. And I have been to New Mexico to visit my friend Mei-mei Berssenbrugge. But that Western mountain was the only one in the book that isn't associated with the East Coast and Europe.

SR: Do you have any associations to the references to narrowness and small spaces in the book?

BG: The small spaces originally were about stairs. There are always stairs in towers. I see all the people in the poems living in these towers, like the De Chirico tower in the first poem.

SR: A lot of these poems mention night and dawn. For me, dawn evoked continuity—the cyclical aspect of days passing—but also the constant new. And dawn is also a time when one is still connected to the visions and unreality of night. Is that how you feel?

BG: No, day and night were the same for me. It was just a continuity. But it was pleasure.

SR: Do you rise at dawn?

BG: No, but I was writing fairly early, by eight-thirty or so. And then I'd write at night, around ten or eleven.

SR: I noticed a number of references to celebration and humor. Pierrot the clown makes an appearance.

BG: Well . . . he's a sad figure.

SR: Here's the word "jocular."[17]

BG: I wanted to hear that word, "jocular." Like the word "jeopardy." In politics you keep reading that word these days. These damn politicians keep saying things like "placed in jeopardy." It's the same thing with the word "marionettes" in the poem "The Gold Tap."[18] I just heard the word, "marionette."

SR: So a lot of times words come into your poems because they're in the air; they're in your ear. It's not that you are dying to talk about jeopardy; it's that you want to say and hear that word.

BG: Yes.

SR: I could pick any poem in this volume and talk about the sounds. For example, "The Trickster" is a short poem, but it's packed with strong sounds: system/seismology/sensibility/visibility; monitors/movement/mountain/mouth/myth. In "Modernism," there's room/chime/modernism/poem; yon/pen/spoon; magic/midnight/modernism/modifies; cloth/magic/carry/ink/coffee/cup.[19] The sounds feel very woven—not hitting me over the head, but carrying me. Do they carry you in the writing?

BG: Oh, yes.

SR: Have they always?

BG: I either want to do it or I don't. But there's always sound; I mean, that's what a poet is—a sound carrier.

SR: Do you put sound above image or do you hold them equally?

BG: I think I hear it first.

SR: There are several mentions in the book of learning new languages: "speaking in other tongues to the imagined room"; "Green numbers, a patois we were learning to speak"; "strangers / who were learning the new tongue."[20]

BG: Yes, and there are references to changing the language.

SR: Yes, "To rearrange rhyme, / while you gather its energy."[21] That seemed to be about knowing the tools of poetry but changing poetry.

Can we take a look at the section called "Hans Hoffman"? Hoffman was deeply influenced by some of the Surrealists.

BG: I suppose he was. Everybody was. I included that section for movement, really. I wasn't going to do it in the beginning, but I feel that it fills in certain things. It gives body to the text. And I wanted it to be a fairly long text. I first learned about Hofmann when his studio caught fire. I was living on Eighth Street, which was a major artery. And one night his studio across the street burned down. I'll never forget that fire. All the artists studied with him; he was a really great teacher. He taught here, too, in Berkeley.

SR: I read some statements by Hoffman in which he said a number of things that crossed over with your work in general and with this book in particular. He said, "[W]hat my paintings say is poetry. I consider this poetry expressed in color." He was trying to interact with color in a dynamic way; color had as much agency as he did. Also, he talked about rhythm all the time; he said that different colors have different rhythms. And he spoke very eloquently about wanting to keep embracing the new.[22] In your poem "Freed Color" in *The Red Gaze* you write, "They hasten to make use of freed color / who bends to no one, / who dwells in a tent like rhythm / continuously rolled."[23] You mention rhythm explicitly in this book, and you bring in color quite a bit, especially in the Hofmann section. And like the title poem in your book *The Confetti Trees*, colors in this section often run the show. They have a life of their own.

BG: Oh yes, they're supposed to. And it's partly because I was thinking of Hofmann.

SR: In the poem "Hans Hoffman," is the part about Hoffman sitting on the park bench true?

BG: Yes. I lived right next to a park. At the end of the day he and his wife would come out and sit on the bench. I wasn't trailing him or anything; he was just there.

SR: Do you know what your next book will be?

BG: No. I'm recovering from writing *The Red Gaze*. I need to come out of its magic. But you know how it is; any book that you're dedicated to, gives to you, and it also takes.

SR: So you're still trying to come out of the thrall.

BG: That's a nice medieval word. I have to write that down.

SR: Is there anything you would love to see done in poetry?

BG: I can't tell you that. I just have my own struggle; you have yours. Each generation has a necessity that it has to work out for itself. And the intelligence will only help you so far in that task, and then you have to reside in your imagination.

SR: My last question is about your experience of the Bay Area writing community. How long have you been back here?

BG: Ten working years.

SR: What is it like to be here? Do you feel connected in any way to something that you think of as a Bay Area experimental writing community?

BG: I had hoped I would feel more connected to the Bay Area.

SR: Are you finding that people are busy with their own poetry careers?

BG: They are. But I do see many people. And I'm doing a number of readings. I've written very well here.

SR: That's a blessing.

BG: It is a blessing. And my relationship to living here is still evolving.

BRENDA HILLMAN

Our Very Greatest Human Thing Is Wild

Sarah Rosenthal: I'd like to focus on *Cascadia*, starting at the end, with the series of poems about the California missions. There are poems like this throughout *Cascadia* which form a spine for the book; they are more airy than the other poems.

Brenda Hillman: Spare.

SR: Yes, spare. In your earlier work, especially *Loose Sugar*, there are tiny fragments that seem to come from an interior, mystical place. Here, in the mission poems, those moments become the entire poem. They are very quiet and prayerlike to the point where, for me, thought begins to drop away. They feel joyful, even though there are words like *hurt*, *pain*, *danger*, and *confusion* laced through them. There are lines here and there that reinforce that seeming paradox: "A blade of happiness cuts like free verse // A breath makes of each hurt a new religion"; "a poet / burst with happiness"; "How did this existence deepen / and get lighter, disaster dreams confused // with hope like those of friars / carrying a saint's bed higher because / the mission's burning."[1] It is so urgent, and yet there is joy, too—and an effort to acknowledge that strange collision.

BH: Thank you for starting with those because I think they are the hardest poems in the book. They seem to me to be about the mission/

mission as a difficulty. The friars had a "mission" to go about carrying the word in an intense sort of way, which produced both beauty and terror. And our feelings about what they did are just as mixed as our feelings—as my feelings—about the mission of the artist.

Those poems were written during a difficult period in my life, and I decided I would just go around California and visit all twenty-two missions and look at the patterns on the walls. What you said about thought dropping away is accurate to the process as well; I started each poem by just sitting in a mission and meditating on the idea of pattern itself, beyond sense. The beauty of those wall-patterns had enchanted me from the first time I'd seen the missions, which was in the midseventies. In looking at the patterns on the mission walls, I felt that the people who had painted them were doing as much "God's work," you know, in big quotes—or the earth's work, or the mind's work, or all those slashed together—as the people who did the actual religious art; they were simply doing a more abstract version of keeping the making-spirit going. There is a particular beauty about the regularity of the way that an artist works in relation to a day. If we are making art, we somehow keep on in a daily, drastic and joyful continuing. How do you continue? That's your job: You get up in the morning, you let some energy get through you somehow, and you put the paint on the wall. That's how it gets there.

You are right to connect the mission poems to the fragment stuff in *Loose Sugar*. They're also connected to the sequence called "Twelve Dawns" at the beginning of *Bright Existence*, particularly the one called "The Servant," which says, "—So you whispered to the soul Rise up! / but the soul was not ready. // —Get up! It's our turn! But that part of the soul / stayed still. So you checked the list // of those who existed."[2] There's a continuation between the idea of soul, and abstraction and geometry, and being at work in the daily, and color—and more specifically, doodling in church and the materiality of language.

When I was visiting the missions and sitting there in these little niches, one of the things I thought a lot was, church can be so boring if you don't expand on the predictable. I had to go to church a lot when I was a kid. You know, you sit there and you just, uurrr . . . so I would doodle a lot as a child. And not well. Not good doodles, just really blunt, stupid doodles because I can't draw.

SR: I know from *Loose Sugar* and from some of your interviews that you were raised in a very rigorous Baptist form. I got the feeling that the poems were in part enacting the childlike experience of being in church, aware that you're supposed to be praying but distracted by others' presence.

BH: I wanted to open my eyes to look at the adults and see if their eyes were open. But I couldn't because I was afraid. So I peeked a tiny bit. Prayer, like poetry, is best when the singular goes toward the collective.

SR: Did you have any instinct of praying when you were a child? Were you spiritual, or was it just sort of forced on you?

BH: Oh, it was a complete mess. So I made up my own little church, in books and in the desert dirt. It's a fairly American, Emersonian notion of spirit in nature and word.

SR: The light is within.

BH: Yes, it's pure.

SR: It ties in so well with your interest in Gnosticism.

BH: Baptists are Gnostics, basically. They are supposed to follow a little antinomian thread. They espouse the privacy of one's relationship to the constructed universe, which isn't controlled by authority, but which is heavily populated. That really appealed to me. I also love the business of visitations. If it had been less morally rigid, it wouldn't have been so onerous. What appealed to me was the investigation into the collective body of received images.

SR: I wanted to look with you at the book's title poem. In "Cascadia," there are faint words sprinkled down the left-hand column: notational details about the road trip to the missions, including, for example, the names of all the tacky hotels you stayed at. I loved "pre-Naugahyde chair."[3]

BH: Do you know the kind? It was on its way to being Naugahyde, as if maybe they hadn't invented Naugahyde yet.

SR: And then there is "post-Naugahyde truth" and finally we get to "true Naugahyde."[4]

BH: I figured we better sort of map out a Naugahyde fantasy . . .

SR: The faint lettering of these marginal notes seems like a geologic gesture: The left-hand part is the part that is submerged, in the way that at one point much of California lay beneath the ocean. There is also a sense of geologic slippage to me in the way that the poem's lines bring in so many different kinds of matter, with sometimes jarring and always evocative interrelationships between them. It is a complex, rigorous poem, which at the same time has a lot of freedom and motion and slippage built into it, and the images and ideas are layered and re-layered, in lines that end up reminding me of rock strata. I was taken by the lines "And what of the unknown where / the inexhaustible plays against form." That play in the meaning of the enjambed "where," between destination/place/noun in the first line, and unknown entity/point of passage/preposition in the second line, very much enacts the idea of the inexhaustible playing against form. In fact, the lines remind me of the Blanchot quote you use as an epigraph, which talks about "the force of the undetermined and . . . the pure violence of being from which nothing can be made."[5] The quote goes on to say that the artist's job is to provide form and boundary in some way, but without tamping down this original chaotic energy.

BH: It's a question that is so upsetting right now. I was talking to Kathleen Fraser a while ago about the opening up of form in the last twenty years, almost to the point of destroying the boundaries of the poem. It is the artist's job to make form. Not even to make it, but to allow it. Allow form. And all artists have a different relationship to it, and a different philosophy of it. I worked on this poem for eight months; it's very carefully structured. But I wanted it to be boundaryless in a way: It's not punctuated, and I wanted it to go back and forth within itself and within time. I thought, "Well, you can have both things: structure and boundarylessness." And in fact I think that when you are trying to open up a territory—in this case I was working with a desire to open the lyric—you have to be greedy, in that you want more than you can do. And you're always bound to fail.

SR: You're trying to let error in, but you don't want error to take over the poem.

BH: I wanted every line to be memorable. Also, I wanted to get at and challenge the idea—not a central idea, because the poem doesn't really have a center—Aristotle's idea of change: that you can tell where something is going because of where it ends up. Final cause, or something like that—which is really kind of an anti-divine notion, and which I love as a philosophy of living. It's sort of like, "I'm not sure where I am going, but I can tell it was my fate to be there because that's where I ended up."

SR: You have been thinking about this problem of form and boundaries in a head-on way for a long time. It's a big theme in *Bright Existence*, in poems like "March Dawn," where you write, "everything has a border doesn't it? the edge where light can not get in // until joy knows the original wound." Or in "Holding On," which I read as about your relationship with your daughter: "wanted to cling to you . . . / . . . so we won't / have to address this problem of the separate you-and-me, / of outer and inner." The word "merge" appears several times in *Cascadia*, as well as the notion of skin as an image of boundary—skin, which strikes me as an extremely tender, vulnerable container and divider. Your work addresses the question of form and boundaries not just in poetry, but in being, in matter. In "Recycling Center" you write, "[we] could tell by the tilt of one / bottle against the next that it's difficult / to be singular, to have identity, to keep / an outline safe in the terrors of space." In "Sorrow of Matter": "suffering invented shape."[6] You seem to be in a long-term process of puzzling out this question, wanting to push the limits of form in the context of a lot of contemporary thinking, while also acknowledging the necessity of form.

BH: Right—the necessity of form and also how it determines so much. I think about the "metaphysical" and scientific aspects of form—for example, just the business of getting shapes made, the idea of a constructed fragment of consciousness in a universe based on change. I also think about the relationship between an individual and the collective. The latter impacts a lot of my thinking about poetry these days. There seem to be a lot of poetry collaborations in the Bay Area right now, and not just collaborations with others but also dialogic forms within single-author texts. So the boundaries have loosened in that sense. That said, I still have the feeling that the task of artists is always going to be a matter of a seeking that is intense and is about a soul at work—"soul" being another term for the seeking of a mind. Boundary issues impact so much of that work: the ideas of shape in a piece of art, your relationship to tradition, how much you can risk, and your relationship to the mysterious and to your future readers—whether you want to call that divine or human, nature or artifice. And language subverts any of our efforts to make boundaries. Our very greatest human thing—which is language to me—musicians would say it's music, but I think it's language—our very greatest human thing is wild. Uncontrollable. It is impossible to put boundaries on your words, even if you make a poem. Each word is a maze. So you are full of desire to make a memorable thing and have the form be very dictated by some way that it has to be. But the poem itself is going to undo that intention. It's almost like you're knitting a sweater and something is unraveling it on the other end. You know what I mean? In this way, it is very strange.

So the idea of boundarylessness sits uncomfortably with the idea of form. I am so conscious of formal technique, and I never want the process and the poem to be so loose that it will just be dropping from a journal accidentally. I would really like the work to go on being extremely inventive in ways that seem process-oriented, but never formless.

SR: The notions of the individual and the singular seem to be part and parcel of the problem of territoriality. Your work asks questions about these concepts without providing closed answers. In "The Shirley

Poem" in *Cascadia* you write, "Nobody works a claim alone. In / 1851 law arrives; government hasn't yet / been invented. Forty feet around a / claim. The need to be unique / has mostly made us miserable." These lines get at the pressure in our society to stake claims on all kinds of territory, both geographic and psychic. I'm led to think about originality, and the yearning of the artist to be original. In that context I thought it was interesting that this book feels much less directly autobiographical than much of your earlier work. There's that mysterious, magical phrase/fragment/poem in *Cascadia*, "(enter: The 'we'—)."[7] I get the sense that the "we" is entering into your work more than ever. I wonder if that is a result of—or perhaps accompanied by—a shift in your ideas about the role of the artist and what you want to accomplish with your art.

BH: Yes, absolutely. The lyric that is also social. Don't you think that this moment in poetry is so interesting because there are so many interesting ideas about subjectivity and the personal? It really does seem less terrifying to write from a form of experience that's not so narrowly construed. There's something about the "I" that is stretchy now; I think of the work of poets like Alice Notley and others. There are so many different ways of being personal. Like Michael Palmer's poem "I Do Not." Who's writing in that poem? It's not a persona, it's not just a "Michael"; it's some statement that goes down a long tunnel of possibility. That much more stretchy sense of "I" really interests me, but one that doesn't lose the depth and feeling tones. Because it's very much the case that at a certain point whatever you think of as the ego project, it's not going to work out. You come to that in art. You can't just stick with that. It doesn't work out in your life either, if you're bound up with ego.

The ego is always worried about its territoriality. In writing *Cascadia*, there was the notion of geology as mind, mind as geology. There aren't that many ideas. I was thinking about this when I wrote "The Shirley Poem." I had been to several conferences and was thinking about how there's no such thing as really inventing something that hasn't been invented, and I was particularly distressed and intrigued by the idea that people need to lay claim to originality. The fact is that a lot of experimental contemporary writing comes out of Baudelaire, Rimbaud, Mallarmé, and of course Stein. The forms in experimental writing come from a lot of different sources. I would never want to say to somebody, You stole my work—unless they actually took my words, which has actually happened on a couple of occasions, without citation to that effect. But people don't own ways of writing, and so it seemed important to kind of get that notion into the world. There are original moments in art, as in everything. But nobody owns those.

SR: But don't you think that is part of the careerism of art? Everybody is their own little company in a way, and that infiltrates our consciousness. It's very hard, I think, for artists to live in a society in which entrepeneurship is so integral and keep that from entering our process and our poetics.

BH: Well, one thing I find particularly distressing for young writers is the idea that everyone has to come up with something. I mean, I think poems come from other poems. They come from lots of different places, and each mind cannot help but contribute. This connects also with the idea of the earth, too: earth as body, earth as mind. Our language is circular. In reading geology texts—and of course when I wrote about geology in *Cascadia,* I messed up hugely and re-did my geology—I saw that there is a conveyor belt under the earth and that one grain of sand takes 200 million years to move from the middle of the Pacific to our coast and then go under and back. So it's all kind of a long process, and words start to participate in a long otherness. And we're talking about language that's being recycled in poetry maybe every couple of hundred years—the whole thing gets remade. That's cool, that you can re-use Keats. For me, the big inspiration behind the mission poems was George Herbert. I love "The Altar" and "Easter-wings," his shapey poems. I always thought those were so cool. I thought, I want to write a girl version of that, with lace around it. And I know that people borrowed things from *Death Tractates* over and over. So the idea of originality is challenging, and how we have to let go of ego to make art, while respecting that there are huge and profound aesthetic differences in a culture of literature as various as ours.

SR: In "The Shirley Poem," Shirley, a pioneer doctor's wife who travels to the mines with her husband, writes in a letter: "I have the vague / idea that I hooked that butterfly comparison from somebody. / If so, I beg the injured / person's pardon, and he or she / may have a hundred of *mine* / to pay for." Then there's a parenthetical that says, "*(italics hers.)*" It's interesting that the parenthetical itself is in italics, so that "her" becomes a completely slippery entity. Whose italics? It's a fine-tuned gesture that gets at this ownership/originality issue. Throughout your work, there are these precise gestures that enact what you are saying. For example, in "Shared Custody," where the daughter goes back and forth between parents like Persephone, the daughter "makes / a roof with her goodbye: //bye\\ mom."[8] In this small typographical moment there is a complex awareness of the ways a child must negotiate her feelings for her divorced parents. I think of Dickinson's ability to funnel big ideas through small yet potent gestures.

BH: There's something about that girlish refuser that is in my work all the way back to *Fortress*, but it really started with *Death Tractates*, with the "what" voice that comes in. And that came from working with André Breton's notion of letting the pen slip so that everything in the margins of the poems starts entering. I've always done a lot of composition using trance methods. There were always unexplainable voices that would come in. I know "voice" is supposed to be a dirty word, and I never quite figured out why. Have you?

SR: There's the idea that something different happens on the page than happens in speech.

BH: But I can't get why one would want to eliminate the trace of a spoken thought in the poem. There are so many moments in which the human "voice" comes in, in Stein's "Lifting Belly," say, or in John Ashbery's poetry, which I love. It isn't *not* writerly. It always seemed to me that one of the great things about poetry was when you would hear *writing* itself, some very specific quality of life that was only possible in that particular expression. There's something really good about the breakdown of the notion of the ego and the accompanying opening up of the page that has come about through literary theory. It does seem to me crucial that we keep in mind that poetry is about states of mind, and about people going through things as selves and as collectives in relation to the earth, in relation to being alive, in relation to becoming. It is impossible for me to enjoy poetry if there is no sense of intense experience. The old autobiographical narrative isn't necessarily going to cut it every time. Yet it seems to me crucial to have a sense that somebody went through something, or the powerful thought of the poem as a replica of that.

So I hope that whatever experiment and opening and wildness and exploration the poem has to go through—and I do mean the poem because I feel like I am in its hands when I'm writing—that it keeps human experience recognizable.

SR: I wanted to talk about gold, a subject your work has taken up several times. You have an ongoing interest in alchemy and the making of gold as an alchemical process, which seems to be a metaphor for the solitary creative process. In *Cascadia*, you also explore gold as money, and you look at the political, economic, and environmental consequences of our historical relationship to gold, and the way gold has been replaced by other means of exchange. The poem "Hydraulic Mining Survey" examines the fact that, a short time ago, we were tearing apart the earth to get gold, and it was a hard process, as if the earth didn't want to yield this metal to us: "Gold just didn't want to."[9]

BH: The earth had it, and kept it.

SR: And only a little while later, we are all using Visa and MasterCard anyway—yet we still live with these deserted mines.

BH: The whole idea of the rape of the earth for gold became interesting to me when I went with Gary Snyder and some other people to look at the hydraulic mines. It must have been almost ten years ago. We just went on a little outing to look at the mountains. And it was quite shocking to see the scars of hydraulic mining still there. It had been a hundred years, and there's no mountain now. For me, the idea that we went to that much work to find gold connected with my interest, which I explored in the central section of *Loose Sugar*, in alchemy as an idea of spiritual process: trying to find the gold of the spirit in a metaphorical sense. And that being impossible, because all mental processes are circular. You don't get to the gold. You don't get to make it. So gold is desirable and elusive at the same time. And now, as a society, we've reached the point where not even paper money stands for gold in the Treasury. Instead, plastic stands for paper money, which stands for gold, which stands for value. It is just so removed, and money itself is somewhat horrifying. It's almost as if gold has lost its value. Who knows what's worth something? I was talking to a friend the other day, who was talking to a mutual friend, a trader, who trades in the thing that comes right after the future of pork bellies. I don't even know what it is called. It's like the wash, the afterwash, the high tide or something. When I started *Cascadia,* the boom was still on. And I thought, people make so much money off imaginary value, and it's going to crash. And how much is it taking out of somebody else?

Of course, there's nothing you can do about it. People will go on hoarding it until the end of time. But it's been very upsetting to watch the boom and then the crash that's based on unreal value. It hasn't really crashed too much around our ears, but there is still something extremely horrifying about things like conglomerate ownerships.

SR: In a sense, conglomerate ownerships represent a highly disturbing version of your phrase, "enter the 'we.' "

BH: Exactly, and one that's got nothing to do with the earth and the gold miner's forty feet around a claim. When I was starting to write *Cascadia,* I read a book called *The Gift* by Marcel Mauss. I had already read Lewis Hyde's book called *The Gift,* and I think his ideas overlap with those of Mauss. The book describes how value should work, or does work, in a culture of art. The gift I give you actually has spirit value in it from its place of origin—the forest, or the mine, or wherever it's from. It has the weight of its history in it. In today's culture, this idea of the gift has totally lost spiritual value. Right now, it's Christmas season; you just order things from Amazon and J.Crew and charge them to your Mastercard. Or look at these poor dioxined apples here: They are called Gee Whiz and they are from something.com and they have their little stickers and they are sprayed. No spirit value passed along.

SR: Isn't this classic Marxism, the alienation between the maker and the product, and between the maker and the user of the object? And the use of money, which is an abstraction—there's no more bartering. This discussion also ties indirectly into a concern you raise in *Loose Sugar*, for example in "Busy Week," about how rushed and busy life has become. That is where a lot of this minimizing of the meaning of objects comes in—we don't feel we have the time any more to sit and make personal gifts for our friends at Christmas, for example.

BH: I'm not this year, but—not to get too Joni Mitchell about it—I'm going to, next year, or the year after. The challenge is to be able to accommodate email and gardening and plastic at the same time—to keep a sense of how things give value to life.

SR: Your work strikes me as profoundly spiritual—spiritual in the sense that the more one is aware of death and the pressing mystery of nonbeing, the more one wants to invest matter with meaning. One becomes concerned with the meaning of our precious time here in relation to the constant fact of nonbeing.

BH: And the fact that everything is constant change.

SR: There's a great line to that effect at the end of the poem "Cascadia."

BH: Oh, "You want to or you don't / want to change but you'll change."[10] Yes, at the time of writing that, I was having some health issues; it was a very hard time in my personal life. That's the private undercurrent of those words. But it did have to do with acknowledging that many of us don't want to admit that we are all about change and decay and falling apart.

I also see spirit as very much connected to language. The other day I was walking into Cody's and I saw a woman walking along the opposite way, wearing a T-shirt that said, "I only do what the voices tell me to do." I think there is some continuum between language and spirit that is absolute and amazing. There's an essay by Walter Benjamin that really helped my thinking about this, even though I have no idea what the essay is saying; it's like a really strange poem. It's called "On Language as Such and on the Language of Man." It's about how we can't get away from meaning and yet we don't know what it is, but there's something about language and the way language relates to the primal that precedes experience and precedes words but is only purely enacted by them. So the language of God is much bigger than words. That made me really think about the connection between spirit and language. In one sense, I don't believe in pure spirit outside of culture, but I do think there are mysteries that we don't know through culture, and in that way it is not all about being human. So that's a contradiction. There's something about the absolute need to insist that every bit of human understanding is a closed system that I don't like. When you're talking to a rock, that is not about human culture; it is about this rock that's going to be here for a long time. There's a reality outside of ourselves. Stevens and Wittgenstein say it is unknowable and that's true; we don't know it; we can't know it. All we can really know is human culture. And to risk the relation to the nonhuman is a nonsense I need to participate in.

SR: I wanted to ask you about the last lines of "El Niño Orgonon" in *Cascadia*: "Weather taught / you to write funny. When it stops / being wrecked, we'll write normally."[11] You expressed a similar sentiment in your interview with Tod Marshall where you said, "I sometimes think sentences have to be screwed up in exactly the same way as we've screwed up the weather."[12] I appreciate the idea that we may feel compelled to write things that don't make logical sense in order to mirror the environmental crisis. At the same time, it seems it is always the job of poetry to move in a nonrational way, even in a joyfully reclaimed, Edenic world. Also, some might say there is a joy, as in the *joissance* the French feminists speak of, in disordering syntax. And then there is the whole question of who ordered the syntax as it is ordered anyway, and to what end.

BH: That's a great point, and asyntactic sentences have been around for a long time as literary devices, for lots of reasons, including the modernist idea that alienation is where we are, so we need to represent ourselves as alienated from our environment in order to be most courageous and because that's how modern cities are. Gertrude Stein's polysyntax is about abutting states of mind against each other in a Cubist way, and her work is the source for a lot of the polysyntax in Language poetry and in the feminist lyric that accompanied the opening of the poem. Syntax scrambling is not only political—as you say, it's also about joy. And it's also about the idea from Russian formalism that the purpose of literature is to alienate us—to make us uncomfortable, for good reasons. Alienation in that sense not being bad, but just separating us from the normal so that we stumble across something we haven't seen before and we see it for the first time. In that particular poem I say that I'm screwing up these sentences because we screwed up the world. I wrote that poem during the scary couple of winters of '92 and '93. We had those terrible storms and I just kept thinking, This is not right; we have got too much water coming down. They say it's this little boy off in the Pacific spinning around, but it's not; it's a mess.

SR: So you didn't mean that in a reductive way; you meant that as one of the many reasons to mess with syntax and sentences.

BH: Yes, one of the many. Since Mallarmé and before, lots of people have been rethinking the sentence in lots of different ways. But I do think there is something different about connecting it with the weather getting screwed up, and with dioxin and other environmental atrocities. And I am probably going to go in that direction somewhat in the next book too, because I feel very concerned about these issues. I was talking with my friend Chris Sindt about the challenge of speaking as a modernist or postmodernist poet about environmental issues, because there's so much sentimentality associated with "nature writing." For many writers, words don't have anything to do with their signifieds. One of my friends noted he was really disappointed to see an actual growing tree after knowing only the name of this particular kind of tree, because of course the relationship is arbitrary. I find it challenging to figure out what language *does* do to reality.

SR: I see *Cascadia* as taking on the environment in a complex way so that it's connected with issues about language, writing, and multilayered states of consciousness.

BH: My approach isn't necessarily going to make a huge hit with the John Muir crowd, but I feel like it is nature writing in the best sense to think the whole idea of nature must be reconceived, and I do feel that you can be a postmodernist and query the very concepts of "nature." What does it mean to have a nature, exactly? It's a long way from me to the pine tree out the window. But there's still a pine tree out the window, even though it's called something else in Japanese.

SR: I'd like to end by asking you about your relationship to the Bay Area and to the notion of poetic community, and about whether those relationships overlap for you. Here we are looking at a book called *Cascadia*, which is a word for an ancient land form that preceded California, where you have lived and taught and written and raised a child for a number of years. *Cascadia* seems to dig into this particular place, perhaps in one sense as an example of place, and perhaps also simply as the location you know best. In what sense is the Bay Area a writing community for you? Has your relationship to the Bay Area as a poetic community changed over time, as your own allegiance has shifted from a more narrative to a more "experimental" mode?

BH: The idea of California has been in my work since *Fortress*; maybe a little less in *Loose Sugar*, but still it comes in. Certainly in *Bright Existence*, *Death Tractates*, and *Cascadia* it is important to think as a California writer about many aspects of California—and now particularly Northern California—as a mode for the universal. I'm never just thinking of it as itself; I'm always trying to think about being on earth, being in the universe. I think of this book as the first in a tetralogy, actually, of earth, air, fire and water. I don't know if I will do it or not, but that's my idea. In terms of California as a geologic phenomenon, I'm interested in the fact that Cascadia in its original land form comprised the entire west of North America. That land form actually subducted in and became a whole bunch of the western form. California didn't exist at one time, and then when Cascadia subducted and became California, it's almost as if it had to sacrifice itself for us. So I was interested in that geological idea of merging—the land being one thing and then becoming another.

That ties into an idea of poetic community that appeals to me. When I first got here in the midseventies, I was fresh from the Iowa writing program and I had very specific ideas about what poetry was, mostly. My first poetry friend here was Patricia Dienstfrey, with whom I've just edited a book of essays by thirty-two poets on the intersection of motherhood and poetics called *The Grand Permission.* She was involved in women's poetry in a way that interested me, and the idea that poetry could accommodate process and uncertainty and show its own evolution was new. Since the eighties, these ideas are much more common, because of deconstruction and all. The Bay Area is also a very exciting place to be a poet right now because there is a growing collaborative spirit. I know a lot of people have to make their living from teaching, and that means you have to compete for certain things, and it's hard to get published. But there's a real acceptance of a lot of different kinds of poetry. And you see a great deal of openness about women's writing, an openness I ascribe to work that was done by a number of people, among them Kathleen Fraser, Frances Jaffer, the editors of Kelsey Street Press, and others. But the main thing that has interested me in the Bay Area for three decades is that it's a community in which writers can feel comfortable exploring the parameters of contemporary idioms, and there are plenty of venues to read your poetry, even if you don't have books out. And I am completely excited about it. It is still really hard to be a poet and there's not a great deal of acceptance of poetry "out there" in the culture. It is still not reviewed much in the *New York Times* or the big literary magazines. But it's a lot easier to be a poet today. Now people are able to honor aesthetic differences and recognize that an art grows as much from transgressions as from positions. I think that makes it more interesting. Don't you?

NATHANIEL MACKEY

The Atmosphere Is Alive

Sarah Rosenthal: The shape of your poetry on the page has evolved. In *Eroding Witness,* the installments of "Song of the Andoumboulou" are gappy and riverine, and the left margin moves a lot. It's the same in *School of Udhra.* In *Whatsaid Serif,* there's a transformation into a more compacted and less aerated shape with a more stable left margin. This latter shape dominates in *Splay Anthem,* where the lines mass into stanza-like clusters with one word pushed out to the right periodically.

Nathaniel Mackey: I hadn't particularly noticed that change but that's a long period you're talking about—something approaching thirty years of writing. It's not unusual for those kinds of changes to take place. They haven't happened at a conscious level. The shape has just slowly evolved, and I think it comes out of my inhabiting a certain way of working with the page that doesn't assume, for example, that you always return to the left margin. From the moment I started writing as a teenager, I've been interested in different ways of putting the poem on the page. I was curious about poets such as those included in the anthology *The New American Poetry*—as well as late Williams, with that radical triadic arrangement he had—who felt a permission not to simply return to the left margin in the way all the poetry I'd read up to that point did. I've experimented with that freedom over the years. The differences that you're talking about are subtle. I still tend to move away from the left-hand margin, even now. Yet what you say about the poems becoming denser and less ventilated is true. It's taken a while for me to give myself the permission of prose in poetry. I think that writing prose alongside writing verse has contributed to that. One of the things that's beginning to come through in *Whatsaid Serif* but is coming through even stronger in *Splay Anthem* is a conversation between verse and prose that's been going on in the work for a while now.

SR: The first letters in your ongoing epistolary work, *From a Broken Bottle Traces of Perfume Still Emanate,* occurred in the context of poems, but almost immediately branched off and became a separate project. I'm intrigued by your description of the relationship between the letters and the poems as a conversation. Do you notice any other ways, besides the recent density that's appearing in the poems, that the two projects are conversing with or perhaps contaminating each other?

NM: Yes. From the beginning they've shared certain kinds of content and certain concerns. Dogon material comes up in both, as does the myth of Gassire's lute, for example. Other bodies of lore and tradition get referred to and made use of in both as well, with recourse to certain areas, geographically and culturally speaking, being common to the two: ancient Egypt, the Caribbean, Brazil, southern Spain, and so on. There's music too, of course, which is primary and pervasive in the prose and is frequently referred to and thought about and worked with in the poems as well. Early on, in fact, I thought of the Angel of Dust letters as a bit like liner notes for the poems, unpacking or being more expository about matters which inform the poems but that the poems, given poetry's musical demand and condensation, tend to be elliptical about. Romance, collectivity, sexuality, and spirituality are some of the concerns the prose and the poetry share. It's worth noting that certain differences in tone are as much a part of the conversation as the similarities and overlaps I've mentioned are, the prose's comic strain, for example, being something the poems don't get into that much. Anyway, in the early eighties I began to include the letters in poetry readings, reading from them as well as reading poems. That's one of the things that got me more involved with and more intimate with the fact that prose has its music. Over the years the prose has come to exert a stylistic influence on the poems, leading me to stretch out and to vary the kinds of locution the poems allow. The increased presence of expository, propositional, and definitional gestures in *Whatsaid Serif* and *Splay Anthem* has to do with that. The increased presence of narrative gestures and the increased reliance on a certain accumulative tack are signs of it as well. I think the greater recourse to wordplay in those two books can also be attributed to the prose. Also, going back to the content level, it even gets to where the band of travelers in the poems appears to be a musical band at points, reminiscent of N. belonging to a band in *From a Broken Bottle.*

SR: Is *From a Broken Bottle* continuing?

NM: Yes, it is. I just finished volume four. I haven't written anything beyond that, but at this point there's no reason for me to think that it won't continue.

SR: The title and subtitles of *Splay Anthem* point in myriad ways to the work. "Anthem" announces song—specifically the song of a nation. This foregrounds the theme of statehood in the volume—a statehood which is constantly eroding, as in this passage in "Eye on the Scarecrow": "momentary kings and / queens, / fleet kingdom. Land fell / away on all sides."[1] The word "splay" announces the splay of images and cultures and musics presented in the book. "Splay" also prepares us for a repeating phrase, "we lay on our backs," which suggests an open, vulnerable, surrendered position. "Braid," the title of the book's first section, gets at the braiding together that you do on every level, from words to images to poems to series to themes; it points to the dreadlocks that serve as a repeated trope in the book; and it connects, via sound and/or meaning, to other significant words in the volume such as "brush." "Fray," the title of the second section, is the braid eroding, as well as more ominous images involving rope, such as lynching. "Fray" and "Nub," the title of the third section, both suggest a wearing away, while "Nub" also points us to Nubia—a rich culture that can't be returned to—and to the idea of the phantom limb, which has long been a central theme in your work. How did you determine what comprised each section and what the titles would be?

NM: I came up with the sections as I went along. I try to make each book a book—a unit of composition, along with the other units of composition that comprise the work. I move intuitively and in the dark, feeling my way. The form or the structure announces itself in the course of the writing. I think I was several poems into the book when I decided that "Braid" might be the title of the first section. The word "braid" came up because I was writing in both of those series—"mu" and "Song of the Andoumboulou"—and letting them weave around one another. But of course, as you've noted, it also has to do on various levels with the content of the poems. "Braid" turned out to be eleven poems, so I said, OK, let's see if I can do a second section that's also eleven poems. I called it "Fray," which suggests not only the unbraiding you mentioned but also conflict. The number twenty-two attracted me because it's got some things going for it—for example, it's two twos, and it's a powerful number in African-American hoodoo. I've been working with numbers going back to *Eroding Witness*—"Septet for the End of Time," for example.[2] Numbers become a way of situating boundaries within the work, a way of adding to the boundaries provided by the books themselves as bound entities. At any rate, for a time it was looking like the book might be comprised of two sections of eleven poems each, somewhat following on *Whatsaid Serif* being more or less twenty poems—twenty-one if you count the half step or half section in "Stra." But toward the end of "Fray," the word "nub" came up in the poems, and I thought maybe there should be a last section called "Nub" and that it should be shorter. It turned out to be three poems. So we've got twenty-five, one of those resonant, landmark numbers: a quarter of a hundred, five times five, and so forth.

I try to keep the conversation open to unconscious impulses and impetuses. For example, *School of Udhra* has three sections. The first section is "Song of the Andoumboulou" numbers eight through fifteen. The second section is "Outlantish," comprising installments of the "mu" series. The third section's called "Zar." A reviewer pointed out that if you take the first section to represent "Andoumboulou," you've got the letter *A*; in the second section, the "mu" poems, you've got *M*; and in the third section, "Zar," you've got *Z*. You've got the beginning, the middle, and the end of the alphabet. That never occurred to me consciously. But there it is.

SR: In "Lag Anthem: 'mu' eighteenth part" you indicate that you've completely overlapped the two series, "mu" and "Song of the Andoumboulou," for the first four poems of the volume: "39 was what it was we / were in, 'mu' no more itself / than Andoumboulou, both, / '8, '7, '6 gone by unbeknown / to / us."[3] How did that happen for you?

NM: Over the years, people would ask me how I knew which series I was in: "Song of the Andoumboulou" or "mu." I had no definitive way to answer that question, and still don't. I have, and have had, some vague ideas of what distinguished the series. But more and more they seem to be coming together. Some of it's arbitrary—we're talking about the names we give things, and the arbitrary relationship between a name and what it names. I'm involved with that question. A self-consciousness and a self-reflexivity having to do with names comes up in the epistolary prose and in the poems: "Fray was the name where we came / to next."[4] So given that this is a haunting concern throughout the work, it follows that it would pertain to some degree to the work itself. I have these two series that started way back, and I started calling one "Song of the Andoumboulou" and one "mu," and they were both based on pieces of music. For a while, one of the ways I distinguished between them was that the "mu" poems tended to be shorter, while the "Song of the Andoumboulou" poems had a tendency to sprawl. Content-wise the "Song of the Andoumboulou" poems had more explicitly to do with the Dogon material. But then I found that, like everything else in serial composition, those walls are very porous. For example, in *School of Udhra*, one of the sections of the poem "Wizard of Ought" is an installment of "mu." So the idea that series could share parts or that they could infiltrate each other began to come into the work. In *Whatsaid Serif* I made a decision to stay within "Song of the Andoumboulou"—or at least to call what I was staying within "Song of the Andoumboulou." When I started *Splay Anthem,* the question had been raised, both in my own mind and by other people, as to what had happened to the "mu" series. So I decided to return to "mu." The first four poems in *Splay Anthem* are "mu" poems. But then we get to the poem that you're referring to, as anticipated somewhat by the first poem in the volume being called "Andoumboulouous Brush." It was already occurring to me that those two series had so much in common that they could share a space. What I came to see is that they're very much part of the same project or impulse. As you noted, the first four "mu" poems in *Splay Anthem* can be thought of as installments of "Song of the Andoumboulou." So you find out in "Lag Anthem" that what you thought was the "mu" series is also the Andoumboulou series, that you've just read 36, 37, and 38, and that you're now reading 39. And then you come to "Song of the Andoumboulou: 40." If you go through the poems you'll notice that the same thing is happening with "Song of the Andoumboulou." For example, you'll see " 'mu' twentieth part" followed by "Song of the Andoumboulou: 42," which is followed by " 'mu' twenty-second part." The idea is that they're both there. I like to think of them as twins, occult understudies. Is "Song of the Andoumboulou: 42" the same as " 'mu' twenty-first part" or is it standing in place of " 'mu' twenty-first part," standing with "mu" in back of it? There's this braiding going on, and one part of the braid is not visible. That began to intrigue me in the early stages of *Splay Anthem,* and that's what then takes over in that book. It has continued so far in the book that I'm working on now.

SR: "[M]u" points me toward the boundary between language and music/sound/noise as well as toward the words "music" and "muthos." Originally "muthos" meant pretty much the same thing as "logos." Gradually the Ancient Greeks made a distinction between, on the one hand, "muthos" as "hearsay—as "whatsaid," to use your word and therefore not reliable, and, on the other hand, "logos" as "law and order." Are you drawing on Charles Olson's use of these words?

NM: The first poems in the "mu" series occurred within a poem called "Poem for Don Cherry," which I wrote in the early seventies.[5] Don Cherry was a trumpeter who played with Ornette Coleman. There are three sections to that poem: " 'mu' first part," " 'mu' second part," and "teo-teo-can." Those titles refer to a couple of albums that Don Cherry put out: *"mu" first part* and *"mu" second part*. "[T]eo-teo-can" is a piece on one of those albums. So music was there from the start.

At the same time, yes, I had read what Olson says about muthos and logos in *The Special View of History*. Olson makes the point that muthos and logos were originally the same, before a distinction got made between "muthos" as "mouth/speech" and "logos" as "word/reason/written discourse." Olson is interested in getting beyond that false dichotomy and showing the ways in which these two things flow into one another. He quotes Jane Harrison's work on Greek religion, *Themis*.[6] I eventually used a passage from that book as one of the epigraphs to "Outlantish," the "mu" section of *School of Udhra*. Harrison says that the first emergence of the word "muthos" was probably the interjection "mu," which she calls a kind of re-utterance or even a pre-utterance.[7] She's trying to talk about an emotional utterance base that is prelinguistic but survives and continues into language and informs language in a way. I was taken with the idea that by putting those two things together—Olson and Harrison's "muthos"/"mu" and Don Cherry's "mu"—I could suggest a continuum between verbal discourse and music.

Historically, the word "muthos" also came to mean "myth." The term carried a pejorative connotation—myth as something whose truth claims, from the standpoint of reason and rationality, are suspect at best. Olson prefers the term "muthologos" because it brought those two terms back together.[8] And of course he considers himself a mythologist, a mythographer. Some of that is also coming through in my understanding and taking up of those terms.

I also had in mind the tradition of the Atlantis myth, which goes way back—you find references to Atlantis in Plato. In the nineteenth and early twentieth centuries, you have people writing about an

Atlantis-like continent/island that had presumably existed in the Pacific called Mu. That comes into the poems. That was one of the ways, early on, that I distinguished between "mu" and "Andoumboulou." "Andoumboulou" didn't have this concern with a mythical lost continent—or at least that's what I thought at the time. But the more I actually did the writing of "Song of the Andoumboulou," it became a figure for lost ground, submerged ground—but also a figure for lost unity in a kind of utopic past that we've fallen from or scattered from or lost. One of the traditions has it that the Atlanteans didn't dream. Think about Freud and psychoanalysis—the dream as harbinger of discontent, the dream as compensation. Well, the Atlanteans apparently were so content and happy that they had nothing to compensate for, so they didn't need to dream. Of course, one of the themes that's coming up again and again in these poems is dreaming—dreamlessness, trying to get into the dream, being in the dream, trying to get out of the dream. One of the epigraphs in *Splay Anthem* is "because to dream is not to dream / if waking up is never finished,"[9] which is taken from Ed Roberson's poem "dreaming has made more strict the terms of dreaming."[10] If waking up is never finished, then the dream is the only reality you have.

SR: Gnosticism, which informs your poetics in many ways, includes the idea that we need to wake up to the reality of our fallen state, a state for which we are not responsible but which is very degraded.

NM: I was seeing the Atlanteans as the state from which we are fallen—a lost, beatific state that they inhabited and that apparently the Muvians inhabited as well.

SR: Wasn't Columbus looking for Atlantis?

NM: When he landed in the Bahamas, he thought that he had found Atlantis. I've heard that the etymology of "Bahamas" goes back to the Spanish *baja mar*, which means "under the sea," because he thought that what he had found was the mountaintops of Atlantis and that the rest was submerged. That comes up in *School of Udhra,* in one of the "mu" poems in the "Outlantish" section. In fact, the word "Outlantish" was playing on "Atlantis." That *baja mar* business appealed to me because my father, though he was born in the Panama Canal Zone, was actually Bahamian. His mother and father were Bahamians and had gone to Panama to work on the construction of the canal, as did many West Indians. It was nice to have a genealogy that goes back to the mountains of Atlantis.

SR: Even though it connects you to Columbus, which isn't such a great genealogy . . .

NM: What's in a name?

SR: You seem to enjoy taking fragmentary bits of myth and history, investigating them to a point, and from there allowing your imagination to inhabit and travel with them—as is the case with your use of the sparse information available about the Dogon funerary ritual of singing a song to the mythic Andoumboulou. You have written about how myth isn't dead and done; it's something that continues to live and breathe and be created. Paul Naylor has argued that you are not so much a mythologist as a mythmaker.[11] Do you agree?

NM: I do. I don't think that's as spectacular an assertion as it may sound. I see mythmaking going on all over the place by pretty much everybody. In *The Special View of History*, Olson quotes Harrison quoting Aristotle as having said, "By myth I mean the arrangement of the incidents."[12] That suggests that pretty much everything is myth, whether you're talking about what we would normally think of as mythological material or not. Certainly it would apply to what I'm doing when I take something said by Columbus and put it together with a trumpet solo from Don Cherry. That's an arrangement of two incidents that in most universes of discourse might not come together. I think that what Paul was trying to distinguish between is that approach, which is syncretic and improvisatory and assemblist, and the attitude that a particular body of myth is a canon that has to be deferred to and is therefore not open to new initiative, originality, and creativity. I agree with that. But like I say, I think it's something that goes on a lot, and not just inside writing. It's a basic human act. If myth is the arrangement of the incidents, then when you go to the family reunion and you hear different versions of what happened on Christmas in 1979, what you've got is a mythology conference. I remember hearing Robert Duncan speak at Stanford when I was a graduate student there. He was invited to read at a conference put on by the Modern Thought and Literature Program. I think one of the topics was "History and Myth." I remember at one point Robert said that he read Freud's case studies as myth. Those patients were mythologizing—were in fact invited to mythologize. And the fact that Freud would then name the complexes that were at work after figures in classical mythology simply underscored the fact that what the patients were doing to begin with was a kind of mythmaking arranging the incidents of their own lives.

SR: I'd like to address various aspects of your relationship to music. In your interview with Christopher Funkhouser you talked about how the serial poem is like improvisation in that it invites further articulation, modification, and variation.[13] I find your poetry highly recursive not just poem by poem or section by section, but word by word.

Reading your work resembles, in certain ways, listening to someone like Coltrane. Like him and other jazz artists, you seem to be listening to ideas and sounds and riffing on them, massaging them, inverting, spinning, braiding, and fraying them. Then at a certain point a new impulse will come in—maybe because you've exhausted the earlier one or maybe because you're looking for some kind of energy that's oppositional or sideways in relation to the earlier riff. In what ways, if at all, do the ideas of jazz improvisation or the notion of composition "under hand" inform your process?

NM: I'm a slow improviser. The slips and slides and variations that you read in the poem, that may have a sense when you hear them of momentariness and instantaneity, something that happens in a few seconds, may have taken a week or two to come together in a composition process which is itself very fragmented. I write in spurts, through a combination of pressure and relaxation. You press and then you see where that can get you, but you can't get everything by pressing. Some of the best things you don't get by pressing. Some things come in a state of receptivity and relaxation when you don't necessarily see yourself as composing. You're in the middle of something else and bam, you'll be hit with it. I've learned over the years to obey those moments and get that stuff written down before it's gone, even if it's only two or three words. It took me a long time to learn that, because I'd think, That's nice, I'll pay attention to that when I have time and when the whole thing it's a part of is ready to present itself to me. I found that if I didn't get to it, I'd lose the little piece that I had. If I can, I'll sit down and see what's knocking on the door. Sometimes those three words will be the opening for something considerably more than three words. Other times that's all it will be, and I won't find out what accompanies those three words until somewhere down the line. But that comes from pressing it: "OK, let's go back to those three words and let's see . . ." And it also comes in conversation with another set of four words that occur two days later. As I said earlier, I write in the dark. I'm feeling my way in a field. I'm feeling one thing here and one thing there and trying to piece them together.

SR: In "Go Left Out of Shantiville" you write: "Music / the breath we took . . . It was only / there we wanted to be, the everywhere / we'd always wanted, ours, / albeit / only an instant, forever, never to be / heard / from again." In "Eye on the Scarecrow" you write: "As / though what we wanted / was to be everywhere at / once, / an altered life lived on an / ideal / coast we'd lay washed up / on, instancy and elsewhere / endlessly entwined."[14] Is there a spirituality for you without music?

NM: I think there's a spirituality without music. But I also think it's no accident that music plays such a central role in the spiritual and religious rituals of so many people around the world throughout time. I talk about this a little bit in my essay "Sound and Sentiment, Sound and Symbol," where I refer to Victor Zuckerkandl's book *Sound and Symbol: Music and the External World*, specifically to the way he talks about tonal motion as motion in the state of in-betweenness. He argues that the space of music is not a place—it's a non-place. That's a way of talking about an experience that's been at the root of all my involvement with music, which is the rapt and intense way that music can take hold of us and create a welling-up that seems to come from inside, while at the same time its source seems to be immaterial. Of course, we can and must take into account the material means of production of music—there's a very physical body blowing into a horn or moving a bow. And sound itself, we know, is physical. But we experience something in music which goes back to some very archaic and primordial human experiences in which the fact of sound as material was not yet evident. Sound seemed to be itself of the order of spirit. What was moving, what was touching people, and what called for these wellings-up was what we called "spirit." We've kept that vocabulary. When we think about it, there's a literal way in which it fits. That ancient vocabulary speaks of spirits as invisible forces that move with the air, move through the air, move the air. That's what sound does. That's what music does. It moves invisibly with the air, through the air, moves the air, and it creates perturbations in our eardrums. We get this very visceral feeling of what we have a deep apprehension of as the immaterial, the spiritual.

SR: So music is a way that we bridge from the physical to the spiritual.

NM: Yes, it bridges the physical and the spiritual in ways that, for me at least, looking at a painting doesn't. When I look at visual art I don't have the sense of visceral movement that music can produce. My guess would be that sound predates visual imagery as a technique of the sacred, to use Jerome Rothenberg's term. I think it speaks of something very primordial. But I may just be picking nits. The cave paintings and things like that suggest a very early point at which visual imagery is doing that as well.

SR: Your talk of moving the air reminds me of "Bedouin wind" and all the other references to wind that seem to blow through your poems.

NM: The spirit has to do with wind. The word "spirit" and the words connected with spirit—"inspiration," etc.—have etymologically to do with the physical fact of wind and breathing, and the fact that one can feel a certain haunting effect when wind moves through a locale. That imagery is very much alive in much of what I write. A lot of the colloquial metaphors that we use still carry some of those meanings that suggest not just physical states but psychic states—"psyche" going back to "soul"—with regard to sound. We talk about "vibes" and there being a certain "vibe" in the air, that kind of thing. That's what sound is. It's vibrations, among other things—the impact of vibrations not only on one's eardrum, as I mentioned earlier, but also on the rest of one's body. Kids driving around in these cars with big bass speakers aren't just listening with their ears. They're listening with their whole bodies. They want to feel the music, and the body becomes a kind of drum. One of the things that they're reaching for is a sense of unity of inside and outside, where it feels as if the pulse of the music is the pulse of one's own body. So again, I think that music evokes the lost ground, or a recovery of the lost ground, the lost unity, that I was talking about before in relationship to "mu." That's one of the reasons that music is relevant to that Atlantean dream of return, that coast in the passage you read a little while ago.

SR: You've used the phrase "monstrous eruption" to describe the music of Pharoah Sanders and others.[15] The word "scream" also comes to mind. In some ways your work is very orderly and contained: It's not splayed all over the page, and it stays within fairly strict boundaries lengthwise. But it too emanates a scream. The jerkiness, the constant disorientation and dislocation, the leaping forward and doubling back of the language create for me a kind of scream, especially when combined with the content about African American displacement and enslavement, not to mention references to other marginalized cultures. Yet the work doesn't continually scream. It constantly finds ways to torque the scream into notes of ecstasy.

NM: The word "scream" is interesting. Coltrane got to the point in some concerts where he would take the horn from his mouth and just start yelling. Rashied Ali, who was the drummer with his last group, talks about an occasion on which that happened. Ali was rather taken aback, and asked Trane about it later. Trane said, "I ran out of horn." I've heard people who do in poetry something that emulates what Coltrane does. They'll actually scream, do things of that sort. Certainly relative to that I'm very Apollonian. My screaming is going on in a different way. It's the fraying of meanings; it's the colliding of sounds that creates certain consternations of meaning that might be the counterpart of the scream, analogous to the scream.

And as you point out, the poems contain a lot of references to some pretty dystopian facts and realities. They are often lamenting wounds of various sorts, and fallings-short of various kinds. But at the same time they are trying to rebound, recover, recycle, go on—trying to outrun in some way the repercussions of certain ordeals and violences and violations. "Fugitivity" comes to mind as a word informing such a poetic. Something is being run away from, and that something is not pretty.

SR: The theme of running comes up throughout *Splay Anthem,* as does the theme of being "hit upside the head." In both of these cases, as in so many of your themes, there's a double edge. The running seems to be a running away from something, but it also has an exploratory quality, a running toward new experience. "Hit upside the head" suggests violence—literal, historical violence—for example "a / big Foot up the sides of our skulls" or "A hammer hit them each on the head." But it also suggests spiritual awakening, as in "Starlight hit us with / headshine" or "Whatsaid sip they lit Eleusis / with it seemed. Barley mold / made them wince . . . Heartrending / sky, held breath held high / as a cloud, / Hoof-to-the-Head knocked hard, / no bolt from on high but their / lips' convergence came close."[16]

NM: There is a revelatory quality to ordeal. That's part of what's being gotten at there. Sometimes spiritual advance comes only because it's necessary. You have to be put in a position where there's really no way out but to advance spiritually. Certainly when we look at the cultural productions of black people in this country going back to slavery, it's been what Hurston calls "making a way out of no way": being in a position of extremity where you had to find a way that you would not have chosen to find. The ordeal made it necessary for you to do that—and not just on large historical levels but on personal, individual levels. We learn from disappointments. We might have learned the same thing without going through that disappointment, but who knows. You don't want to say that therefore the suffering is necessary and ineradicable, and therefore it's a good thing, or any of that. You want to work toward eradicating those sorts of things, but at the same time you must record the fact that they have been the occasion for people moving on in important and indispensable ways.

SR: In your interview with Edward Foster you said, "How do you lament loss without investing in loss?"[17] But, fortunately or unfortunately, there's so much loss to deal with that that doesn't seem to be a real problem.

NM: It's an academic question: Are you to the point where you're seeking it out? Well, my experience has been that you don't have to seek it out. It'll find you. And when it does find you, you need to be able to take it somewhere else. That's part of fugitivity too. It's not just that you're running away, but that your running transforms the loss. Part of the recursive quality that you mentioned is the revisitation that wants to transform. One classic formulation I think of is Ralph Ellison's discussion of the blues in his review of Richard Wright's autobiography, *Black Boy,* which he sees as a blues text. Ellison describes the blues as an impulse to finger the grain of a wound in order to squeeze a lyricism out of it. He says that Wright revisits his childhood in order to reopen wounds and extract a certain lyricism from them, and that that lyricism takes the wounds to another place. Ellison is talking about a poetics—a poetics of therapy, a poetics of transformation. These figures of movement, of drift, of transit of various sorts, especially throughout my poems of the last several years, have had a lot to do with that—with, in a sense, taking that trite and colloquial phrase "a better place," and then, without actually using those words, getting at the impulse to move on—but without avoiding difficulty in an escapist way.

SR: You said a few minutes ago, and you said a number of years ago in your interview with Christopher Funkhouser, that you're not really into image—that you're much more focused on music.[18] Yet your poems are loaded with aleatory images—momentary, fragmented images in motion. You're always pulling up some kind of picture, and then it mutates. One poem in *Splay Anthem*, "Song of the Andoumboulou: 56," focuses on imagery—visual art in particular. Were you looking at work by Irving Petlin?

NM: Yes, his *Lake as a Furnace* pastels. I probably overstated my attitude toward the visual in that interview. Obviously mine is a poetry that's filled with images. One of the things that attracted me to poetry early on was the phanopoetic, to use Pound's term—the casting of visual images and pictures. Melopoesis and music are part of it, but I was drawn to imagery. Imagery as I encountered it wasn't necessarily at odds with or divorced from the music. One of the first contemporary poets who I was really into, as I've mentioned elsewhere, was Amiri Baraka, specifically his early work such as *The Dead Lecturer* and *Preface to a Twenty Volume Suicide Note*. He's certainly someone who's into music, but one of the things I was attracted to in his early work was the imagery. What strikes me about the formulation that you pursued in raising the question is your emphasis on movement, because Baraka could just pull up images one after another. He wasn't meditating on a single image which became a unifying symbol or metaphor—he was moving on. He wrote some liner notes in the sixties for an Archie Shepp album, *Four for Trane,* in which he talks about the playing being characterized by the images changing, and changing quickly. In the movement of images, the visual and the sonic come together. It's striking to me that we talk about pieces of music being divided into movements. That's already in the vocabulary of the music. So yes, I work with the movement of images, the switch from one image to the next, the variation of images so that you'll see an image that you've seen before but you'll see it slightly differently.

SR: Sometimes you create a superimposition of images. In *Splay Anthem* you have the couple in the bedroom and then in comes the image of the bar/lounge. Sometimes it seems as if the people I'm seeing in the bar are still the couple, while other times they seem to be a whole group of people. This superimposition draws my attention to what different images share. For example, both the bedroom and the bar are sites of a search for an altered state, which can be brought about by alcohol, or verbal or physical intimacy, or dreams. The mixing of pronouns furthers this sense of simultaneity or braiding of images or locations.

NM: It's palimpsestic in that sense. The images are atop one another. But they're also revising and erasing one another to some extent. I like the phrase "altered state." They're altering one another. There is a desire in the poems for steadiness and the everlasting, yet it's complicated by the desire to move on and not let things simply devolve into the status quo, the static, stasis in some stultifying sense. There's a lot of emphasis on movement in the poems, and there's a lot of questioning about ultimate arrival, about whether there is such a state or place. It's a poetry of seemingly endlessly altered states. The endlessness of those alterations is by turns a source of joy and a source of lament—ecstatic but haunted by the fact that one then moves on, that ecstasy doesn't last forever.

SR: Paul Naylor has written that "the desire for [a] state of 'two-ness' is the driving force behind . . . *Whatsaid Serif*."[19] I think of your poetry as pursuing a dialectic between oneness and two-ness, or between oneness and multiplicity. Your figure of the archetypal lover couple seems to enact such a dialectic. Couples want to merge and can momentarily achieve a feeling of merging. Yet that feeling inevitably dissolves and the two are back in their separate places again. This movement between merging and separating seems to come up often in your work.

NM: It's one of the dimensions of the way I've been working with the pronoun "we" in recent years. That "we" runs the gamut from the he/she couple to larger groupings—you mentioned "nation"—that the title *Splay Anthem* evokes. One of the things that makes the anthem "splay"—an awkward anthem, a disturbed anthem—is the fact that one is of more than one mind in this desire to be a part of a "we," whether it's a couple, a nation, or some other collectivity. This ambivalence splays the anthem, the unifying song of whatever the collective is. The collectivity that these poems seem to be about or to chronicle in some way, the lost tribe that sometimes goes by the name of the Andoumboulou, seems to be some renegade group whose relationship to established collectivities is a fugitive one. This lost tribe is in flight from such established groups and seemingly in search of some alternative way of bonding. The alternative that they seek is marked by the word "splay." This is an anthem that wants to open out, that is ungainly—I think "ungainly" is one of the synonyms for "splay"—that is wary of the harmonies and the symmetries of conventional, bonded ways of public belonging. Again, a musical reference suggests itself. I always think of Albert Ayler's music as a kind of anthem for a collectivity that doesn't exist and maybe can't exist. Ayler was one of the avant-garde jazz saxophonists of the sixties. There was an old New Orleans marching band quality to his music. He'd have titles like "Truth Is Marching In" or "Our Prayer." There was a very millenarian sense of expedition and arrival in his titles and in the music, but also a strangely backward-reaching quality as well. One of the things that's always stayed with me is some critic referring to Ayler's music as sounding like a Salvation Army band on acid. I think the critic meant it pejoratively, but I thought, That's an interesting possibility. Because when you think about the mission of the Salvation Army, that's certainly a laudable thing. And on acid, I mean—if the Salvation Army band on acid isn't a splay anthem, then that title means nothing.

So that oblique, outward-bound impulse toward some alternate collectivity, some alternate form of bonding and belonging, informs the perturbations that we've talked about, which take place on the individual male-female romance level but also in the sense of lost or diminished possibility that comes across in the sense of having moved into the republic of Nub at the end of the book, where the collective seems to be diminished and insufficient and stifling. That last section of the book is very much informed by the atmosphere in this country over the last several years post-9/11—the sense of diminishment—"diminishment" being the term that keeps coming up when I think about the contraction and the circling of the wagons that we've suffered and continue to suffer and that the leaders of the country continue to inflict upon us. Hence that sense of "nub"—the "[n]ot yet / nation of Nub" and all that stuff that's coming into those last poems in *Splay Anthem,* which I had no way of forecasting when I began the book.[20]

SR: Did you begin the book before 9/11?

NM: Oh, yes. I must have begun *Splay Anthem* somewhere around '96. I was finishing "Fray" in the summer of 2001 and going into the fall. And then the "Nub" section came.

SR: So the poetry is your own form of direct response to world events.

NM: It has always been that. It doesn't announce that in a topical way, but again, the atmosphere is alive. One of the things that that figure you mentioned earlier, "we lay on our backs," is trying to get at is a state of receptivity and reverie that is returned to again and again and again. The phrase is speaking, among other things, of that intuitive openness that I talked about earlier as being something that I want to keep in the writing process, that sense of feeling my way. And feeling my way, I'm imprinted by what happens. I'm multiply imprinted. Again, it's a palimpsest.

SR: I'd like to explore your use of the word "muse" in *Splay Anthem.* It shows up in different ways. There are a couple of moments where it seems to be a female lover/goddess—the muse as it's been configured in the Western, male-dominated canon. For example, in "Lag Anthem" you write, "Psalmed her hips' high / ride, the fall of cloth / across her jutting / chest . . . Monk's po metathetically / spun, recounting one morning leaving Eronel's / lair." "Eronel" is "Lenore" spelled backward. Lenore was the girlfriend of one of the musicians with whom Monk wrote the tune "Eronel." In "Beginning with Lines by Anwar Naguib," a couple are sitting in a bar talking about poetics: "Talked muse, / told who he / called muse the muse redresses, decks / her in alternate cloth, draping her / hips, / just below ass-crack, ass / absconditus, broadcast / weft." I struggled with such images of a highly sexualized female muse, who in the case of Eronel/Lenore seems to play the traditional role of inspiring the male artist to create. At the same time, I appreciate the fact that you deal directly with sexuality in your work. In addition, I see a number of ways that much of your language about the muse complicates traditional connotations. First of all, taking the second passage I quoted, it's not clear who the muse is exactly, who the muse is redressing or why, and so forth. In addition, in other passages it's "we" whose bodies are suggestively draped in cloth, for example "the imprint of crevice / and curve the admission of cloth / that we wore nothing underneath." Further, it's obvious that music and myth are in some sense your most important muses. And finally, you also talk about "muse" as a state of mind or concept: "muse / made of wished-it-so"; "muse / meant / lost in thought."[21] Yet a lot of contemporary poets won't even go near the word "muse" because it's so freighted with sexist baggage.

NM: I know that. Those poems have to do with sexuality. They have to do with the lure that sexuality triggers, the idealizations and wishful thinking, the reverie that sexuality can lead to. The poems also have to do with expectations that can be set up and the disappointment of expectations, the blues, that results from that. These are all real things that come into the poems, as do other real things. But muse *is* a state of mind, among other things. "Muse / meant / lost in thought." There is an awareness in the poems of the possibility of being led astray by thought, led astray by music. That's certainly been brought to light in the critiques of the male tradition with regard to the misapprehensions of the women in question or of women generally. Those passages acknowledge and wrestle with such misapprehensions—there's a complicating impulse, as you've noted. I'm not ready to abandon a word that means so many things, that is rich in so many ways, that relates to the constellation of concerns and impulses that we've been talking about. Yet I do recognize that it's a term that's been rendered problematic. That's one of the reasons that I've been intrigued by the fact that I continue to be drawn to it enough to use it. It's one of the things that's led me to ask myself, What else is going on in that term that's making me want to use it? You've talked about some of the meanings of it that I've explored. But I think that the sexual magic that goes on between people, which, like any magic, is subject to misleading the people involved, is something that hasn't gone away.

The sexual theme in the poems goes back to some of my formative experiences with poetry. When I first started reading poetry as a teenager, I was interested in what it had to say about romance and sexuality. When I teach creative writing, I find that that's what beginning poets write about for the most part. The initial poetic impulse is very much bound up with sexuality, sexual coming of age, romantic expectation. Young poets are rightly sensing that sexuality is something that's in the repository of poetry—the tradition is filled with it. I mentioned Amiri Baraka's *The Dead Lecturer* earlier. You have lines in there like "Who am I to love / so deeply?"[22] It's hard to imagine Amiri Baraka writing lines like that, but in the early sixties he did. Many of his poems from that period are love poems.

It should also be pointed out that there's also a tradition of women poets having muses. H.D. certainly is a poet of muses, including male muses such as D.H. Lawrence, Paul Robeson, and the Haitian journalist Lionel Durand, who figures in the writing of *Hermetic Definition*. Sappho had muses. Sexual fascination is a human fact, and it's reciprocal. There have been social structures and social regimes that have suppressed that reciprocity, so we get a distorted tradition in which it's male poets musing on female bodies. But there's evidence that male poets can muse on male bodies, female poets can muse on male bodies, and female poets can muse on female bodies. Musing seems to me to say something important about this story that we're involved in and that poetry wants to speak to.

I should also note that "mu," in addition to suggesting "music" and "myth," suggests "muse." In fact, muse figuration occurs in "Poem for Don Cherry" and comes up throughout the poems within the "mu" series. My interest in the idea of the muse goes way back.

SR: In your interview with Peter O'Leary you said, "Duende, as Lorca talks about it and as singers and musicians in flamenco talk about it, is . . . that quality of discontent, it's that refusal to be satisfied with mere material achievement—whether we're talking about technical elocution or technical virtuosity—so I think there's something very spiritual about it. It is a spiritual discontent with the very nature of material achievement, no matter how exquisite. These figures of ghostliness and absence and incompletion [in my work] are meant to suggest a spiritual supplement to the world that both invests it with a certain urgency and divests it of any ultimacy."[23] Could you talk more about how spirituality creates urgency and lack of ultimacy at the same time?

NM: Lorca makes a connection between duende and death—something to the effect that the duende appears when there's the presence of death. I think in the same interview you quoted we talked about mortality and the fact that "Song of the Andoumboulou" is a funeral song among the Dogon, that it harks back to these pre-human or failed human figures known as the Andoumboulou. One of the reasons it does is that with the Andoumboulou, death came into the world. Death, mortality, deprives life of ultimacy. It seems to suggest a destination beyond this form. But at the same time it charges it with attachment and gives it a certain urgency, makes it something of a test or a rite of passage. "Not going to be here forever. Got certain things I've got to do." Isn't that what this positing of a realm of the spirit, a realm beyond death or a realm to which death is the door, is all about? The spiritual supplement is another way of talking about this really quite archaic idea that there is another realm or dimension that outlives this one—not only outlives this one but drives it.

SR: Is duende the effort to contact that realm, or is it an inhabiting of an awareness of death?

NM: I would say it's more the latter.

SR: What in your opinion pushes anyone to reach beyond technical virtuosity?

NM: Among other things, it's that we're the thinking animal. It's the philosophic impulse. Montaigne writes about death and philosophy. Wallace Stevens talks about death as the mother of beauty.

SR: Do you feel that for art to really move you, for art to really be worth its salt and take a permanent place on the shelf, it has to deal with mortality and death?

NM: I don't think art *has* to deal with death. There's a variety of subject matter for art. Williams's "The Red Wheelbarrow" and "This Is Just to Say" are not about death. They are about the joys of everyday life. But I would not characterize them as poems that have duende.

We're talking about a particular aesthetic embodied in *cante jondo,* flamenco singing, and flamenco artists aren't singing about how tasty the plums in the refrigerator are. They're singing about first and last things. They're singing about love: Will it last forever? No, it won't last forever. In fact, it's over already. They're talking about death. One of the stock lines in flamenco singing is *cuando yo me muera*—"when I die." It's like in the blues—"My baby left me this morning"—which is also about a kind of death. This agonizing over the ending of things is a particular aesthetic, a particular thematic that does not exhaust the scope of valid, legitimate art, but is what we talk about when we talk about Lorca and duende.

SR: And you're saying that you tend to be pulled toward that aesthetic.

NM: Yes. I think I've always been disposed in that direction, even when I was a kid, and it's certainly been strengthened by the fact that I'm in my fifties now. *Splay Anthem* and *Whatsaid Serif* come out of the nineties and into 2000 or so. Those poems reflect the fact that the nineties were brutal, in terms of losing family members. My mother died in 1990; I lost a brother not many years after that; I lost a cousin, I lost an aunt, an uncle. It's been the experience of losing people of whom your initial apprehension was that they were going to be there forever. They were your gods and goddesses. When you came into the world, they were the terms of your reality. And those terms, you thought, would not change. There's a way in which you never outgrow the child who looked at them that way. Mortality is certainly something one knows to be a fact of life, but it becomes more pressing as you get older. That may have something to do with why the kinds of reflections that started this question have become more salient.

SR: I want to end by asking you about your relationship to the Bay Area experimental writing community.

NM: It was in the larger Bay Area that my earliest bondings with people on the basis of being an aspiring writer took any significant form. When I was writing as an undergraduate at Princeton, I didn't have a sense that I was part of something. When I lived in Southern California for a year after I graduated, I was writing, but I was pretty isolated. Stanford, where I did my doctorate in English, was the first place where I had some sense of a community. I met both younger, aspiring writers and writers who had established themselves in some way. At Stanford I met Al Young, who was teaching there. He and Ishmael Reed had a magazine, *Yardbird Reader,* which published my work. I met Michael Harper when he read at Stanford, and Adrienne Rich, who was a close friend of my dissertation adviser, Albert Gelpi, when she read there. I took a course from Donald Davie, the British poet-critic. Jon Eckels, who had published poetry with Broadside Press, was in the PhD program at Stanford. William J. Harris was a grad student there as well. He's written a book on Baraka, and he's one of the editors of the Riverside anthology of African-American literature. I don't think he's writing poetry anymore, but he was writing at the time and he published a couple of books in the seventies. Reginald Gibbons was also a grad student—he later became editor of *TriQuarterly* and is a novelist and a translator as well as a poet. I met Robert Duncan at Stanford when he was there for a reading.

But it was really my trips to San Francisco and the East Bay that were most formative. I went to the memorial readings for Kenneth Patchen and Ezra Pound. I remember a reading in which Robert Duncan, Robert Creeley, and I think Diane di Prima and Phil Whalen read. I attended a Ted Berrigan reading. The night before I took my PhD orals exam, I went up to hear a reading by Robert Duncan and George Oppen.

I was at Stanford from 1970 to 1974. Then I taught for two years at the University of Wisconsin. I wanted to come back to California, and I got a job teaching at USC. But I had my eyes on Northern California. I found the atmosphere conducive to writing. Fortunately I got the job here at UCSC in 1979. By that time I'd gotten to know Robert Duncan a bit better and we got together regularly. The Poetics Program at New College opened up at that time and he was teaching there. Duncan McNaughton was teaching there—I had met him at an Olson conference in Iowa. Robert Duncan introduced me to a number of people—Michael Palmer, David Bromige, Michael McClure. I met Bob Callahan through Ishmael Reed—he was involved in the Before Columbus Foundation. I met Cecil Taylor at Bob's house one night.

SR: The people that you're mentioning are all over the map in terms of their poetics—from Adrienne Rich to Michael Palmer is a pretty big stretch. It seems you were open to a larger conversation with the literary community, rather than limiting yourself to a particular school or movement.

NM: When I first moved up here, I wanted to live in San Francisco. That didn't work out, for various reasons. But I came to see that as a good thing, because there were a lot of turf wars going on which I was able to stay outside of. I would go to events and there would be two people I would talk to who weren't talking to each other. There was a big rift in the late seventies and early eighties between the Language poets on the one hand and New College on the other, with Michael Palmer kind of straddling the two. It eventually subsided, probably because a lot of people left. Bob Perelman is at Penn; Barrett Watten and Carla Harryman are at Wayne State; Ron Silliman lives outside of Philadelphia; David Levi Strauss lives in upstate New York; and so on.

SR: It sounds as if you think it's healthy that those turf wars are over.

NM: Yes. Maybe it's just my temperament, but I didn't have any use for being in the fray. I didn't feel affiliated. I had more basic concerns: I was spending all this time in academia and I was worried about whether the writer in me was being gobbled up by the academic, the critic. For me, it was good to meet a range of writers. One of the things I appreciate about the Bay Area literary scene is that it has a variety of persuasions, aesthetics, schools. The other scenes I've been to have been much more homogenous and constricted. That was the case in Madison, Wisconsin, and to a lesser extent in Los Angeles.

SR: Do you interact with younger poets? Do you see younger poets facing anything that's different than what you've experienced?

NM: I teach some creative writing and I do have contact with younger poets who I meet, for example, at readings. I get submissions of work from younger writers for *Hambone* and I publish some of them. So I feel somewhat in touch. There's a whole world of poetry on the Internet that I think is a fact of life for the younger generation, which it isn't for me. There may be new turf wars that I don't know about; there's another generation or two of poets that may need to go through that process of self-definition.

MICHAEL PALMER

The Recovery of Language

Sarah Rosenthal: Starting with *Company of Moths,* your most recent work—how did you go about putting it together?

Michael Palmer: I always attempt to wait for some kind of architecture to emerge, and it often emerges late in the process. In this case, it was a struggle to find the shape. Until the last poem in the book came to me, the one for Gozo Yoshimasu, I wasn't sure how the work would be sectioned. The sections I arrived at are in chronological order, though I moved a few things around within sections.

SR: The section called "Scale" stands out formally. The eight poems in that group are all short and have monosyllabic titles.

MP: I was commissioned to write in response to the paintings of Gerhard Richter. It was a sequence of paintings called *858*: eight small abstractions that Richter painted right after recovering from his severe stroke several years ago. David Breskin, a friend of Richter's who has written about him, borrowed the paintings, which were later shown in the Richter retrospective here though not shown in the New York version of it. David asked a group of thirteen poets and one composer/performer, Bill Frisel, to respond to the work. I ended up responding as much to Richter's own writings, the history of his work, and the play between abstraction and representation and the undermining of expectation that runs through his work—the built-in paradoxes and contradictions that he revels in—as much to those elements as to the sequence of paintings. Except that I did do eight small poems in response to the eight small paintings.

Often events like that can creatively turn a work. I had felt a little bit impeded in what I was doing, and working on this series of poems helped free me up. They function structurally as a turn in the book too, a *volta*.

SR: I didn't know they were in response to Richter. I saw them as trying out, on a smaller scale, certain gestures and tropes that are present in your longer poems.

MP: Yes. And then of course there was the play on the Richter Scale. Richter himself has always been fascinated by earthquakes.

SR: Two of the earliest poems in the volume have very solemn dedications. The poem "And" is to the memory of a suicide. "The Thought" is to Faraj Bayrakdar, who was a Syrian political prisoner. Bayrakdar has spoken in an interview about what he calls the "Nazi chair" or the "German chair," one of the forms of torture that he was subjected to while in prison. The chair would bend his shoulders back to the point where if he took a full breath he would die. He had to teach himself to take half-breaths.[1]

MP: I'll have to look that up.

SR: It's interesting that without knowing about that, you referenced breathing: "We breathe in, we do not think / of it." Some of the poem's images are perhaps evoking solitary confinement: "where the light does not differ from dark"; "where we fashion a calendar from a wall."[2]

MP: That poem was also commissioned, by an international committee that was trying to bring attention to his plight. A special book was made about him to try to help free him. The earlier poem you mentioned, "And," is for Walter Benjamin. His *Passagenwerk,* or *Arcades Project,* is a kind of bedside reader for me. The poem represents an immersion in the textures of that book, its examination of the commodity and also its wonder at the commodity, and the hallucinatory character of emerging commodity culture which Benjamin was looking back to in the nineteenth-century Paris of Baudelaire.

SR: "[T]he shining ornaments / for ankle, waist, neck and wrist" . . .[3]

MP: "[D]ioramas, cosmoramas, pleoramas"[4]—it's looking at this culture of commodity in the *passages,* the arcades of Paris, the precursors to our malls.

SR: I was getting a bleak feeling from the reference to suicide and to imprisonment. The "Scale" section also feels dark. But after that second section, I broke out of that feeling. Like your other books, *Company of Moths* does not have a dominant affective tone. Yet it does feel different in its more cohesive use of rhythm, rhyme, form (couplets), and syntax.

MP: Yes, formally it's more consistent than my earlier books.

SR: I wondered if you were interested in taking on or inhabiting figures of speech—turning them inside out—rather than resisting them.

MP: In the evolution of my work, I've had an increasing interest in what we think of as ordinary language, perhaps like Wittgenstein's evolution toward looking at things as they're said. I have an ironic relationship to figures of speech as they are in the world, and a fascination with the mystery that occurs as we reframe them. We let them pass as everyday-life words, and yet if we pull back just a step, they acquire a kind of poetic estrangement. Not that I approach this systematically, but enough people have talked about it, that I think that in *Company of Moths* there is an evolution toward that kind of focus—particularly with the last two sections, where of course we're facing the utter bleakness of the Bush years. I finally began to realize that the only possible response to this was some sort of Dionysian laughter. I'm convinced that George Bush doesn't exist; that it's actually Terry Southern doing an impersonation of the President of the United States; it's the only possible explanation. The Magic Christian is back, and he's been almost-elected President. It's that ludicrous and primitive. And I think therefore I've started once again—as we did in the Vietnam era—to attend to the strange language of hypocrisy and prevarication that we face, and to include a relationship to that speech in the work.

SR: In an interview you did with Peter Gizzi in *The Exact Change Yearbook* you said, "I worry that a certain kind of theoretical overdetermination of vanguardist gestures or moves in itself becomes as airily dismissive or as enclosed a space as art for art's sake, and as limited in its address and in its horizon as art for art's sake. It becomes a conversation for those refined enough to know the terms."[5] I wonder whether in this book you wanted to approach the conversation with the reader in a different way.

MP: I wanted to have a more open and generous conversation with the reader, and I don't mean by that to begin to write "transparent" poems, which are condescension, an insult to the reader. But my work was moving toward another form of voice and address—it just has done that. There's less of a focus on, let's say, syntax, and more of a focus on figures and on the strangeness of rhetorical gestures of public speech.

SR: I got the sense that you're trying to take the thinking that you've always done and find ways to help it reach people in a different way—to begin more with where they are and lead them into your thinking, rather than confronting them with all the things that you've thought about and read, when they haven't necessarily had that kind of access.

MP: Well, that's certainly true. But it's something that's also a natural evolution in the work, in that that was an area that was opened up to me *by* the earlier work—that I couldn't have arrived at without the earlier work. Every time you finish a book, or maybe even a poem, you think, What did I not manage to include? I think of that wonderful dream of O'Hara's of a poem that would include everything. The effort to allow more breathing room into the work is part of it too. I remember a conversation with Edmond Jabès, when he was out here in '83. He and his wife, Arlette, were staying with us for a week or so and we would have these long conversations in the evenings; he was a wonderful conversationalist. He talked about respiration in the work. I said to him at one point, One of my problems is that I keep trying to go deep into it, yet I keep bobbing up to the surface. He said, If you stay under, you'll drown. He then talked about his early correspondence with Max Jacob. Jacob had been a mentor to Edmond, who was then a sort of proto-Surrealist poet in Egypt. Edmond would send Jacob a manuscript and Jacob would write back and say, You're not breathing. And then the next work would come and Jacob would write, You're breathing too much—you're panting! So there was this series of gnomic instructions about learning to breathe and learning the breathturn of the work. There's a sense in this of breathing in the world (breathing *in* the world), which is also Celan's notion. After you breathe the world in, there's a turn, and then you exhale, you let it out, and there's a moment of stillness where the meeting of inside and outside occurs. People interpret this in any number of ways. I was struck some years ago when I'd been talking about the breathturn and someone came up to me and said, That's exactly the term my singing teacher used to use.

SR: The Buddhist meditation teachers talk about it all the time. They think that when you reach the breathturn, you contact the void; it's a *bardo*, a space between.

MP: Yes, I have a very serious Buddhist friend, a former dancer with Margy Jenkins's company, with whom I've talked about just that.

SR: This book works with couplets of an even length, and many of the poems are about a page or so long. Your earlier work does more experiments with the page as an open field, in the sense in which Olson described it. In this book you seem more interested in "verse," in the sense of the ancient origins of that word—the furrows, the tight turns of the plow.

MP: I think there's an increasing focus on the strange mechanism of interiority mixing with a kind of antilyricism and bringing the congeries of unpolished material of the world itself into the midst of it.

SR: So the form provided a reliable container in which you could make these experiments?

MP: The form just seemed to be endlessly flexible. Sometimes, as the OULIPO people say, if you establish a limit that's stern enough, it allows for continual possibilities. The form maintained its viability through the range of the book. It became something to explore. And the moths whose company I'm keeping in this book, such as Mandelstam and others, seemed to be able to inhabit this form in an interesting way. Mainly those "moths" are lyric poets—if we remove the term "lyric" entirely from workshop poetry and from the saccharine sweetness with which it is so often associated.

SR: So let's talk about moths. There are moths not just in *Company of Moths* but in *The Promises of Glass* as well.

MP: As it turns out, all my work is moth-eaten. My Japanese translator excitedly wrote to me saying that he had found moths in the first poem in my first book. I looked and sure enough, there were moths, munching away on the fabric of my being. As these moths continued to eat away at my pages, I began to use them as the focus of my part in an ongoing collaboration with the artist Augusta Talbot. It would be far too simple to describe Augusta as a representational painter, but representations, objects, come into the work. As I began to focus on moths, a lot of work started to explode for both of us. Then a friend of Augusta's, also a painter, asked, Have you read *Austerlitz* by W.G. Sebald? I had had it since it had been out but I hadn't read it. She said to Augusta, There's a beautiful passage on moths in that book. As such things happen, I pulled out the work and it opened to that passage. Sometimes there's that little wink of the gods.

Many poets responded immediately and strongly to Sebald's work. Sebald and I had the same editor at New Directions until Sebald left for Random House. I had been hoping to visit Sebald on a trip to England, and then we received the news of his death in December

2001. It was devastating—the removal of someone in the prime of the work, with whom you think you're in conversation, and from whom you're waiting for the next message. The thing that can't be replaced. So a poem in *Company of Moths*, "Arc," became an elegy for him, quoting fairly liberally from the passages in *Austerlitz* about moths. Anyway, that became a further confirmation that one of the thematic ties in the book was moths.

But it came to me gradually, it seems, that that is the company we, as poets, keep. I think of going toward the flame and all of those clichés, with that brief moment that we have to do our work, in a crepuscular world that the light shines rather weakly on in American culture. We're in the shadows. In fact, in relation to that, the poet Bei Dao said a wonderful thing. A lot of people had thought that he was going to receive the Nobel Prize a couple of years ago, and instead a Chinese novelist living in Paris got it. Eliot Weinberger, who's one of Bei Dao's closest friends and has translated him, commiserated. But Bei Dao responded, No, I'm too young for that and it's better for a poet, at least at my age, to be in shadow rather than in the light.

SR: In the first poem in your book, "And," the moth gets tied in with the image of a ship. "The ship—what was her name, its name? / Was it The Moth?"[6]

MP: That was long before this became *Company of Moths*. But obviously that had begun to settle in my mind in some preconscious way.

SR: The section called "Company of Moths" starts with a quote from Montale's "La primavera hitleriana": "Whirls the white cloud of mad moths / above the parapets' ashen lights . . ."[7] This image links up for me with the frenzied dance that comes up repeatedly in this volume.

MP: Yes, a death dance, or carnivalesque. I knew that poem of Montale's very well, and had always liked it as a response of the basically interiorized lyric voice to the political circumstance. People who misunderstand the lyric don't realize that that's constantly there, whether in Dante or elsewhere.

SR: You're talking about the lyric being bigger and better than the way that it's been used.

MP: Oh, of course, better than the weekend verse about sweetness and light and sadness.

SR: In the poem "The Phantom of Liberty," you seem to be inhabiting that voice to mock it: "We began, I remember, with the ordinary— / sips of juice, strips of bacon of a morning, // eggs over easy."[8]

MP: Yes, I was parodying the "middle voice" poem. Insofar as these poems are "about" anything, that poem is about the return of the ghosts of fascism in the midst of the ordinary, in the sleep of reason or whatever you want to call it. "[A]nd the ghosts we thought long gone / bearing fresh robes it's true, // and the sheep in the fields wandered up to the fence / and greeted them, come anew."[9] This is about the return of the horrors, into our midst, of what is basically fascist behavior. That's one reading.

SR: In that connection I think of your poem "The White Notebook" in *The Promises of Glass,* which speaks of the erasure of history: "But we have painted over the chalky folds, / the snow- and smoke-folds, so carefully, / so deftly, that many (Did you bet // on the margins, the clouds?) that many / will have gone, unnoticed, / under."[10] I'm curious whether the images of "over" and "under" in that poem are related to the theme of "above and below" which manifests elsewhere in your writing. For example, you have written about going to a cemetery in Roxbury and being struck by the sight of unearthed tombstones. You could see the "practice alphabets" cut into the lower part of the stone by stone-cutting apprentices.[11] This image comes up again in *At Passages*, "Letter 2": "Belowabove: hum of the possible to say?" "Song of the closed mouth? / Of an alphabet underground?"[12] The poem "Arc" in *Company of Moths* also revisits that language.

MP: "There is the above and the below of each."[13] There's the above and the below of the conscious and the unconscious, so to speak, and the intersection or conversation between these realms. I think that's something one constantly revisits in making work. *Company of Moths* also evokes what the French call the *entre chien et loup*—between dog and wolf, between quotidian, civilized behavior and night, the wilderness of dream. The transitional move between those—waking from a dream and so forth.

SR: I also think of conversation and its obverse or underside: silence, mishearings, absence. For example, you thought you were going to be having a decades-long conversation with the novelist W.G. Sebald and now he's gone.

MP: Yes, and I got word this morning from Pierre Joris that the great jazz musician Steve Lacy has died. He had been ill for a while and had taken a bad turn a few weeks ago. So there's another instance of irreplaceable loss. I first heard him when I was a teenager, and I've been listening to him and in conversation with his work ever since. He was an unusual jazz musician in that he had a very intense relationship to poetry. He set all sorts of poems by American, British, and Russian poets to music for his wife, Irène Aebi, to sing. He did a score for a piece of mine. I don't know if he ever recorded it; if he did, I haven't heard it.

So that's also part of the company that circulates through the work. It's not just the company of poets. It's the company of voices—including the voices, as Williams says, of Polish mothers. So the company should be understood, I think, in the larger sense of voices in the street, voices of readers, singers, demagogues, necromancers, psychotics, hierophants . . . who did I omit? Readers, of course, because the poem only exists when the book is opened. It exists by their grace. They establish the present and the presence of the poem, and the now and the future and the past. They confirm the "time" of the poem, even as the poem articulates a time of its own.

SR: When you said you inhabit certain figures of speech, I got the feeling that it was to point out their absurdity. But at other times you seem to inhabit common figures of speech in a more intimate way.

MP: Not just their absurdity but their polysemy. We tend to take clichés and commonplace figures, the metaphors of our daily speech, for granted. And when we allow them to resonate out, to breathe in their own way, they acquire an interesting depth. So when they're recontextualized within the poem, of course, we see them very differently.

SR: You end the poem "Company of Moths" with the words "Outline of stuff left behind." Often you put more common words and phrases into your poems. This casual, even sloppy word, "stuff," comes in one sense as a surprise but it also makes sense given the rest of the poem, which names "The Book of Poor Text," "Streets of the Poor Text," and "Faith in the Poor Text."[14] There's an awareness here of the inadequacy of language to connect.

MP: Well, the limits. One lives the truth of skepticism, but one also makes a path to language to allow it to occur. That's what we do, we make an agreement, since it's the only one that's going to work. It's a social agreement, a negotiation, maybe. But at the same time, as poets, in any case, and maybe in everyday language too, we come up against the limits of expression and the limits of reference: The fact that words are *not* things, they're not the same as things. It's a problem that philosophers have forever wondered about, not just poststructuralists. It's almost the opposite of, let's say, bourgeois realism or whatever you want to call it, which is not problematized by that question. It's the opposite of the language of the page turner. For example, there's a novelist named Michael Palmer who writes pulp fiction. I read an interview with him in *The Boston Globe* a few years ago and he said, The first thing I try to forget about when I go to write is language. I thought, What a wonderful idea: language as pure transparency! My satanic Doppelgänger!

SR: In *Company of Moths* you're testing out some new ways of getting at the meeting ground between language's limits and its capacities.

MP: After all, that has to be negotiated too. Poetry is a perverse thing in that it gestures both toward the world and toward a self which also, in a sense, is the world. At times it wants to bring the world impossibly close, and at other times it wants the world to go away so you can do some thinking.

SR: Isn't there also a way of recognizing distance that perversely makes one feel more connected?

MP: I think that's what Williams called "contact." Poetry, even if it is involved in a certain kind of dialectical negativity in relation to things as they are, still calls to people and things, even as it acknowledges the space in between. It's a critical and productive relationship, an endless traversal.

SR: I'd like to ask about all the appearances of the words "no" and "not" in your poetry. I thought about your coming up during the Vietnam War and feeling angry at what was being handed to you, and that circumstance generating a political "no" of resistance. But then there is something about the innate nature of language that is a "not."

MP: With a *k* or with an *n*?

SR: Good point; it's both. I was thinking about the "not," as otherness, and the work of the poet being in part to open oneself to that other, which is a different, more invitational sense of negation.

MP: Of course, because it's not about solipsism, after all; it's about contact. And so the "no" is a positive refusal, a critical refusal and one that's historically part of the role of much poetry. Not the poetry of sentimental assuagement, of course, with its adhesiveness to the mushy cultural center. In fact, such work represents the negation of the critical force of poetry; it's a poetry in fealty to a debased expectation. And that's been true of a lot of writers since the beginning of industrial society. After all, the hatred for Shelley and Keats and those poets was monumental until a way was found—not so long after their deaths—to appropriate them into a harmless lyrical canon. In the summer of 1822, the Courier, a major Tory newspaper in London, ran an obituary that began: "Shelley, the writer of some infidel poetry, has been drowned: now he knows whether there is a God or no."[15]

SR: I didn't realize there was such a vitriolic response to the Romantics.

MP: Absolutely, and in differing ways. Now, of course, Wordsworth, after his apostasy, his abandonment of Romantic resistance as well as his return to the Church and abandonment of the political left, became quite literally a poet laureate—and wrote dreadfully, in the main, for the rest of his life. He should have had the grace to die young too.

SR: So there's a refusal which is actually an invitation or a hope or a request to be read more complexly.

MP: Yes, and to read the world more complexly, or at least more skeptically. To counter the mendacious drivel. To be, in other words, as far as possible, what the current administration (of George the Second) and the cultural arbiters would consider a bad citizen. We work toward consciousness, after all, and conscience, against oblivion. Conscience: con-scientia: to know along with another.

SR: There's a continuum in your work between political resistance and investigation of language.

MP: I'm not a political poet, in the sense that let's say Amiri Baraka or Adrienne Rich are, or Allen Ginsberg was. Their poetry is instrumentalist by design; it's meant to incite direct action. I suppose I'm in the polis and in relation to the polis in a different, if often sympathetic, way. And that illustrates the necessary range of voices, as Wallace Stevens said, between inside and outside, between a poetry that incites to action and a poetry that incites to reflection. But that puts it far too simplistically, since reflection is necessary to responsible intervention. We're speaking of active reflection, naturally, a form of unmasking, of bringing to light, beyond the means readily at hand, beyond habits of speech and thought.

SR: You do a lot with repetition and variation, within and between poems, and within and between books. You seem to be teasing out all of the different ways that that can add to and support your project.

MP: Recurrence and variation have fascinated me since I first read Gertrude Stein as a very young person. Or perhaps I should say: since I first heard nursery rhymes and incantations as an even younger person. Likeness and difference and their dance—isn't that the ground of the poetic project and of our signifying capacity? And metaphor: a thing in terms of another thing, a bearing across between a one and "an other," or self and other.

SR: Or between the self that I am in this moment and the self that I am in the next moment.

MP: Voices stream through many of my books—voices of poets and people in the world. They are books of echoes; echo chambers. I've always felt that poetic voice is a mutable entity, rather than that odd creative-writing construct of "finding your voice." There is that, to my ear, Keatsian line (I once misremembered it as coming from Keats's letters), "the voice that is great within us," which Hayden Carruth borrowed from Stevens's "Evening without Angels"[16] as the title for his very popular anthology, first published in 1970. The anthology itself is quite a mixed bag, as most are. The lesser work seems to misapprehend the phrase as "the voice that is trivial all about us," reflecting the hoary workshop cliché of "finding your voice." As Keats and Stevens both might have put it, the voice isn't a signature but is in fact an enigmatic construct of many voices: of the conscious and unconscious, of endless echoes and prefigurations, and so on. It's constituted *de profundis*, if you will. Frequently that is mistranslated into finding, in the worst sense, a style. Style itself is very fascinating, but it has to do in the best sense, paradoxically, with depth, the dynamic interior, as revealed upon the surface, as in great architecture. I think that's one of the differentiating points between a poet of momentary and one of enduring interest.

SR: At different times repetition and variation seem to operate in your work as translation, jazz, conversation, and a stutter.

MP: It's interesting that you bring up the stutter because my earlier work talks about the poet's and the philosopher's stutter: the stutter of the effort of articulation, which is part of the articulation. You hear it—the stutter or the hesitation, they're part of the same thing—if you listen to a Gilles Deleuze or a Jacques Derrida speaking—improvising philosophy. You may also see it in the improvisational steps Wittgenstein takes in his work toward whatever goal is there, letting the fly out of the bottle, let's say.

SR: I'm glad you've raised the topic of improvisation. I know you don't just compose improvisationally and leave it at that; your work is very layered. But nonetheless you seem to be after an improvisational feel.

MP: I think in the layering—which has become more intense over the years—what you're trying to arrive at is not some proposition of the well-wrought urn, but rather, in fact, immediacy. But there are different ways of interpreting the word "immediacy." In Beat poetics, for example, immediacy is "first thought, best thought"; pure improvisation on the surface. For me, the improvisation is one that occurs at many,

many levels, including the palimpsestic construction of the text and the listening—not just the speaking, but the listening. It's oddly enough a process of arriving at something that's more immediate than I'm gifted to give at the beginning. I think one of the problems of Beat poetics—whatever the virtues may be, such as spontaneity, etc.—is that you are too prone, as with some aspects of free improvisation, to fall into certain habits of composition. So you get a sameness of composition which is *not* immediacy; it's habit in the guise of immediacy. For me, paradoxically, to arrive at the now, the immediate, I have to swim in these strange channels, shifting currents.

SR: Just because a poem hasn't been written in ten minutes doesn't necessarily mean that it's not improvisational. We're talking about slowing down and expanding the idea of improvisation to include the perhaps quite lengthy process of layering and shaping. Do you learn from paying attention to pure improvisation in other forms such as dance or jazz?

MP: I've learned not just from improvisation but from the development of alternative structures and compositional possibilities in contemporary music and dance, structures and possibilities that were largely unattended to when I was a young person in school, being exposed to the canon of academic verse of the time. That verse simply wasn't answering to the needs of the work. On the contrary, it seemed to be building monuments to an exhausted nineteenth century neo-romanticism, stuffed with homily, strained artifice, and posturing. So it was really to the other arts—painting, etc.—that I turned.

At the same time, of course, I was exploring that alternative tradition in American poetry that extends from Dickinson and Whitman on to the present, through the great modernists and some of the lesser modernists too, who may not have been fully able to realize their projects but who were really trying something out—Mina Loy, for example. I just had a conversation with someone who's making a film about Mina Loy. She's someone who, for whatever reasons of personality, discipline, etc., never fully realized the incredible gift that she had as an artist. But you look at some of that slashing, proto-feminist satire and you learn something from it. You see all these concerns that were not being attended to then, all the currents that were really condescended to in, let's say, official poetry.

So modernist poetry, along with the other arts, was really helpful to me. Also, when I was still young I met the poets of the outside, so to speak, in all their variety, and realized that I was not alone in my interests. I "met" Stan Brakhage through Bob Creeley at the age of twenty. I "met" Louis Zukofsky through Bob as well, though as Clark Coolidge recently reminded me, I'd already read a bit of his work before. So there were these worlds opening up.

And of course I was out here at a very fruitful moment in poetics. When I first arrived, in '68 or '69, there was a bit of a lull. The Spicer generation had scattered. The San Francisco Renaissance was no longer in its moment, although some of its poets were doing great work. Then suddenly in the early seventies, as for instance Lyn Hejinian, Bob Perelman, Johanna Drucker, and many others began to gather here, as well as those in opposition to what they saw as the Language movement, there was a lot of very interesting contention about theory, about performativity, about all of those questions, which was extremely useful. Whether you were a card-carrying Language poet or not, it was a useful time to be around the discussion. So that kind of boosted the public nature of poetry. There were readings at the Grand Piano and other cafés, talks at Natoma Street, Langton Street and other venues. These events were full of an eagerness about "What is so-and-so doing this week?" They reproduced the vitality of, let's say, the jazz clubs of an earlier time, where you would hear that John

Coltrane had just taken up the soprano saxophone and you'd go down to the Five Spot and hear him working it out. There was some of that excitement in a very different cultural landscape here, through the seventies and into the eighties, that helped all of us articulate something like a poetics and a relationship to performance. Let's not forget filmmakers, like Nathaniel Dorsky and Warren Sonbert, and numerous people working in music and the visual arts.

And then dance, my work with Margaret Jenkins and her company, also helped me think about the space of performance. That can be the space of the page, where the words and the silences are performers, but also the public forum where the work is presented. Public presentation has become so much part of the life of poetry in this country. Sometimes (not that often), I read in front of a thousand people and sometimes (more often) I read for twelve, and those are both very interesting occasions, though I must always overcome a certain *dread* to make it—no, to allow it—to happen, however many may be present.

SR: You seem to treat reading to audiences as a zone of creativity in and of itself.

MP: I think it's part of the art, in a good sense and a bad sense. The good sense is that at a reading, people can hear the musical logic of the work in a way that often they can't hear by themselves. A lot of people aren't so good at finding the music on the page, and so a poem becomes more available to them if you voice it. What seemed impossibly strange becomes less so—sometimes, anyway.

But in giving readings I've never been too interested in artifice and theatricality. I've always tried to speak the work with a minimum of stylization or affectation. There are some very interesting ways of constructing a performance, but I try not to do that. The readings I enjoy most are the ones where the poetry surprises me with its information; where I discover something in the poem I didn't know was there when I wrote it. I can't really get at that if I self-consciously project a persona. I think that type of artifice can always be interesting as part of the art, and some people do that in very fascinating ways, whether we're talking about early Dada or postmodern play. And that thought in a funny way takes me back to the distant rhetoric you hear when you listen to recordings of Tennyson or Yeats reading, with that oratorical artifice that they both employ. Pound had it too, almost certainly from Yeats. There's something fascinating about hearing them read, but I don't want to be there at all, with that construction of the vatic persona.

I was talking about this the other day with the South African novelist John Coetzee. He said, Who then do you admire in the performance of poetry? I said, Well, George Oppen and Paul Celan, among others. Celan reads the work without unnecessary stylization or posturing. And I don't mean it has to be serious—I mess around at readings too. I talk a lot more between poems now than I used to, because I've found that the density of the poetry is such that a little conversation in between allows the air to circulate better. So I'm more relaxed about doing that nowadays. I don't mean the kind of pandering and bad faith where you explain the poem and then read the poem. But sometimes the context out of which a poem arises can be illuminating for people in terms of process. It can be relaxing to have that conversation and be reminded, Oh, it's not church, it's a poem. Whatever traumas you've had in English class, please forget them. This is not a question and you don't have to answer it at the end on a piece of paper. It's also a way to demythologize the poetic persona.

SR: Isn't there also a way in which it's impossible to avoid performance? I'm thinking of the page as much as the public reading. One is "putting on" words.

MP: Of course. The theater of the page, as well as the stage, is very real. So I'm not positing in some impossible way a "pure naturalism," which would be after all a mode of stylization in itself.

SR: We're getting to the tricky nature of the word "authentic." Each person has to arrive at their own negotiation with that word.

MP: It is a negotiation. We've long ago deconstructed the myths of authenticity. I take that back; they're still with us. In any case the term, justifiably, has been destabilized.

SR: What about the figure of Quod in the poem "Q"?[17] There you were playing with a persona.

MP: Yes, and obviously my work has many voices pouring through it, often in a theatricalized way. It's not just the textbook lyric voice by any means; there's a ludic aspect to it. Quod was an instance of this impossibly conglomerate character that I built out of many, many people. Roman Jakobson is in there, particularly his book *My Futurist Years*, but also my memories of him as a teacher. Georgio Agamben puts in a cameo appearance, as does Jacques Roubaud. Maybe Quod is my clownish version of Monsieur Teste (Monsieur Texte?). At any rate, this comic figure of abjection in relation to the century just sort of arose as I scribbled this piece, which was written somewhat en route, the way *The Danish Notebook* was written. I was writing it on a bus going to Cambridge, England for a poetry conference they had there; I was writing it in Paris in a borrowed apartment. I was writing it in the room where we're talking.

SR: Quod reminds me of the philosopher in the doorway, a figure who comes in and out of the "Autobiography" poems in *The Promises of Glass*.

MP: That particular philosopher in the doorway started with a review I read of Joseph Brent's biography of Charles Sanders Peirce.[18] He was a philosopher whose range of pursuits, which included mathematics and semiotics, has always fascinated me. He was extremely eccentric—today he'd be diagnosed as bipolar. His work was full of a kind of poetic logic. And at points ungraspable. He never attained the public renown of a Dewey or a James. He was more a philosopher's philosopher. In any case, this biography, the first of its kind, talked about the strange, tragic career of Peirce, who, because of his very erratic and perverse personality and temper, never got an appointment at Harvard, for example. He went from making quite a bit of money at one point in his life to, I think, bankruptcy and virtual homelessness. So that was the beginning of the figure of the philosopher in the doorway.

SR: I'm also reminded of "Letter to a Vagrant" in *Company of Moths*, which evokes the Jabèsian sense of the outsider or the foreigner.

MP: In relation to that, I sent Anne Waldman an email yesterday when we knew Steve was dying. I wrote about an anecdote that Merce Cunningham had told me years ago. He'd come here for lunch sometime in the seventies and Steve Lacy came up in our conversation. Merce told me the story of how his company was touring in South America and Steve showed up at one of their events and told them he was marooned. The gig that was supposed to take place, for which he had paid a lot of money to fly down, hadn't materialized. He was broke and couldn't get back to the States. And so Merce and John tried to help him in various ways. I wrote to Anne in this email that I'd always been haunted by that vision of ending up in a doorway. As poets, even if we're doing OK, that vision of the homeless person lurks in the back of our minds, because we haven't spent our lives earning money as primary purpose. And we *are* homeless, in a way. I don't mean to be melodramatic about that. But we are homeless in the Jabèsian sense of being at home solely in the book. And that goes not just for the diasporic Jew but for the poet.

SR: I'm interested in blindness and deafness as they appear in *Company of Moths*. In the poem "Finisterrae," you write, "The eye on each wing, for example, / many have mentioned this. // That it sees nothing, / no one has mentioned this."[19]

MP: And there's the epigraph at the beginning of the volume from Carlos Drummond de Andrade: "Enter the kingdom of words as if you were deaf," which is fascinating to me.[20]

SR: I don't know if I get any closer to it, but I keep circling around it.

MP: I think it's something to circle. It has a certain enigmatic quality to it. What's interesting here is the word "deaf." I did worry that the citation might be taken wrongly by people focused on disability issues. I just had a conversation with Michael Davidson who, as he has gradually lost his hearing, and faces the possibility of deafness, has come into contact with the signing world, the world of the "hearing-impaired," and been alerted to the extraordinarily rich relationship to language and speech that the deaf community has. And so that's another way of thinking of entering the community of words as if you were deaf. It can be as if you can't hear, but it can also be as if you were more alert to language issues and limits than the general community of language-users.

SR: In "The Turn (May 2003)" you write, "What is that turn you took in Beltà, in Beauty? / A blind man is staring out at the sea."[21]

MP: The first line is an address to Zanzotto and his book *La Beltà*, which was a real turn for him and his work, a turn toward the later, experimental phase of his work. The figure of the blind man has to do with an article I read, I think in the *New York Times*, about Ved Mehta, a prose writer whose work is extremely visual, and who's blind, having a house built for himself on an island off Maine. There's a photograph of Mehta sitting in an Adirondack chair next to this beautiful house, and he's staring out at the sea.[22] It's a wonderful metaphor for blindness as insight.

SR: In "The Merle Asleep," you write, "Who are these blindered travelers // choiring Amazing Grace, Haunted Heart, / All the Things You Are, // while I can only speak."[23] Here we have blind people being gifted singers. Again it seems you're getting at the idea that the absence of a sense can make one attend in a different way.

MP: And of course the merle, which is a European blackbird, can't sing. It squawks. I often think that those of us who come to this impossible task of poetry come out of a disability with language, a lack of fluency rather than dazzling fluency. I think dazzling fluency leads to other media and other uses of language, rather than the impaired fluency of our squawkings.

SR: Deafness can also mean turning a deaf ear, and the same goes for blindness. In "Company of Moths" "a child's gaze falls // on the corpse of a horse beside a cart, / whimpering dog, a woman's mouth agape // as if to say, We must move on, / we must not stop, we must not watch. // For after all, do the dead watch us? / To memorize precisely the tint of a plum, // curve of a body at rest (sun again), / the words to each popular song, // surely that would be enough."[24] I'm taken by this child who hasn't learned to avert his or her eyes from death and suffering. And the adult figure, as most adults do, has distanced from that immediacy, in favor of an obedient attention to digested culture and digestible images of beauty. Perhaps that's narrativizing the poem too much. But you seem to be getting here at the "denial white" you speak of in "The White Notebook" in *The Promises of Glass:* the whiting out or erasing of cultural memory.[25]

MP: There's certainly the monstrous side of forgetting, a historical forgetting that allows us to reenact the depravities of the past. After all, how far are we from the monstrous events of the twentieth century? Not far at all.

SR: We're already mired in the monstrous events of the twenty-first century.

MP: And who knows—maybe we can outdo the last century. We have a president who's a cynical halfwit who thinks God is giving him instructions. Imagine a god stupid enough to tell Bush that he should be president. But as the historian Daniel Boorstin said, Those who try to predict the future without a knowledge of the past are like people planting cut flowers. So this kind of forgetting is monstrous—and murderous.

SR: But there's another side of forgetting which is creative and which acknowledges process.

MP: Of course all memory is forgetting too. It's a creation of the moment. So this past that comes to us in fragments and fictions is a curious thing as we try to imagine a future.

SR: I want to ask you about your experience of the San Francisco writing community. You came here in '69 or so and met Robert Duncan?

MP: After a couple of years, yes. I had met him briefly at the Vancouver Poetry Conference in '63 but I had been most friendly with Bob Creeley and others. Robert was a rather bristling presence there, an intimidating figure. But really only in '71 or '72 did we begin the extraordinary conversation that lasted until his death in '88. And Jess, the painter and assemblage and collage artist who was Robert's partner, was often part of that.

SR: And then there was the gathering of the young Language poets?

MP: Not only Language poets. There were many others. Leslie Scalapino was doing her own highly distinctive work. There were writers such as Norma Cole and Aaron Shurin, who enormously enriched and expanded the scene, some through the work we were doing at New College with our poetics program. I taught there intermittently for a while and then for several years I was a core faculty member. That was great fun in many ways. If we could have been paid a little more, that would have helped to make it even more fun. I can still see the bouncing checks, bouncing down the street. But it was great to run our own program, teaching not just what we loved but what we thought was needed and desired by the students.

SR: Who were the other core faculty?

MP: David Meltzer, Diane di Prima, Tom Clark, Duncan McNaughton, Robert Duncan, and Louis Patler.

SR: So that was a locus for you.

MP: It was one locus that created an interesting dialogue. Then there were a variety of younger writers testing things out. And this wasn't happening in isolation; there was, for example, a constant dialogue with New York. This was before the time of the virtual communities that have been created by email, which dramatically reconfigures notions of groups and space, such that you're no longer dependent on geography for your site. But at that time it was still much more actual-site-specific, as opposed to virtual-site-specific.

Then there was a partial dispersal of that community in the mideighties or a little earlier as people went off to take professional jobs in universities. Their lives, as they made families, became materially more demanding, and they couldn't hang out in the same way. So the nature of that communication changed, and of course a couple of generations of younger writers now have come through, with that characteristic diversity of poetics that we see now in the American scene, where it's very hard to define one or two directions or schools. This reflects, not necessarily in the negative sense, a kind of culture of drift that we see in other areas as well, for example in the diversity in the visual arts and musical scenes, in which it has also become difficult to define genres or movements. It's dramatically different than it was a couple of decades ago. Also we now have the phenomenon of the professional school. Many more of the writers have gone through MFA programs and are looking toward the profession of teaching or what have you. That's the cultural sociology of the contemporary scene. The effects of it are fascinating to contemplate. It includes the institutionalization of the experimental, for example. These days, universities often have a slot for the experimental poet, just as there is an "ethnic" slot and a slot for an academic formalist. Very bizarre. It becomes all about slots. In a funny way, that remains the eternal problem as a poet, not to be slotted. Maybe just the terms have changed.

SR: It's a different ballgame. For perhaps a mix of good and bad reasons, there's been a splintering, and each poet is to some extent an island. There's a sense of positioning that is disturbing.

MP: Well, with the MFA training comes a strategizing of career and of the nature of your work.

SR: How do you gauge the relative importance of the San Francisco poetry community to you now?

MP: San Francisco is the place I return to, and it's been fine in that way, but it's very much enhanced by other sites. I mentioned earlier the Japanese translator who found a reference to moths in my early work. The foreignness of another eye on your work is very interesting. Maybe because I come from an immigrant family, I think I've always by disposition been internationalist. It was not solely the Anglo-American canon that was central to my development; it was very much a broader vision. And part of that was my own discovery and part of it was due to people like Ezra Pound. There are a lot of things *not* to thank him for, but that particular opening to the Provençal poets, the early Italian poets and the Chinese poets, et al., however skewed it may have been in many ways, was enormously valuable to me as a kid. And certainly the eccentricity of his early critical writing was interesting. His publisher, James Laughlin, was busily suppressing the racist and anti-Semitic bits, so you didn't have to face all of that as a young writer—until later. "No Ezra, that's bad, we can't publish that, Ezra, we don't say 'kike' in our poems." Jesus! Maybe Laughlin was doing us a service, since his act of suppression allowed us to absorb the more benign and generative aspects.

SR: It sounds like you've always had an orientation toward the far-flung and the experimental.

MP: Since poetry became a fact of my life in high school, it was always pulling me outward. I remember talking at some point to someone who wondered how I cultivated all these international connections. I didn't "cultivate" them; they just evolved because I was interested. I lived for a time in Europe, particularly when I was underground during the Vietnam War, moving from country to country one step ahead of the draft people. That was for me in part a counter to the cultural isolationism and xenophobia which is such a sickness of this country. I've always thought that one of the important functions of poetry is to stand against the monstrous aspects of nationalism. Which is not to criticize American poetry per se. I'm all for the particularity of a national poetry, but it's one thing to celebrate that particularity and another to laud blood and soil, as we all know. Those are the two sides—the dark and the light sides—of the Romantic ethos. And so crossing those boundaries seems to me a gesture of great actual and symbolic importance. An example of this is when Lyn Hejinian opened up the conversation with the Russian poets while we were still in the "Cold War." Establishing those connections was a refusal of the dictates of power, just as when the Palestinian and Israeli poets refuse not to speak with one another, they are doing something of great symbolic importance. It doesn't stop the slaughter, but it leaves a "no," which is a "yes," imprinted on the culture. It's undeniable. It refuses the hatred and the stereotyping and the racism on both sides. And that's the recovery of language.

STEPHEN RATCLIFFE

Artifice and Accident

Sarah Rosenthal: I'm struck, on reading your more recent work, by the way you use and re-use simple words, many of which have a certain permeability or lend themselves to multiple allusions. As you use them in different combinations and contexts, a meditative, layered complexity emerges.

Stephen Ratcliffe: I think you're right. As I use words again and again, they become little markers or signatures. They become filled with possible sense. But I'm not using them to make allusions to things, but because I like the presence of a particular word in the text. You know, on the page.

Rosenthal: As an object.

Ratcliffe: Yes. Some words, like "yellow," enter every page. So the question becomes, what does it mean even to write that word? How precise can it be? I used to think that you should never repeat; you should always say something different. But now I am fascinated by this effect of repetition. I think that it connects to a whole tradition of song; it works like a refrain. These poems are like song—they're so shaped in various ways, and there is a music that goes with them. And the repeated words and phrases accrue a certain power. In my current manuscript, *HUMAN / NATURE,* the unmade yellow and blue bed is almost like a character because every five or six days I put it in there.

In fact, all the books in the series I've been working on for the past few years—*Portraits & Repetition, REAL, CLOUD / RIDGE,* and the current one, *HUMAN / NATURE*—are marked by the use of a simple, recurring vocabulary. I see my work as an investigation of structure and form and what appears to be a surface which doesn't have any depth to it: perceivable phenomena, things going on in the immediate present tense, or very often things recalled. Not recalled from distant memory, but from yesterday or something like that—somebody saying something, or somebody telling me something. In *HUMAN / NATURE,* there's often a man in a blue shirt who is recalling, so the word "recalling" comes in over and over, but there are other words that repeat, like "cloud" and "ridge" and "sky" and colors and things from the ocean, surfing and water.

But I did want to note that in my early book *Distance,* I used a much more varied and "esoteric" vocabulary, which was all coming out of a found text, a dictionary.

Rosenthal: Yes, and then there's *Present Tense,* which I group with *Distance* in that the vocabulary is much more varied.

Ratcliffe: That's true, although unlike *Distance,* it's composed through observation of daily life and popular culture, not taken from a found text.

Rosenthal: Yet both books contrast with your more recent work, where the field of diction has radically narrowed. This narrowing seems to allow for a deeper exploration of nuance.

Ratcliffe: I like that idea, like Voltaire's notion that we should cultivate our own back yards. Which I do. I sit there in my house in Bolinas and write. The landscape there is essential to my work.

Rosenthal: Could you describe that a little?

Ratcliffe: I live in a house that looks out onto an 85-acre field, and beyond that the Mount Tam ridge. Above the ridge is the sky. There is a road where cars go by, but it's on the other side. I sit in the morning and write, looking out my kitchen window. And in every poem in this series of four books, the first section of the poem—and in the case of *Portraits & Repetition,* the entire poem—is based on looking at things as perception. Either looking out the window, or looking at postcard images or objects that are on the windowsill, that sort of thing. But it all comes out of writing in the present moment. And doing it over and over. I am aware that I am repeating a lot of the same words. I'm fascinated to see how a word can be different depending upon its immediate context. Because in fact, as Stein said, it isn't so much repeating as it is a kind of insistence. Hence it's exploring facets of something. And maybe you only want to read a little bit of it; that's fine. I think with my work you can open to any page and just read that page. There can also be a spell-binding quality for listeners when I read twenty pages or so; it takes you off on a visual/mental excursion.

Rosenthal: Did you plan these works to be a series before you began them?

Ratcliffe: No. When I started the first one, *Portraits & Repetition,* I thought, Well, maybe I'll go for a year. Then when I got to the 365th poem, I didn't want to stop. I thought, It's just getting good. So I kept going, and then things were going on in life, and I thought, This has to stop, it's getting ungodly long, it's ridiculous. So I got to the 474th poem and there was a certain symmetry in that number, like a 747, a big jet. So then I thought, Well, maybe I will write another one, and maybe I could go on that long, and maybe I can do a triptych. I'll do three. So *REAL* was next, and *CLOUD / RIDGE* was the third one, and then I thought I would stop. But I didn't want to. So I started the current one, *HUMAN / NATURE.*

Rosenthal: All of these works have exactly 474 poems in them? There's a poem for every single day for 474 days?

Ratcliffe: Yes. And they are all the same length on the page; that is, the poems in *CLOUD / RIDGE* all have fourteen lines, though some of the lines drop down so they look to be more than fourteen lines.

Rosenthal: So there is an echo of the sonnet form.

Ratcliffe: Ron Silliman calls them sonnets, while Tom Raworth would say they're fourteen-line poems. I think of them as fourteen-line poems. But the form is influenced by my study of Renaissance poetry so, yes, there is a trace of the sonnet in them.

Rosenthal: I think a lot of writers would feel deadened by the practice of looking out and describing the same scene day in and day out, year in and year out. They would feel they had exhausted the possibilities of that scenario.

Ratcliffe: Yes, except I'm not really focusing on description. Merleau-Ponty said something like, "What we want is to give a direct description of our experience."[1] Stein, in "Portraits and Repetition," says she became excited by the discovery that the words that made something look like itself (and then later she says that words "made something *be* itself") were not words that had anything to do with description.[2] I think she is talking about "Tender Buttons." In that work, she gives the name of the object that she's making a portrait of, like "Mashed Potatoes," but the text itself doesn't seem to be a description of mashed potatoes at all.[3] I think my work does appear to be description, but it's trying to test the boundary of what description could be. There is always a gap between writing something down as words, and the world that's out there being described. The world out there can't ever be exactly reenacted. But through working in these repeating forms over a long period of time, I'm exploring how the things of the world can be enacted in language.

Rosenthal: When I read your work I am not even worrying about what's out the window; I'm engrossed by what's on the page. The more I read, the more I slow down and become aware of the immediate sensations and perceptions I'm having in the act of reading. Every little moment begins to matter, from letters to punctuation to spacing. So I assume you are aware of these things too?

Ratcliffe: Yes, I'm completely focused on the words on the page and what's happening in the form.

Rosenthal: Can you describe some of the formal elements at play in your current manuscript?

Ratcliffe: Sure. In every poem, there are four stanza units totaling ten lines. The first stanza has three lines, the second has two lines, the third has three lines, and the fourth has two lines. The three-line stanzas have two commas, which means there are a total of three syntactic units in those stanzas. In the two-line stanzas there's one comma, so those stanzas have two syntactic units. The lines can only be five inches long. I use Courier typeface, which is non-proportional, meaning that every letter and space and mark of punctuation has the same width. For example, a *w* is as wide as a period. In Times Roman, Palatino, and many other typefaces it's proportional. So I don't count letters, but I do set up a margin. There's a lot of mathematical measuring; it's about measure. Figuring out the relationships between things.

My procedure for writing the poems is also very precise and formalized. The first unit of every poem in this book and in the previous book, *CLOUD / RIDGE,* is always being written in the present moment, looking out the window in the morning. The following three stanzas come out of notes that I've written down previously. I use two notebooks. I have a small notebook ("A") that I keep with me at all times to jot notes in. When I sit down in the morning to write that day's poem, I write it in a second, larger notebook ("B"). I start by writing a direct observation. Then I flip through the small notebook ("A") and look for recent notes, and when I find one I want, I put it into the poem I'm composing in notebook "B."

Rosenthal: These are notes on things you are reading and thinking.

Ratcliffe: Reading, seeing, overhearing.

Rosenthal: Do you copy the notes verbatim from "A" into the poem you're composing in "B" or do you rewrite them in the process?

Ratcliffe: I've gotten so I can write things down in notebook "A" that I will be able to use as closely as possible. But there are often extra words that I have to pick and choose—when you're overhearing something, you have to catch it on the fly. So there is still a lot of pruning. For example, here's a note in notebook "A": "Red finch landing on rose branch next to feeder in right foreground." When it entered a poem in *HUMAN / NATURE*, it became "Finch landing on rose branch next to feeder."

I should add that what happens with the right margin is an important aspect of that pruning. As I type a poem, there's something that pleases me about seeing a certain visual pattern emerge along the right-hand margin, a visual relationship created among the line endings. That visual relationship helps dictate what's being written down in the line. So the shape of the right margin is crucial to me in the process of composing the poem. It has nothing to do with what's in the notebooks.

Rosenthal: It's a further restraint.

Ratcliffe: Yes, it's like a rule or a game. Each one is different, and it comes about only when the actual materials of the words come into the poems. I pay a lot of attention to the sounds of the words, but also to spacing on the page.

Rosenthal: Has the right margin always been an important element of composition for you?

Ratcliffe: Absolutely, going all the way back to my book *MOBILE / MOBILE*. In that book, all the poems had right-justified margins, which I created on a Courier typewriter—not by counting letters, but by adjusting the words to make it come out that way. But that was letterpress typeset, and the person who typeset it, Les Ferriss, used a different typeface, so it shifted. It caused me anxiety, thinking no one would know that I had worked to get this right. But then I thought, Well, it doesn't really matter because it served its purpose; having that constraint helped me to write the poem. Now I use a computer and I use Courier typeface to approximate that pica and elite type that old typewriters used. But again, when these books are typeset in different fonts, things shift. *Idea's Mirror* was set in the same font as the one I'd composed in, so I could preserve the look of the right margin.

Rosenthal: Why do you think working with the right margin is so important for your creativity?

Ratcliffe: A poem isn't a picture, but it is like a visual abstraction. It is like an abstract painting, perhaps. I just attended a slide show at the San Francisco Art Institute by James Siena, a visual artist from New York. He works with metal plates, maybe 18" x 13" or somewhat bigger. He thinks of them as being on a human scale, like the size of a head or something. He fills the two-dimensional plane right out to the edge with very minute, detailed work—nesting, repeating forms that create a sense of complexity and shape, yet there is also a simplicity. The shape of the poem, the physical space that the line occupies on the page, is for me a dimension of the poem. I wrote about this in an essay, "... *sound* ... *shape* ... *meaning* ..."[4] There is the sound of the words, which is potential when the words are on the page, until they are actually read aloud. In other words, you might hear a sound in your head when you read to yourself, but there is something about speaking that puts it out into the air, where it becomes an acoustic shape. And then there is what we've been talking about: the physical shape of the words on the page. The relation of sound and shape to meaning, whatever "meaning" might be, is, I think, crucial in poetry. So I pay attention to it.

Rosenthal: Do you feel that focusing on the length and shape of the lines is a way to keep the quotes around the word "meaning"? To continually demonstrate to yourself, and perhaps to others, that conventional meaning is only one factor, one element in a dance that includes sound and shape?

Ratcliffe: Yes, I think it's a way of acknowledging the provisional, elusive quality of essential meaning, whatever that may be. It's also a way of celebrating the process itself. James Siena said in his lecture, "My work is a celebration of work." I thought, I can get what he means by that. There's something about the sheer dint of effort to get this stuff to come out this way that is a lot of fun.

Rosenthal: When we talked a few years ago, you described using a similarly rigorous and elaborate process while writing *Present Tense:* You had a precise line measurement, and you even completely reconfigured the lines and stanzas at one point. I seem to remember you used to work as a carpenter. Do you see this work as a carpentry-like craft? Hammering, sawing, sanding?

Ratcliffe: I do. It is like building stuff out of words.

Rosenthal: I haven't seen the books in your recent series but I'm getting the picture that while many formal constraints are repeated throughout, each has its own signature formal elements as well.

Ratcliffe: That's true. For example, both *HUMAN / NATURE* and *CLOUD / RIDGE* include one stanza unit drawn from a note I've written the prior day about something observed while surfing. I go in the water every day, and when I'm out there I see something, and when I get back to the house, I write it down in notebook "A." But an element unique to *CLOUD / RIDGE* is that the fourth of the five stanza units is always an excerpt from Virginia Woolf's *To the Lighthouse.* Every day I would turn to one page and find something and put it into my poem. I went through the book several times. I wasn't using it during the early part of the manuscript, but then I started to read it and make use of it.

Rosenthal: Maybe you could read a poem from *CLOUD / RIDGE.*

Ratcliffe: Sure. I'll read the last poem in that book. It's number 10.18, because it was written on October 18, 2002. [Reads poem; see page 224.]

Rosenthal: I get the sense that you were very aware of saying goodbye to this book: "I have had my vision."

Ratcliffe: Yes, definitely. I know it is almost too much, but . . .

Rosenthal: It speaks of your deep personal involvement in the project, and of the loss involved in finishing it.

Ratcliffe: Oh, yeah, it was really powerful. I knew that I was going to come to the end, but I didn't know what would happen, what I would do next.

Rosenthal: And in fact you moved right on into *HUMAN / NATURE.*

Ratcliffe: I did.

Rosenthal: You mentioned that you surf every day. Part of the ritual and skill of surfing involves becoming highly attuned to changes—often minute ones—in the conditions of weather and horizon and ocean. Do you see a connection there with your writing practice?

Ratcliffe: I do. I think about how this writing is like life. Our lives are made up of little incremental changes, and if we are fortunate, things go by and one day follows another and another and another. These poems seem to be trying to enact that. They are recording what happens.

Rosenthal: I came across a passage in a book called *Deconstruction: Theory and Practice* by Christopher Norris that made me think of your writing. The passage is summarizing Derrida's critique of structuralism: "Structuralism and phenomenology are locked in a reciprocal *aporia* from which neither can emerge with its principles intact, but on which both depend for their moments of maximum insight."[5] Your have a highly structured writing practice designed to release a phenomenological, moment-by-moment experience involving lots of chance and accident. You take in—in a way you're flooded by—sensations and memories and perceptions, and you find a way to let them flow onto the page, but within a very defined structure. There's a phenomenological side and a structural side to your practice, and these two sides are at odds yet are also dependent on each other.

Ratcliffe: There's this ongoing flood of phenomena that's happening in the world, and in our perception of the world—it's just incessant. Even when we are asleep, we're dreaming, and, whether we remember it or not, there are cars going by outside on the street. There's all this life. There is this continuous present. The future is always becoming present, and the present is always receding into the past. My work is an attempt to articulate that by giving it a shape, finding a structure.

There's a lot of artifice; the shaping hand of the maker is at work, in the work. But there's also an awful lot of accident that comes into it. So there's a tension between the contrivance of the shaping power and the accidental. One way accident enters is that I don't really have a plan of what I am going to say in any poem. When I actually sit down to look through notebook "A," maybe there's something there that I already know I want to put in the poem. Sometimes I don't know, and then it's harder.

Also, this is all done very quickly, because I'm busy. I don't have all day to write these poems. I'm often up and out of the house by ten or ten-thirty in the morning, off to Mills. By that time I've already done the writing, the surfing, the typing, and some emails. I get up early and I do all this stuff, you know. I have this habit.

Rosenthal: What time do you get up?

Ratcliffe: I wake up with the light. And I go down and I have my tea or coffee and toast and I write in the notebooks.

Rosenthal: Right away?

Ratcliffe: First thing. I live alone, so I have this time to do it. The writing really comes out of the space of being asleep. There's something very powerful about looking out the window first thing and getting those fresh perceptions. That's what I write down for that first stanza, into this notebook "B." Then if I have to go to Mills, I get into my wetsuit and go surfing, and I write the surfing note when I come back. Then I shower and dress, and then I type the poem. Then I leave. I've gotten to the point where I can make these poems come out quickly and make them work. It used to take a long time.

Rosenthal: What happens when you travel or your schedule gets disrupted? Do you get disoriented?

Ratcliffe: Yes. But I am pretty intense about making time for writing. In these long works, there wasn't any interruption. And I did travel. Over winter break I went to New York. For twelve days I couldn't go in the water. So that I gave up. I found that there were still things in New York that would work for those parts of the poem. There was still sky, there were birds, there were clouds.

Here's one I wrote in New York, dated 12.29. [Reads from notebook.] "triangular green plane of weathered green roof in right / foreground, whiteness of gull flapping across below it, / high thin white clouds against pale blue sky overhead"—this was at a big hotel where I stayed a couple of nights on Mills business, Le Parker Meridien on 57th Street looking up toward Central Park; I was looking up at these big buildings, but there was a gull, you know—"man / on right claiming that the Mayan calendar was accurate to within / three seconds, woman across from him recalling Saudi Arabia // Balanchine telling Stravinsky the dance would be 'about two- / and-a-half-minutes,' Stravinsky thinking 'there is no such / thing as "about," give me the exact time please' / sunlit / silver body of jet passing through to the left behind black edge / of building in left corner, cloudless blue sky above it."

Rosenthal: It's interesting, in light of your own preoccupation with measurement, that the man in the poem is obsessing about the Mayan calendar being accurate to within three seconds, and Stravinsky is saying that "about two-and-a-half minutes" is too vague.

Ratcliffe: There is humor in a lot of these. A lot of the time I'm creating odd gaps, so that parts of the poem enter into an ironic or commenting relationship with each other.

Rosenthal: I wanted to make sure we talk about your use of lines and line breaks. I was looking at a poem in *Mallarmé: poem in prose* that spoke to me about that aspect of your work:

> leaves, no doubt the chill
> 'I forgot' an aesthetic
> you know? the text in isolation
> for instance on the part of people
> who claimed it, the heard phrase
> after the verb you understand
> thinking of night, a road
> in the sound initials
> stopped, called in the gap
> between sleep and the position
> of the friend of a friend I drive
> reflection aground, progress
> in the concern to leave
> this obstacle of land, a bridge[6]

I notice the phrase "the text in isolation" and later "the heard phrase," and I become aware of a rocking motion, an overlapping, between the line in isolation and phrases that wrap to the next line. The lines both press forward and refer back. The words are often appositives for something that has just occurred and at the same time looking forward to something that is coming up. This kind of play is one of the prime ways poetry makes itself, yet your work seems to foreground or heighten that effect.

Ratcliffe: That's true. In *Mallarmé: poem in prose* the units of words in the line are both standing as a line and also wrapping forward and back; often there are words in apposition to other words and so on.

Rosenthal: And it is true of *SOUND / (system)* as well.

Ratcliffe: In those books, and also in *Idea's Mirror*, I wanted to have the sense that each line was an independent unit—that's why I put so much space between the lines—and also that each line fed into the next.

Rosenthal: In *Idea's Mirror* you heightened that effect further: Every line has a comma in it. So I'm reading each line in isolation but I'm also looking at the unit of words that's formed between any two commas.

Ratcliffe: Also, in that book, the number of syllables after the comma in one line is the same as the number of syllables before the comma in the next line. So there is an interlocking of materials from the end of one line into the beginning of the next, which creates a little poem inside the poem. But there is also, as you say, the independence of each whole line. The effect is an interesting music. Also, in *Mallarmé* there was a sense that each of these was just one statement that would go from the beginning to the end of the page through the poem's fourteen lines. You know, the way things kind of hang, but also connect into larger units.

Rosenthal: In the poem I just read aloud, there's discussion of progress and driving and obstacles. That brought up for me a line in your essay "Notes on Sound": "Sound in the line the syllables one after the other next the other trailing head to foot as if along a road one travels one's way."[7] I also thought of Creeley's poem "I Know A Man," which can be taken to be reflecting on navigation through the lines of a poem, the forward motion and the obstacles or interruptions, as much as, or more than, it's about driving a car. In an essay called

"Form," Creeley talks about the importance of the silence at the end of every one of his lines.[8] I think of that silence as "the darkness surrounding us," the void. I've heard that Creeley developed this halting quality in part by in a sense misinterpreting, perhaps deliberately so, Williams' approach—that when Williams read his own poems, he read right through the line breaks.

Ratcliffe: He did, yes.

Rosenthal: Whereas Creeley, whose lines bear such close relation to the older poet's work, stops for every break. Yet in Creeley, there is still that motion that propels one through. I feel that in your poems: a through-line with distinct ruptures.

Ratcliffe: I feel that too. I think there's a tension between going forward and stopping. And the line break creates stops, as does the punctuation mark. Often I just use the comma. The lines don't begin with capitals, and in the recent work, there aren't periods. If there is a punctuation stop within the line, it causes a pause, and the line break causes a kind of pause. But these same elements cause an impelling drive forward, because sense isn't complete. So there is this tension between wanting to move forward and an impulse to stop.

I am also struck by how fast all the syntax seems to shift in that passage you read: "called in the gap between sleep and the position of the friend of a friend"; "position of the friend of a friend I drive"; "I drive reflection aground." It shifts faster in this than in my more recent work.

Rosenthal: I think it shifts very fast in *SOUND / (system).*

Ratcliffe: It does. In both *SOUND / (system)* and *Mallarmé* all of the words come out of previous texts. *SOUND / (system)* used a volume of Henry James's letters, and *Mallarmé* used Mallarmé's prose poems. That makes such a difference.

Rosenthal: The last lines of the poem from *Mallarmé* are, "progress / in the concern to leave / this obstacle of land a bridge." The word "bridge" hangs there, and I find myself wondering how I will bridge the space between this poem and the next. The words seem to invite an acute awareness of the present moment of writing/reading.

Ratcliffe: Yes, there is a kind of open jump to the next poem, because I was writing these on consecutive days. I think there is a continuity, and it does come out of the body, out of present circumstance, present experience. You're writing a different poem every day, but the cellular makeup of the person writing today is roughly the same as that of the person who was doing it yesterday.

Rosenthal: Did you look back at the previous day's poem before you began writing a new poem?

Ratcliffe: I can't remember if I did with *Mallarmé*, but I don't think so. In *Idea's Mirror*, I built even more of a bridge between the poems—I repeated a word from the last line of one poem in the first line of the next poem.

Rosenthal: That motion from one poem to the next brings up something else that recurred for me in reading *Mallarmé*. The book seemed to address the joining of the past to the present and to the future—in the context of literary history, relationships among writers across time—in a way that challenged for me the notion of any author's ownership of his or her work. Sometimes words from Mallarmé's text seemed recontextualized, recast, in a contemporary light. For example, "parents" becomes a possible verb in today's diction. Or "lit," which in our era could be "drunk" or "literature" in addition to "illuminated." On page eleven there's the phrase "contemporary, she emerged from the head." It's like Diana emerging from Apollo's head, or it can be a woman coming out of the bathroom—and the word "contemporary" underscores that we are using these words now. On page eight you write, "an ear the remnant of the sum / of words, potential / thinking." I think about how we have an ear that remembers these words—whatever words we remember out of the totality of the history of a language, but also the history of one's personal relationship with the language. But in that remnant that our ear hears, lies a potential: to think, to write, to create. So you're collaging these words out of Mallarmé, taking remnants out of his texts, but there is this potential in hearing them, and that potential creates a new poem.

Ratcliffe: Absolutely. I like to think about poetry and language, and to investigate that in the writing of poetry. All of these works that make use of found text were for me a way of continuing to do literary research, because I spent a lot of time doing that in graduate school. In the academic and scientific worlds, one does research as a way of investigating material. I think about poetry and how it works and what it is to write it, and with teaching, one thinks about these things all the time too. Clark Coolidge wrote a book of poetry called *Research*, which I thought was a great book title.

Rosenthal: I found myself thinking about the interrelationships between books and between authors when I was reading *SOUND / (system)* too. The very first poem in the volume, "Knowledge," raised these issues for me:

> [A] for "atmosphere"
> or way of adding
> what is said
> to be information, letters
> addressed to the person "outside"
> (the same) in other words
> fiction, writing
> submerged as a picture
> as immediate the second time
> it appears as absence
> when it begins
> or action itself, certain
> other places (ways)
> translated to the world[9]

When I read "letters / addressed to the person 'outside' " I think about how you were using a volume of James's letters addressed to others. "Outside" can be in quotes because if somebody is writing a letter, who is the person they are really writing to? Are they truly writing to someone else? Or are they still writing for themselves, to themselves? Then it says "in other words / fiction." Letters are fictions. One puts together one's experiences—this happened and that happened—and it's a story. But also, "what is said to be information" is a fiction: We can organize reality and describe it in factual, rational language, yet our sense of reality and the way in which we describe it can still be called a fiction. It's *said* to be information, but maybe it's just a story we're telling ourselves, telling each other. "Writing / submerged as a picture": When we read, we immediately make what we're reading into a picture we visualize. There's something there about the way that we generally assume that writing points to the outside.

Ratcliffe: Yes, as reference. Creeley says, "[P]oems are not referential, or at least, not importantly so."[10] There's an idea that poems and words point to things, which isn't necessarily so.

Rosenthal: We can forget that we have words; a picture is what pops up in our heads first. But then "the second time / it appears as absence / when it begins / or action itself." I'm radically simplifying because these poems aren't meant to yield linear meanings. But it's interesting to think of "the first time" being James's writing, and "the second time" being these same words, but now marked by absence. James is still present in the words, but he's dead, so he's only present through absence. This poem is a space separate from his work. It's the same words, it's writing, and it's action itself—we're in the moment of creating, of reading/writing.

Ratcliffe: That sounds great to me. The writing is enigmatic and you're saying, "You can go in this direction or in that direction with it." You're making a reading.

Rosenthal: While we're on the subject of *SOUND / (system)*, I'd like to ask you about the table of contents and the titles. Neither of those are typical gestures of your work to date.

Ratcliffe: Ron Silliman mentioned in a blog he wrote about that book that the one thing he had questions about is the use of titles. He questioned whether they are necessary, and said they don't seem to be connected to the poems. I agree with him in a way, but I still think the title is a crucial part of each poem—its first word, the poem as "definition" of it, etc.

Rosenthal: In your essay "Notes on Sound," you write, "typographic devices . . . [call] increased attention to the material fact of words as the medium at hand."[11] I see the table of contents and titles in *SOUND / (system)* as a way of foregrounding your interest in this materiality—the titles make use of a lot of typography and punctuation marks. It also becomes a catalog of concerns in some way. For example, the first title is "Knowledge." Then in the poem there are the lines, "what is said / to be information, letters addressed to the person 'outside' / (the same) in other words fiction." This reads like a definition of knowledge, so it's an accurate title. Also, if you read the table of contents aloud, it starts sounding like a piece of music, with its repetitions and variations. "ECHO, POSITION, *POSITION,* ECHO, MOUTH, MOUTH, MOUTH, MOUTH, C, D, *(C),* D, *D,* E, F."[12] I know that you're engrossed in both Renaissance and contemporary experimental music, and I can hear both of these genres echoed here.

Ratcliffe: I like that idea. Those were all words or parts of words from the James book. They were of great interest to me at the time, so I kept reusing them. Some of them have to do with sound and some have to do with the body, and some are letters of the alphabet that had private significance. They do foreground the material quality of words.

Rosenthal: What is your relationship to the authors whose works you use as sources? Do you pick authors whose work you know intimately? Or do you deliberately pick authors you haven't read closely, so as not to have a predetermined notion of the work's significance?

Ratcliffe: In the case of Henry James, I had never really read him. I always felt that was one of the many holes in my education. My then-wife and my daughter Oona and I were living part-time in an apartment in San Francisco while Oona was going to high school there, and I found a volume of James on the shelf. A very nice Harvard publication, Volume III of his letters edited by Leon Edel. The book covered the years 1870 to whatever date; James was in London at that time and he sometimes traveled to Italy. So I picked it up—it was a nice book to handle. But I never really read it. I would underline words and use them to compose my book. I went through the James volume several times, just picking out a word here or there, or sometimes parts of words.

Rosenthal: What about your relationship to Woolf and to Mallarmé?

Ratcliffe: The same thing with Woolf—I hadn't even read *To the Lighthouse* before but had started it once, and took it with me on a backpacking trip to the mountains early in the time of writing *CLOUD / RIDGE*, and so it started to come into the work and soon enough became an important part of it. And I'd always had a great interest in Mallarmé, going back to studying French in high school and college—there was a class in translation at Berkeley where I translated some of his sonnets and "L'Apres-Midi d'un Faun" ("The Afternoon of a Faun"). Anyway, I had a little Penguin edition of his poems, with translations by Keith Bosley on the bottom of each page. I used that; I didn't make my own translations. I hadn't particularly read the prose poems before I picked up that book. I don't know how that started, but it started.

Rosenthal: How do you think about characters? Your books are filled with characters that keep reappearing, but often they are just pronouns, or a man or woman associated with a particular color or item. Maybe there's a particular "she" who's the same every time she shows up, but then again, maybe it's a different "she" every time.

Ratcliffe: I am very perplexed about it too, and curious about these people.

Rosenthal: Do you make them up, or are they people you are thinking of?

Ratcliffe: They are all real. And if they are famous people, like Pound or Stravinsky, they sometimes come in by name. But "man in blue shirt," for example, might be a friend of mine. The man or the woman on the phone comes in a lot. And I should mention that for me, "email" means "phone." I do a lot of communication through email, living out there in that isolated world, you know. I realize readers are going to think I am talking on the telephone all the time, but I'm not.

Rosenthal: Do you use "phone" instead of "email" because you consider the latter too ephemeral, too contemporary?

Ratcliffe: Yes, too contemporary. I mean, "email" is like a brand name or something. A few years ago I didn't even know what "email" was. But "phone" I know. Also, "email" seems too "revealing" somehow, too "personal." Beyond that, I like the word "phone" because it has to do with sound. Like "phonetics." I like the way it sounds, too—that long *o* sound.

But back to your question about these figures, "man in a blue shirt," "woman in black." Bob Grenier once said it's kind of like the Homeric epithet. You know, "the gray-eyed Athena." I think it's a way of identifying someone with a generic descriptor that doesn't pay any attention to individuality, but does locate the person and create a character. By the way, I almost never appear in my own poems as an "I."

Rosenthal: Do you describe yourself with one of these generic descriptors?

Ratcliffe: Once in a while. Sometimes I am the man in the red jacket. But usually, in these more recent poems, I don't even bring myself in. I am usually looking at somebody else. And if I am involved, as I am in the first section in these poems, I just look out the window and I see something; I don't describe myself doing the seeing. Someone said the other day, "I saw an 'I' in your poems; it was so nice to see that because it almost never comes in." And I said to her, "That was someone else talking; I was quoting someone." But then I found myself saying, "Well actually, all of the people in these poems are really me." Which I had never thought of before. And I don't think it is quite true. But there is an odd mystery when you write a character. It is you creating that character—Keats's idea of negative capability. Yet these are often things that people say or that I see people doing.

Rosenthal: Well, it is all being filtered through your selecting consciousness.

Ratcliffe: Yes, my own consciousness and my writing.

Rosenthal: I'd like to ask you about your relationship to the Bay Area writing community. You've described your isolated life out in Bolinas, which I assume contrasts rather markedly with your job as chair of Mills' English department, where you are in a sense a figurehead in a larger community. I remember from a previous conversation that you got involved in experimental writing in the context of the Bay Area. You met Bill Berkson . . . ?

Ratcliffe: I knew Bill in Bolinas; he was a friend. He introduced me to experimental writing. I was just telling someone about this—you know Scott Bentley? He's now getting his MFA at Mills. Leslie Scalapino has published one of his books. He teaches at Cal State Hayward. Anyway, he said to me, "Man, did you ever have a conversion experience in writing? Did you ever write more traditional kinds of poems?" I said, Oh yes, I did. I told him how, right after I finished working on my dissertation on Thomas Campion at UC Berkeley, which was 1978, I think, Bill Berkson was clearing out his bookshelf, and he gave me this little stack of *L=A=N=G=U=A=G=E* magazines. That publication was pivotal in the early days of the Language poetry movement. It was a real eye-opener to see writing by poets like Charles Bernstein and Lyn Hejinian and Bruce Andrews and Ron Silliman. These were obviously serious thinkers writing about poetry, but they weren't in the academy at that time at all, except maybe Bruce Andrews.

Rosenthal: Did you take to it immediately?

Ratcliffe: I did, because I had just been released from this "penance" of writing my dissertation, and I could get back to writing poetry. Shortly after that incident, Bill said to me, It would be interesting to write a work that makes use of a found text. This is one of those ideas that came out of Bernadette Mayer's experiments at St. Mark's Poetry Project. So I thought, That is a great idea, I'll use the dictionary. And I wrote *Distance,* which I originally called *Random House,* because the Random House dictionary was the source. It was a great title because the work was all about accident and randomness—I composed it by going through the dictionary and having words just jump off the page, which I learned how to put together in complex sentences. But I had to change the name because a lawyer friend said, Have you ever thought about the fact that there's a trademark on that and you could get sued? So I wrote to them, like an idiot.

And they said, Oh yes, we guard our trademark zealously. So I decided to rename it *Distance.*

Rosenthal: Did Bill Berkson introduce you to other writers?

Ratcliffe: Somewhat. I met Clark Coolidge, who was an old friend of Bill's, and I met John Ashbery, because Bill would invite him to read at the San Francisco Art Institute and we would go out to dinner sometimes. Bill knew a lot of people and he would have parties. I never met Creeley when he lived in Bolinas, but I met him afterward.

Rosenthal: What about Joanne Kyger?

Ratcliffe: We're good friends, although I didn't really know her until I had lived in Bolinas for a long time.

Rosenthal: Do you feel that the Bay Area writing scene is a vital part of your writing life, or is it secondary to your writing practice and your teaching work?

Ratcliffe: I do participate in a little poetry community in Bolinas, but it consists more or less of Bob Greiner, and Joanne, and her husband Donald and me. We get together for dinner and we read things. We've read Charles Olson, Whitman, Shakespeare, Pound. For a while, particularly after my divorce, I came into the city a lot to attend readings and hang out. But I've gotten so busy lately, I've cut way back.

Rosenthal: You are too busy and self-motivated. You just kind of do it on your own.

Ratcliffe: I have my habits. This obsessive writing practice, and my surfing, and I have to go to Mills three days a week. I really feel this kind of withdrawal lately from the world of people who live in the city.

Rosenthal: Branching out into a larger notion of writing and community, I wonder how you think about your writing within a political context. Your poetry brings me into a fresh, wonderfully alive awareness of the moment. Yet the moment in which we find ourselves is occurring in the context of a very fearful world facing all kinds of trauma—environmental disaster, economic downturn, and the war in Iraq, for example. How do you negotiate these issues with regard to your writing practice?

Ratcliffe: I read the *San Francisco Chronicle*, and I listen to the news a lot when I am driving—NPR, KPFA. I like the "Democracy Now" program in the morning. I was riveted to the news during 9/11 and the weeks following. My daughter lives in New York City and she witnessed people jumping from the towers. There is stuff that comes into *CLOUD / RIDGE* that is directly political—for a while I was putting Rumsfeld in there, and Bush, by name. But I don't want them in there anymore.

Rosenthal: Are you going to take them out?

Ratcliffe: No. I like having that political reality in the book; I think it is important. But at the same time, there's this other part of my life experience which comes from living out in Bolinas, surrounded by parks and Mount Tam and the ocean. Political issues are immensely far away from my immediate present moment, except what I hear on the news. In the poems that I am writing now, the format limits what can appear. So in the first stanza unit, I'm looking out the window at what's there, and there isn't any Rumsfeld out there, or Bush. There's a jet airplane that comes over a lot; that's a recurring thing. "Sound of jet passing overhead." "Jet passing overhead." "Jet trail slanting across ridge." But I banish politics from my immediate attention in the writing. I am more interested in writing about aesthetics, painting, perception, and popular culture.

Rosenthal: Do you think political reality impinges on your writing even if it's not subject matter?

Ratcliffe: I think it does. It conditions my sense of the value or fragility of things. So I am not writing about political reality right now, but I am definitely paying attention to it.

10.18

grey-white streak of cloud above ridge in window
opposite the unmade yellow and blue bed, song
sparrow calling from lower left foreground

woman on phone looking at center of circle
passing through vertices of triangle, noting
"proofs are in the heart of mathematics"

man
in green shirt wondering what it means for words
to be concrete, Pound claiming Chinese presents
"pictures of actions and processes in nature"

Lily Briscoe drawing a line "in the centre,"
thinking to herself "I have had my vision"

line of white water moving across flat grey
plane in the lower right foreground, circular
green pine on point against grey plane above it

ELIZABETH ROBINSON

Falling Is the Safest Thing to Do

Sarah Rosenthal: I've been tracing some of the themes that cycle through your work: rain, along with fog and dew and air; house; wound and incision; boundary and map; eating and food; and garden, along with weed and tree and vegetation. There are references to fall and gravity—I'm sure you're aware of those. I also noticed nakedness, and hinge and joint, which seemed connected with all the limbs in your poems.

Elizabeth Robinson: Yes, I was told by one friend to stop putting hands in my poems. So the last couple of years I've been amputating the hands. I am really aware of the body imagery and of trying to make an anatomy out of language and poetry. I'm also aware of the house imagery and the rain, and the gravity. The other ones I wouldn't have been so aware of. Although now that you're naming the garden imagery, I can see that. I think I'm fairly preoccupied with creating an environment in my poems that can function in a broad sense as a tonal landscape, but also as the embodied environment, since clearly the two overlap.

SR: I'd like to start out by looking at *Apprehend.* The book's cover shows a huge bird scooping up a stick person. The image of this fragile figure in the mouth of the winged beast is so striking. It looks medieval, but it speaks to the urgency of our time. Did you have anything to do with that?

ER: Yes. I wanted to convey the idea of "apprehend" as understanding and grasping, but also as disquiet and fear. I was looking at pictures by contemporary children's-book illustrators, ones that were clearly oriented toward children but that had a kind of uneasiness about them. But all of the children's illustrators have agents and they're exorbitantly expensive. I couldn't afford the permissions. So I got one of those Dover clip-art books, and that's where I found this image. All that clip art is in the public domain, so it was free. I don't know exactly when it was made because it is just in this book of woodcuts. But I am completely happy with what it reflects.

SR: The poem "Topple" is about 9/11.

ER: Actually, I started writing that poem two days before 9/11. It's so tainted by what happened immediately afterward that I feel uneasy about it. I tried to tone it down. My concern is that it would seem to grandstand a more politicized position, whereas I tend to feel that poetry is most effective when its politics don't whack the reader over the head, but show some understanding of the inevitable ambiguities that inhere in any circumstance. A friend of mine, Beth Anderson—whose work I really admire and who has been incredibly helpful to me editorially—said, Just take it out; it's too resonant with 9/11; you should put it in a different collection. I also talked about it with Ed Smallfield, who did a lot of editing with me, and he really thought it should go in. In the end, I included it, because I decided it would look even more emphatically "9/11ish" in a different context. Here, at least, the "Chicken Little" material comes through and puts it in sync with the other material in the book.

SR: But it resonates beyond 9/11. "Why would the world / be disobedient / and the sky hunch / over with its sickening bravery."[1] For me, that brings to mind the anger and frustration that we Westerners feel when we want our environment to bend to our wishes and it doesn't. I associated this feeling both to the micro level—the fury one can feel being stuck in a traffic jam, say—and to the macro level of our political leaders insisting on controlling the world, and responding with fury when they encounter resistance.

ER: For me it was more the macro level: a sense of impotence combined with the vast control the United States is exercising over the rest of the globe. I remember Bush saying that the people who attacked the World Trade Center and the Pentagon were cowards. It seemed odd to use that kind of language, because I don't consider him particularly courageous. So I was thinking (somewhat ironically) about the way the United States has behaved in the world in recent years.

SR: I'm looking at the fifth stanza: "Not the sense / of loss, but actual lostness / should not commit to response / to the feather falling from dust / until the sky merges / again with itself. / The gravity of itself / is what it regrets."[2] This said to me, We are lost—that is what we need to admit. Instead of rushing in and doing more damage, we should wait for the dust to settle, and try to understand. "The gravity of itself is what it regrets": That's a complicated phrase, which I read in part as addressing the fact that we take ourselves so seriously. It is perhaps asking, What is this thing, this self, that we are trying so hard to protect?

ER: Originally it ended, "Until the sky merges again with itself." I decided that that signified too much a sense of reconciliation and closure, and I wanted to land on a feeling of irrevocability and continuing rupture. I had the sense that the rifts in the universe are not healed, and the sky, or the ground beneath us, may be breaking open without our completely apprehending why, or what's going on. There is a lot of misapprehension about the construction of the world, but there is an irrevocability to action sometimes that we nonetheless have to live with. And there's the foolishness of this little creature who is us. The overarching tonal quality of the "Chicken Little" tale is, for me, absurdity. It's pathetic and comic at the same time. So "The gravity of itself is what it regrets" seemed apt.

SR: Speaking of creatures, I was fascinated by the poem "Whose Monster's Noise and Weather." The opening lines are, "From what language does this beast extend, / joints like bracken."[3] I found it generative to see this beast, this monster, as the poem under hand—or conversely, to see the poem as a body in motion. It's interesting that the poem is set in motion by a question, but one which doesn't end in a question mark. So there's a space around the word "what." It's that big "what" that's never going to be answered.

ER: Yes, and it can become assertion also. I like the idea that something can be queried and asserted at the same time. I also like your sense that the poem initiates motion. That speaks to my idea of articulation as hinges or joints that extend a range of motion. Now as I'm looking at this poem, I can see what you mean about some of the recurring themes. There is the theme of things being consumed, and there are these joints.

SR: The joints appear right away. The phrase "joints like bracken" is directly followed by a joint in the form of a stanza break. The references to joints helped me see a certain poetics about breaks in poems. If we are going to talk about the body of your poetry, I started seeing joints as two words coming into contact with each other, as line breaks, and as stanza breaks.

ER: That makes sense to me. I enjoy in poetry that there are abrupt turns that also leave the aftertaste of what preceded, a tenuous continuity.

SR: The next lines continue, "that it / eats what it finds / in its nest, even // the amniotic, / the cliché."[4] This is such a crude, utilitarian monster. It grabs and consumes whatever is around, including its young. You set up "the cliché" as an appositive to "the amniotic," creating an equals sign between them. That made me think, What do we start with when we write a poem? We start off with clichés—familiar words, familiar narratives—and then we have to build them into something or find a way to renew them.

ER: Yes, a lot of this material is so familiar that it is constantly verging on cliché. The image of the parental figure consuming the child is a familiar one (strangely enough!). So I'm writing a cliché and at the same time addressing that fact, saying, How to plunge right in and go after it anyway? The ongoing struggle with cliché seems a central part of writing—an ethical process—undermining groundless assumptions, querying or displacing. To continue the earlier metaphor: putting it out of joint. It is a way to create or recirculate, remodel an epistemology.

SR: And rewrite it. In "Hansel and Gretel," you say something like, Well, the stepmother was really just frazzled, and the father was just tired, and if I'm the one telling this story, I can say the witch was just a nice old crone.

ER: It *is* my story—I'm just frazzled!

SR: You have such compassion for the evil parents.

ER: Or a Hannah Arendt sense of the banality of evil.

SR: A little further in the "Monster" poem you write, "In a world posited as graceful, / where light makes shape, / why be bilious? / This is a variant of birth."[5] Obviously "grace" is a big word in Christian faith, and the Protestant work ethic ties grace to the notion of constant striving. If we have been raised on the idea that we'll reach perfection if we just try hard enough, then why would we be bilious? In this question I hear the implication that one might deliberately choose to be bile-filled and imperfect. How and why be bilious? Because we have to be; because we are. And maybe that biliousness is its own route to grace . . . but I can tell from your facial expression that you are thinking something different.

ER: Since you're raising Christianity as a theme, I want to say that my Christianity is a vehicle for me. I like the categories and I use them elastically. But I'm not a traditional Christian. I have had the experience of people reading my work and saying, Well, that's Christian, or, You're a Christian, or, I don't want to read this Christian material. So I feel constrained and typecast by that response. There was even a review of *House Made of Silver* saying something to the effect of, People who aren't churchy are probably not going to be interested in this book. I don't think the book reflects traditional religious thinking at all. All my work is suffused with doubt and ambiguity and struggle. I see the struggle as one of trying to bring some element of gracefulness into a monstrous world—a world in which we consume our own progeny as a way of surviving. When I write, "Why be bilious, this is a variant of birth," in an extremely reductive way I'm saying: Maybe the untidiness, the monstrousness, can give pleasure and texture, and be a way of perceiving. I wouldn't want my work to reflect an attitude of striving toward perfection because perfection (or, say, the Western religious vision of "heaven" or "paradise") has always sounded arid to me. Rather, the monster in the poem, despite its monstrousness, is endowed with the ability to make decisions. That crux moment between decisions, and then the act of deciding and its movement-toward, is what engages me. Deciding is not, in my experience, a clean process. It's untidy, and sometimes ugly, but fascinating.

SR: I do see your work as deeply engaged with certain Christian themes, but not in a reductive way. My sense is that you are interested in the ancient, defining stories of Western culture. Your poetry aims at the heart of these stories, and tries to see what is useful in them. When I say "Christian," I don't mean it in a limiting way, yet I don't want to shy away from something that deeply informs your poetics.

ER: It is of concern to me, because the word "Christian" has such an incredibly pejorative ring to it and immediately results in people stereotyping you and then limiting your query. I was at a conference where I was sitting on a panel about spirit and word. And the other people were saying, Well, I don't really *believe* or anything, I'm just *interested* in Christianity . . . so I stood up and said, Well, I'm a Christian. Because, I mean, it's incontrovertible—I attended a seminary. And afterward, someone came up and said, I can't believe you said you're a Christian; that's like saying you're a smoker. And you know, it really is. It's worse!

SR: But also, the word "heretic" comes to mind, in the sense that one believes deeply, but in a way that stakes out a highly individual, even marginalized relationship to the belief system. I think of people like Simone Weil, who was deeply engaged in Christian belief, yet refused to be baptized, because she felt that identifying so firmly with Christianity would reduce her ability to connect with the larger human community.

ER: I've read her work extensively. She's extraordinary and set apart from so many other thinkers, though I do think that resulted in an isolation that is counter to what I've found as the vexed best that any practice (artistic or religious) can offer, which is a *communal* experience. Even so, I love Weil's refusals and the gritty, sometimes obnoxious way she insists on sorting through her distinct senses of gravity and grace. I think in my case, my relationship to Christianity has to do with the idea of usefulness you mentioned earlier—usefulness as in ingenuity. I feel our (specifically United States) culture lacks what I would call a religious imagination. Our religious practices are bizarrely literalistic and anti-imagination.

SR: Can you define what you mean by religious imagination?

ER: I probably can't completely define it, but what I'm looking for is a practice and an attentiveness that are untethered from any specific tradition, but also untethered from our assumption that all that there is to be known has some empirical, material basis. I'm interested in trying to engage rigorously with what I've been given, and seeing where it can take me. If I had been born into a Jewish family, I'm sure that given my temperament and other similarities of context, I would probably have used that material in a similar way. Those traditions endure because they have vitality and can be repeatedly excavated.

SR: You're talking about adaptability, which is a kind of shape-shifting. "Whose Monster's Noise and Weather" is also concerned with shape-shifting: It says, "Creature *is* rain," as if to say, You *can* redefine the terms—you can look up at the rain and see a monster.[6]

ER: I think that is one of the miracles of poetry: You can make the world change with words. You can put things together that just don't belong together, yet they do, because you decided that they do. In my recent writing, I've been transfixed by ideas of pronoun and persona, and by the notion that a writer can simply, through an act of language, take the discrete entities of the "I" and the "you" and merge them into "us." And when you juxtapose things that don't match, some kind of third entity emerges through the friction of the dissonance. It's alchemical.

SR: And in the poetic process of juxtaposing words, one discards many of those words. In the poem, the morphemes are still clinging to the back of the monster, as if saying, We want to come along for the ride!

ER: They're the progeny that never were.

SR: This lusciously ugly, denuded monster makes such a racket: "What is ringing out," "pealing," "wrecking and / bellowing," "[t]he bluster of the universe, if it were / a bell."[7] There's a lusty call here for us to loosen up the hold of narrative and reconfigure things in fresh ways.

ER: Or that's me, demanding that permission for myself. I definitely identify with that monster.

SR. It seems you do take that permission. From book to book, your work appears to be refining an understanding of the hinges, while staying malleable and naked in the process.

ER: There's definitely a tension in my psyche regarding form, aesthetics, and how the process of the poem actually plays itself out. I like clean lines and clean language, but I am attracted to the messiness of experience, and the way that language can reflect that. For example, I love a lot of the New York School writers. I remember reading O'Hara's work—which in spite of its casual surface is actually very elegant and formally adept—and thinking to myself, Wow, you could just talk to your friends in a poem. And then reading Ted Berrigan's sonnets, which are, you know, about what drugs he's taken, and they're messy and repetitive. I thought, Look what he did, a person could do such a thing! It was a wonderfully shattering experience to see that. So I want to claim that possibility for myself. But then once I get to it formally, I like it to be a little more lyric and I want to underline the openness of the page where nothing is said—the listening, but never passive, part of the space. I was saying to some friends that I like the exuberance and lyric untidiness of Eleni Sikelianos's work. And they said, But you don't do that. And it's true—I'm always taking out words because they seem cluttery. But I'm attracted to poets who can let things be more sprung across the page.

SR: When I read your writing, I'm often caught off guard by the way the lines unfold. On the one hand, there's a carefulness, a lyricism, and a use of traditional syntax, all of which set up certain expectations. On the other hand, there's often a jarring quality to the juxtapositions, an asserting of unusual links or associations. One of the results is a sense of mystery. "As Betokening," in *Harrow*, demonstrates this. The second half of the sixth poem, for example, reads, "Suddenly ready after protracted withdrawal. / A brew, it does have this. // Said: even if all, not I. // Said: that shall twice bay and thou / Said: Before it bay twice today // first shalt thrice / thou shalt thrice."[8] At first take, some of the phrases seem to promise that a certain kind of traditional sense-making will take place. Yet ultimately that expectation is thwarted. The part that I read is less about making sense than about hearing the biblical-sounding chant of a mysterious diviner-bird-housewife-icon who emerges in the poem. She seems like the figure of the female priestess or divinity who was silenced during the formalization of Christianity.

ER: There isn't biblical material on women. There's only what imagination can supply from tiny fragments. I wanted to inhabit those fragments and create my own query and mystery and narrative. That's similar to my process in *Apprehend,* in the sense of having some resource and interacting, even fighting, with it—and claiming imagination as a form of logic. For me, the pleasure of writing poetry is in some sense the pleasure of solving the problem. I have some preoccupation I'm grappling with, and the process of making the poem is a way of solving the problem. "Logic" could be a vexed word because of what people think it means, but you try to make a process that has some kind of continuity, some kind of solidity from which one can proceed—or depart! And maybe that's what logic can be. But that doesn't mean that it has to reveal all mystery, or lead to resolution, or make juxtapositions that one can anticipate. Part of logic is what one can't anticipate, and learning to encompass that. I've written two or three essays in which I refer to Pound's phrase, "points define a periphery."[9] I like that sense that a poem can be both inclusive and full of gaps, and that it's possible within those conditions to create a grace or process that can take you somewhere. Where, I don't know. I would say that making a poem is akin to making a hypothesis—you play out one possible set of relations or causal chain, but it's equally possible to return to the question and set out another hypothesis that can be worked out differently. Doing this is not only obsessively enjoyable, it's also necessary, in the way that Joan Retallack, in *The Poethical Wager,* discusses the necessity of fighting our way out of ossifying constructs that limit our ability to act as positive agents in an imperiled world.

SR: I'd like to ask you about the words "fall" and "gravity." "Fall" is traditionally associated with the terrible burden of guilt that our culture carries. Yet I wonder if you are trying to renew these words, or shift their emphasis in order to speak about human experience from a different slant. I think of how we are constantly in the midst of falling, in a certain sense—we are always sinking more deeply into our human condition.

ER: That preoccupation means lots of different things to me. It was interesting to me that on the back of *Pure Descent* the publisher put, "The poems of this collection understand gravity or 'The Fall' as an agent that acts upon both spiritual and social experience . . ." I haven't really thought about it in terms of a fall from Eden. I think of it more in terms of the precariousness of existence. On the back of *Apprehend*, Robert Creeley wrote something about safety, and Patrick Pritchett wrote a review saying something to the effect that, in Robinson's poetry, the world is broken but it's still a safe place to live. Yet I don't think the world is safe at all. That's not my experience. Poetry works for me at times as a wedge against a sense of complete endangerment, a psychic and political precariousness. Bodies are fragile, and even spiritual states or spiritual processes are contingent and dangerous. So falling in some sense denotes the worst that could happen, the ultimate danger, but it also denotes finally reaching a place below which one cannot go, which is a place of solidity. My poetics is ontological: I'm trying to find out something about being, and how being occurs in experience. I grew up within a very dualistic atmosphere. Like many Protestants, I was taught to be ambivalent about my own embodied experience and about sexuality. Then I made the great discovery that bodies are rich and in some ways always *beyond* their own limits; that it's good to be in a body. And I discovered the possibility that embodied experience could have metaphorical meaning.

My MA in Ethics had to do with creating bioethical narratives of the body. So embodiment becomes an ethical process as well. That's the kind of solidity that makes falling the safest thing to do.

SR: Can you say more about how embodiment becomes an ethical process?

ER: If you try to have a dualistic, transcendent mind making the decisions, and deny that you're in a mortal body, you're outside of a real ethics. You can't rise above your own contingency and endangeredness. So it's powerful for me to think there could be a story that gets made within the body that has to do with physical processes and with living in a world that has solidity. The main thing that has kept me from getting completely fed up with Christian practice is the whole idea of word as flesh as word as flesh as word . . . the idea that the immanent and the transcendent are intimately, sensuously, inextricably braided together. Language comes from the body: We feel it in our mouths and we perceive it in our ears and we see it on the page. But it also conveys meaning and the way meaning gets lofted on time as we say the words we say on breath and air, and this can take a writer or a reader through experience that is not completely limited to the way the tongue hits the palate.

SR: In "Term," in *House Made of Silver*, there's the phrase, "the word you wish to join."[10] This phrase recognizes words as something other, that one wishes to draw close to. Yet ironically, in order to express this desire the speaker utters words, generates words in a physical process. The words are coming right out of the body—

ER: —and going away on its breath. Transient.

SR: So that's an enactment of the braiding you speak of. Your talk of endangerment adds another reason for your attraction to fairy tales: They're stories of peril and of seeking shelter. The house trope ties in here too, because houses are a symbol of shelter, and they also imply the obverse—the way in which we are shelterless. The poem "Manna" in your book *in the sequence of falling things* describes a state of homelessness. The biblical story you're echoing is a highly disturbing one.

ER: Someone made the mistake of telling me that story in Sunday school when I was seven or eight, and it haunted me.

SR: The Jews, who are following Moses, complain that they are sick of eating manna and want meat. What they get in response is a cloud of quail raining down on them. They are doomed to eat the quail until they vomit and die. It's so punitive.

ER: It's so punitive, and they're so vulnerable already, because they're homeless and wandering and lost. Why tell a young kid that story? As an eight-year-old, it made perfect sense to me that no one wants to have macaroni and cheese every night, no matter how much they like it. The divine who's portrayed in that story is all about domination and obedience—ick. I wanted to subvert it in some way.

SR: Up against this disturbing image I think of "Passage" in *Apprehend,* where you write: "[A] child nearby earnestly explains // that in dreams the fall is exciting / and does not result in injury."[11] The sense of endangerment in your poetry—falling, wounding, incisions, violence, homelessness—can be seen in relation to the Stevens quote that you mention in your unpublished talk for a conference called

"Twenty-First Century Poetics": "Poetry has a violence from within that protects us from a violence without."[12] In poems, as in dreams, the fall is exciting but does not cause actual harm.

ER: When I found that Stevens quote I thought, That's just right; he's got it! Though obviously, in my work, violence and rage are very modulated, because that tends to be how I conduct myself. It's not that I'd want to cause harm, but at the same time, poetry makes clear that, often in the most nuanced ways, something is at stake and we may well be in jeopardy.

SR: Often I think it's just a matter of the jarring syntax or word juxtapositions we spoke of earlier. There's a subtle violence to the act of violating assumptions about how words go together.

ER: I discussed this some years ago with the poet Robert Kocik. He was talking about the pleasure of metaphorically breaking into a house in order to rearrange the furniture rather than to damage or steal anything. That is a perfect evocation of what I like to do. The way I experience anger and violence in my work is, as I said, through subversion. Not wholesale destruction, but subversion, and exploring what power emerges from that. I like to disrupt expectation, not for the sake of doing it, but to make a point or at least open to an alternative. I enjoy reading some of the more transgressive work being written. Some of the material is interesting formally. But then beyond the shock effect or the figuring-out-the-device, I admit that I ask myself why I should continue to read. I don't at all think that meaning is docile or stable or eternal, but still I embrace the possibility that through all the shifts and uprootings of daily life, meaning is shape-shifting along with us.

SR: You appear to be seeking an active conversation with the reader, asking, What is actually happening in this act of reading and creating? Is it a body or is it a process? Your poetry invites the reader to inhabit the edge between shape and shapelessness.

ER: Order addressing chaos and chaos addressing order, in an ongoing, demanding process. It's frightening to relinquish control of the work to a reader, but writers don't exist alone; they only exist in the interchange, the conversation.

SR: There's a passage from "The Book of Apprehension" in *Apprehend*: "It's my creator who / follows most furiously / and least well. // Who knows better my scent. // The elements of my making. // But no one can plumb what I pursue."[13] The creator knows her craft—words, lines, stanzas, form. Yet she is chasing along behind the poem. The poem is much closer to the imaginary—it *is* the imaginary. The creator is trying to keep up with that bounding creature.

ER: Yes, the manifestation of the created thing outstrips the creator. In the poem you're quoting, the gingerbread man completely evades the little old lady who cooked him. She never gets to taste; she never gets to interact. He has his own quest, and he's gone. But it's an unfulfilled quest. He gets consumed.

SR: But he can go back again: "Any race run / can be run again / to losses / and gains." The poem enacts the idea of re-running the race by repeating words and phrases: "His legs are brown, / his arms are brown. / His beauty was vegetal / as it sped by. // His beauty sped by / and the clarity / of his body / amended what // relation."[14]

ER: Those lines ask how we stand in relation to what is pursued and what pursues us, and if there is any stable place (I think not!) along that progression. That poem is principally about desire and the inversions that occur in response to desiring.

SR: "His face is simple and fine. / He makes the onlooker hunger."[15] Is the hunger a desire for permanence?

ER: I think it's just the desire to pursue. In a way, the desire to desire. There is something beautiful and so compelling about running toward.

SR: The notion of desire takes me to "Hansel and Gretel," where you hint at incest: "Brother and sister / share a tentative kiss. // Not of passion, / but of its many alternatives / they choose security."[16]

ER: There I was playing with the idea of necessity. You have to live to eat, and you have to be safe to survive, even if in some kind of marginal way. So the idea was that they can do this transgressive, somewhat incestuous thing as a mode of securing themselves—that there are positions that are granted under extremity. And in fact, we're always in a state of extremity.

SR: The idea of transgression in turn brings up the words "boundary" and "limit," which appear throughout your work. In "Hansel and Gretel" you write, "Now side by side they lay / innocent of each other, / but parallel as their bodies / line the boundaries / of a path."[17] I think of the assertion of boundaries here as in one sense a desire for tidiness and order that in reality is transgressed all the time.

ER: I'm attracted to the idea of order, and to the idea of tradition, which I see as an ordering strategy. But those are just constructs. For example, the whole idea that countries have boundaries is absurd in some sense. So boundaries just become a certain guideline which one is welcome to destabilize. In fact, it's incumbent upon us to transgress at times; it's a sign of curiosity and vitality. That's one reason that poetry as a craft is so appealing to me. Poetry has a lot to do with patterning; it imposes order on chaotic experience. But if it's too orderly, it's not interesting. You have to disrupt the musicality of it to make it musical; you have to disrupt the logic of it to make it an interesting solving of a problem.

SR: Rain or moisture in your poems often serves to penetrate and dissolve boundaries. In "Entry for Song," from *Harrow*, you write: "This is the contour / that I'd deliquesce."[18] In "Immolation," from *in the sequence of falling things*, you write, "From up above he spit down on me with a particolored confetti. As I crossed the street, rain. What body do I have by my gender? Excuse my interest in this. The line or circle of sight poured out on me. // The markings fell out of me. I could not keep up while trying to make division by what I could see. This all permeated my skin. Like white sand, I tried to set out a circumscribed yard of the sightings."[19] We have a "he" above, raining confetti down on the speaker. This leads to multiple crossings of boundaries: The speaker apologizes for voicing an interest in gender as it relates to her own body, as though she is crossing a line in raising this issue; sight is poured onto her; and markings (words, perhaps) fall out of her. I got the sense that in the aftermath of this permeation, she's engaged in trying to reestablish boundaries of seeing and saying, but that it's kind of hopeless—and that that hopelessness is actually a good thing.

ER: Yes, I agree. You're identifying some processes that I haven't been consciously paying attention to. Yet I know rain comes up constantly, and I think partly it's in the sense of gravity; of being soaked with something, some inevitability. But there is also the boundary-crossing you're speaking of. One is porous; one absorbs something that is imposed upon one. One is suffused. Also, I like the idea that rain—as fluid—is itself an element in a transitional state: a liquid between solid and gas. It is versatile as an element, and our being bathed or sodden with it indicates something about our potential for versatility and inventiveness.

SR: In "Badiliyah," from *Pure Descent*, the rain is washing away the birds' nests. "Adobe, mud, mortar" underscores the connection to human homes. "[A]nd then, when the hard rain comes / and quenches their hold— // Mud-and-stick / is nest-building material, // but we are en route, on our way. / If we ameliorate what is missing, // wall's solidity or stance, / another might come in and stay // while we are gone."[20] What is the point of building back up the walls, if we're going to be moving on? We're like birds—we migrate, we travel, we wander like the Jews did in the desert. But we might be providing shelter for the next group, the next generation.

ER: I'm also expressing ambivalence there. We have lost this house; if we repair it, we'll lose it in a different way or it will be reclaimed in ways we hadn't anticipated. So we're condemned to be dispossessed, no matter what. I realize that sounds pessimistic, but it's how I see our experience.

SR: In the same poem there are the lines, "The way water wanders, and the doctor says, / 'Amnesia // is a good way to begin the cure.' "[21] Water wanders—not keeping to a track, not keeping track. There's a way in which we, and/or our poems, can be like water, forgetting what has been.

ER: Shape-shifting.

SR: And that can be a good thing to do.

ER: It's resourceful.

SR: It's a good way to read a poem. You need to double back, but there is some way in which you need to move on and let new images unfold, let the monster become a cloud.

ER: Or the rain can evaporate and return as cloud and then rain again. I think that's something else that draws me to rain and to weather: its cyclicality. It consumes itself and repeats its process. The patterning of weather, like the patterning of a poem, is very interesting to me. There can be many iterations, but their variation itself perturbs and rearranges meaning.

SR: The hydraulic cycle is amazing—the fact that this is the water that we have. It doesn't go anywhere; we don't get more; it just goes through this cycle endlessly.

ER: There's a finitude but there's also an endlessness. It really is remarkable, especially in relation to the concepts of pattern and boundary we've been talking about.

SR: The word "downfall" also appears in your poems. It occurs poignantly in the poem in *Pure Descent* called "The Playground," an elegy for a toddler.

ER: That was written for my son's friend Marjory; she was three. And there "downfall" has a sense of tandem processes, of going up the steps of a slide and then the downfall—both falling, i.e., sliding down, and a literal ceasing to be.

SR: In the poem "June" from *in the sequence of falling things,* you write about being "in downpour": "Part of me is not happy but // in in house in downpour."[22] This seems to be getting at the idea that it's not necessarily our job to be happy, but to be engaged.

ER: Yes, exactly. I think writing is a very ethically oriented process, and that our ethical obligation is to be engaged and alert. And that has political ramifications for me. Yet I don't know if my politics are always evident to readers of my work.

SR: I do see your work as political, but I'd like to hear more about how you see it.

ER: I look at the Bay Area writing community, and I see an overt politicization of a lot of the work. I can read that with interest, but that's not what I want to do. So I think there is a way that I give myself permission by saying to myself, I *am* engaged in the conversation—on my own terms. That's a defiant statement, but also hopefully an ethical one. Even to insist that I require a space for my own strategy is my way of insisting that there need to be many strategies in order to constitute a healthy community. Whether or not you are engaging in a larger politics in the polis, there is an ethical possibility in engaging with language, engaging with relation and possibility in language, that is important. Even the most radical community or paradigm can eventually lapse into assumptiveness.

SR: I agree. But I think your writing does address the polis, as exemplified by the poem "Manna" which we talked about earlier. In that poem, Moses and God are essentially complaining about the whiny masses. Moses says, I didn't ask for this; I didn't want these people. And God says, All right, I'll give you a break this week; I'll do the punishing. Your sympathies clearly lie with the "we," the wandering people who are following Moses because they're hoping he'll help them survive. I see that poem as emblematic of the way you try to identify yourself with the raw, humble, human condition, saying, This is *my* condition; I share this; we all share this.

ER: That would be my ideal.

SR: This cycles back to the notion of usefulness we touched on earlier. Your work poses the question, Given that we're stuck with these stories, how can we use them, even relish them, and at the same time rewrite them?

ER: Yes, I feel there's an insubordination in working with what you're given—not just chucking it away—yet not following the rules of the given. There is a suppleness and generative friction in that. In a sense, it's a form of "cheating." I follow the rules to a certain point, but I am not aiming toward the traditionally intended ends. It has to do with tools and processes rather than outcomes.

So I'm both retaining and disrupting elements of tradition. And sometimes a narrowing of a resource or boundaries helps to channel energy. So, for example, I think it would not be so useful for me to try to become a Buddhist, because I wouldn't be chafing against my intimacy with my given tradition. It's interesting to try to figure out how to channel even my distress about some of these deeply disturbing biblical narratives.

SR: Yes, like the story of Miriam, which you refer to in "As Betokening," in *Harrow*. She talks back to Moses.

ER: And then she is booted.

SR: God gives her leprosy, and she barely survives.

ER: There's a story in Judges that I'm never going to get to in my writing, and I don't even want to, but it's about a husband and wife who are traveling. They come to a town and the man is threatened. So he throws his wife out of the house where they're staying, and she is basically raped to death. He's angry that the people of the town would transgress his property that way. So he hacks her into thirteen pieces and sends one piece to each of the thirteen tribes and says, See what they did to my property, now we must have vengeance. Even though he had utterly betrayed her. That starts a war and there is a slaughter. It's a completely appalling story, but it is part of the canon. For that reason, I think you have to fight with it, at the very least. It would be remiss to ignore that something so repugnant is still part of the Western canon. In *Harrow*, I was appropriating and fighting with the stories at the same time. I was using external resources that could function as a kind of hermeneutic on the available material, and interpolating them.

SR: What kinds of external resources?

ER: Things like the pseudoepigrapha and the apocryphal texts—things that are not accepted as part of the canon but that might have more to say on behalf of women. Also, there's a lot of good feminist scholarship that talks about how radical the New Testament materials really are. Evidently what happened in that utopian, early Christian community opened up atypical possibilities for women—even though from our perspective it still looks very constraining.

SR: H.D. comes to mind because she was trying to retell the bible in a way that would breathe new life into Mary the goddess.

ER: Oddly, I've read more about her than I have read her work. Some people have read *Harrow* assuming that I'm steeped in H.D.'s work, but that's not the case. I anticipate that I will get to her work at some point and that it will give a lot of pleasure.

SR: Another figure that crops up a great deal in your writing is the map. One example is "Site Legend" in *House Made of Silver*. I was drawn to the image in this poem of the speaker examining the creases of the folded map. The image forces me to contemplate abstraction and materiality at the same time: A map is an abstraction but it's also a physical, foldable, readable entity.

ER: That's exactly what it means to me: You impose a pattern on material. You're patterning the page of the map, and you're also imposing a pattern or a grid on a landscape. But that abstraction is arbitrary. For example, who says what the border is between Berkeley and San Francisco? You get on the Bay Bridge and there's a certain point where it says, "Now you're in San Francisco." And you're in midair over water. I love the weirdness of that. We decide something is so, and it is so.

SR: "[E]xamining the creases" of the map in a way says, I'm enlarging the frame; I'm acknowledging the map as an object in my world.[23]

ER: I also wanted to express the fallibility, the quirkiness of the "constructions" and their enactment; that they themselves have creases, can fray. And then there's also the word itself as an object. Like that Sausserian question: If you say "tree," does it really mean the thing that grows in the ground, or is it just the word, "tree"? You can say, "Tree, tree, tree, tree. . ." Did you play that game when you were a kid?

SR: Right, until it's just an incredibly bizarre sound.

ER: You abstract it from its meaning by the process of making the sound in your mouth.

SR: I was thinking about Celan in relation to your vocabulary, not only because like his work, yours often has a haunted quality, but also because he too used a simple vocabulary of tree and stone and such: simple words he kept excavating and making his own.

ER: And they always retain a strangeness. They are never simply trees.

SR: Do you feel a kinship with his work?

ER: I do identify with Celan in the sense of the world being a foreign place and the poet inhabiting the foreignness to make poems. When I was in college, I took German just so I could read Celan. As soon as I sat down with my German dictionary to "translate" one of his poems, it became clear that, not just through his eccentric compound word constructions, he was pressing on the multiple layers of each word within a very sparse lexicon. His poems are mostly extremely terse, but they are dense. They weigh a lot. Any reader could learn a lot by participating in this work. Clearly, I never went through anything as catastrophic as what he went through, but I identify with that willingness to collide with pain, to move toward the space that is haunted. I don't know if that is what I do in my work, but I find it powerful in his work. He goes places he doesn't want to go, because he is called to go there.

SR: He felt a kinship with Dickinson, and I felt her presence in your work also, partly in the sense of taking on form and then working both inside and against it.

ER: I do feel a deep bond with Dickinson. The first book of poems I received as a child was her work. Everybody knew that I liked to write poetry, because I started when I was really little, and that was all I ever wanted to do. In Orange County in the sixties, there was so little poetry by women available—I was given lots of stupid Rod McKuen books like *Listen to the Warm*. My mother gave me a hardback book of Dickinson poems when I was in grade school. That was a really important gift. I haven't read Dickinson as much as an adult, but I have lots of those poems memorized. I experience her work as balletic and awkward simultaneously, creating its own tactics for movement.

SR: Your work also resonates for me with that of both Howe sisters: Susan Howe's investigation of marginalized histories, and Fanny Howe's spiritual-feminist nexus.

ER: I discovered Susan Howe's work while I was in grad school. It was like breaking through the glass ceiling. I was amazed at what she did in her vocabulary and her process, and the way she spliced things together, and above all the intelligent investigation—the discoveries she could make by truly paying attention and constructing a history. In the last couple of years, Fanny's work has become more important to me. I admire her ability to be so straightforward and to undertake writing projects on their own terms. I came of age as a poet in an experimental writing milieu where certain things, such as confessional work, or even traditional syntax, were impermissible. Using first-person pronouns was a no-no. Even now, some taboos are in place. Yet I have always had a strong affiliation with lyric. I was at a conference where Jennifer Moxley said, "I write lyric poetry, but it's not fashionable to say that." I'm in the same boat. Lyric gives me pleasure, and pleasure is a really important part of writing. Of course there's plenty of work to do every day—write your congressperson, clean the toilets. The pleasure of writing is multidimensional and it dignifies and stretches me, so that I can pick up the Ajax and scrub brush with goodwill.

I see that practical imagination in Fanny's writing—her work is politically and emotionally direct, in such an unabashed way. And she's prolific. She writes her way through processes, through experience. So in terms of praxis, too, she is an exemplar for me. Susan and Fanny have very different approaches, but they are probably my most active exemplars in some ways. I love Cole Swensen's work also, and I admire her willingness to grapple with difficult concepts and with her own process, while retaining a level of accessibility. I find some of the experimental processes constraining. There's a de rigueur attitude that says, Don't make it too easy for them to read—because maybe accessibility is anti-intellectual or Republican. Do you feel that sense that there's a "way" to be experimental, and that we're the "us" and they're the "them"?

SR: You are bringing up questions of access, and perhaps wanting more conversation, both among experimental writers, and between experimentalists and more lyric poets. Your own activities seem based on a desire to be inclusive: Your reading series mixes emerging and established poets, and your EtherDome Press publishes first chapbooks of emerging poets. It seems you're working to enact a politics of access and openness among writers.

ER: Yes, that is really important to me. When I was an undergraduate, I worked with a poet named Robert Kelly who said, Don't worry about getting published; make magazines, and publish each other, and set up reading series. So, early on, I got into that. I am ambitious—I want to be published and I want my work to be read. But what I really want is to be part of a larger conversation. I love the idea that you don't have to wait to be invited to the party; you can have a party and people will come. After my children were born, I felt isolated, until I came up with the idea of doing a reading series in my back yard. And everybody I asked to read, said yes. After a certain point, they started calling and asking if they could read. I didn't want there to be any sense that some people are more welcome than others, or that there was an "in" crowd. So anybody is invited, but the readers have to do their own publicity. It was an experiment to see how, with limited resources, I could participate but also create a provisional model of community.

SR: I noticed that you do the lineup alphabetically; not the emerging poet followed by the established poet, as is often done.

ER: Yes, I wanted to follow a different possibility that wasn't status-oriented or hierarchical. And I make it potluck, because people are more comfortable if there is food and drink.

SR: Do you perceive an active Bay Area experimental community that you feel you're a part of?

ER: Well, I first moved here in the early nineties, on the heels of a period in which the community seemed in one sense more defined and cohesive, but also very feisty in a way that had left some people shell-shocked. Now it's more fragmented, and there are a lot of contested approaches. Even so, I started to feel constrained by that in the last few years.

SR: You felt constrained by . . . ?

ER: The sense that I wasn't Marxist enough, or that I'm too Christian or too lyric, or whatever label was implied, or even directly applied. I just want to explore what I want to explore. But I read everything. I would like to find a way to make more conversation between people who don't have the same strategies. Some of the people most willing to talk to me are doing work that is more conventional than I would have read in the past. But I'm also close to experimental writers like George Albon and Avery Burns, who I've known since I first moved here. We were putting out the magazine *26* together, along with Rusty Morrison, Brian Strang, and Joseph Noble, who I met more recently. Editing a magazine is a great way to be in conversation, because we were all soliciting different kinds of work and then arguing about what was good, which I found enormously fun. And I work on Instance Press with Beth Anderson and Stacy Szymazcek. In the last couple of years my students have become an important part of my sense of community. EtherDome, which I run with Colleen Lookingbill, did chapbooks by Valerie Coulton, Megan Pruiett, Susanne Dyckman, and Amanda Field, all of whom were students of mine—and now they have become my peers. The reading series also gave me a way to meet people I wouldn't get to meet otherwise. I find it frustrating and unnecessary that there are so many poets around here and yet we become factionalized. But at the same time, it's just amazing to live in a place where there are so many good writers. I place an extremely high value on community and I would argue that poetry-making is not a solitary but a communal activity. Part of our ethical work as writers, if you will, is to engage with that, to be good readers and responders, to participate in some way. I do complain that this very fine and rich community of writers isn't utterly perfect, but the truth is that I enjoy myself hugely and I always have interesting things to wrestle with. I remember those horrible poems from Rod McKuen and Jonathan Livingston Seagull from my childhood and look at where I've ended up—it's like, you know, that Frank O'Hara poem in which he says, "And here I am, the / center of all beauty! / writing these poems! / Imagine!"[24]

CAMILLE ROY

Experience Is a Demanding Mistress

Sarah Rosenthal: What does it mean to you to be an "experimental" writer?

Camille Roy: I'm not into experimentation for its own sake. For me, experimentation is about accepting that in order to represent experience, you need to break the conventional mode of representation. I teach a creative writing workshop, and I find that my students are often people who are in some way marginalized. I tend to be drawn to people who have a personal need to find tools that help them represent their lives, because the conventional ones just don't do the job.

SR: How did you first encounter avant-garde artistic practice?

CR: My first exposure to experimental work was through the jazz community in Chicago. Growing up there in the sixties and early seventies, I went to a lot of concerts by the Association for the Advancement of Creative Musicians. The AACM is a Black Nationalist organization committed to the intersection of avant-garde jazz and community practice. Joseph Jarman, an AACM member and a leading jazz musician, came to teach at the camp I went to, Circle Pines. AACM's jazz is a radical artistic practice that is completely understood in relation to the African Diaspora and the contemporary

African-American community. For me, that connection between experimental work and community has always been strong. I think some of the theoretical poetry of the last twenty years has wandered off from that.

SR: What do you think it has wandered off into?

CR: There's a lot of it that I really love, so I'm not bashing it. But I think that in terms of community practice, in some sense experimental poets talk the talk, but don't walk the walk. How do you do experimental poetry workshops in prisons, or for homeless youth? What is the value of these tools in contexts that are not defined by privilege, by layers of social insulation? I think that there hasn't been much of a commitment among the original core group of theory-based poets to finding out how to make those connections. On the other hand, it has been interesting to see how in the last fifteen years, a lot of the theory-based experiments have proliferated outside the boundary of the original white, upper-middle-class, largely heterosexual group. Experimental poets of color have used these experiments as tools to decode postcolonialism and gender issues. Renee Gladman comes to mind, as do Tisa Bryant and Tan Lin. This discourse has migrated across class and racial boundaries. That development validates my sense that these tools are helpful in discovering representational strategies that actually function to enact one's own experience.

SR: It's interesting that you have foregrounded your teaching so early in our conversation. Teaching seems to be a way for you to get out of the world of theory and see what actually works in practice.

CR: That is really true. For me, teaching has always been enjoyable—partly because I only teach a workshop and am not overwhelmed by teaching four classes, as I would in a university. When I first came to San Francisco, I found the writing workshops at Small Press Traffic and I took a couple of them. The one that really changed my life was taught by Robert Glück. There were a lot of people in that workshop—Dodie Bellamy, Kevin Killian, Mike Amnasan, others. I got schooled in a community of writers. My degree is in computer science, and though I took some writing classes at San Francisco State, I never really filled up my tank with poetics in a university setting. So when I teach, I feel that I am participating in the community that taught me what I know.

SR: I would think that growing up in a communist household where intellect was an important part of people's political and community life, part of their lived ideals, would also have provided a training ground.

CR: Also, Chicago is just so challenging, or my experience there was. You needed to have all your resources, including your cognitive tools. You needed to develop a set of ideas in order to navigate. One of the great things about Chicago was that understanding your environment was not a luxury; it was a necessity.

SR: In your play *Bye Bye Brunhilde,* you named a character "Fear." That is a profound gesture from a psychological as well as a feminist point of view. Fear runs us in so many ways, yet mostly it goes unnamed. Our response to 9/11 is a perfect example of fear running the show yet not being named as such. So just on that level it was interesting, but on top of that you make the character, Fear, so intriguing and desirable and full of imagination and power. As a reader, I loved trying to enter and understand these seeming contradictions.

CR: I find it compelling to write the story of a character whose "I" has been exploded as the result of experience. Narrative makes a whole set of assumptions about the narrator, including the notion that in order to narrate a story you need to have a coherent and stable identity as a prior condition. That becomes a problem if the narrator is, for example, a multiple personality. Then what happens to reality? How can you represent something that is recognizable? That's an example of what I was saying earlier about breaking convention in order to represent experience. Experience is like a demanding mistress; it demands that people continually invent new aesthetic strategies just in order to represent it. In the case of the character Fear, she wants to hide in a little hole in the ground precisely because she lives in a state of total exposure. She is completely unable to shut down, and her mental states wobble a lot, from one extreme to another. For me, those are representational challenges. One of the interesting things about Fear is that she is kind of a hysterical clown, the type of woman who often is not taken seriously. Yet as the play goes on, it becomes more and more clear that she is at the heart of everything. The people around her—in this case, Technique—continually have to strategize ways to placate or subdue or restrain her. Fear is an origin, it is the original condition, and everything else is a reaction—that's something the play is arguing. That is one reason that Fear, as the play evolves, becomes the character who is in a way supreme. You understand that the relationship between Fear and Technique is characterized by struggle and neither ever "wins the war." But Fear has won a battle by the end.

Fear as a character has reactions that one would associate with being a victim, yet actually it's more appropriate to say she's seen combat. Women get cloistered into domesticity in a way that leads to a misunderstanding of feminine experience: Domesticity replaces extremity in some sense. I like to break that up. Some of my female characters have been in abusive or scary situations, and I write about that as though it were combat. Some of their emotional reactions would have been the same had they been soldiers. Women are not supposed to see combat, even in the army. Yet women see combat all the time, and it's a formative part of making a character. And though the person who's seen combat may not appreciate those experiences, the result may be really interesting. People tend to see those kinds of things as blemishes that need to be treated, for example with therapy, whereas I think that if it doesn't kill you, it can make you more interesting. I look at those extremes as situations that require aesthetic strategies.

SR: Your writing embraces rage and conflict in a way that is unusual in women's writing. I think of the moment in *Craquer* when Camille, who's white, sees the black girls fighting in the schoolyard.[1] Instead of shying away, her instinct is to jump into the fray. She sees it as something exciting to participate in. Not only your content but also your form embraces conflict. You wrote in your introduction to *Cold Heaven* about how the lines almost propel each other through dialogue; it's as if a certain kind of dialectical conflict produces the words.[2]

CR: I'm interested in some fundamental questions: What is real? What is happening and where am I? It's not possible to have a satisfying experience in relation to those questions without action and conflict, because conflict is how social beings reveal themselves. Conflict doesn't have to be motivated by a desire to hurt; it can be motivated by other forms of energy. Also, I think there's a larger picture which conflict is just a part of, and that is the—for lack of a better word—"performativity" of being in society. I see social life as like theater in the sense that, for anything to happen at all, there has to be a commitment to acting. We operate in a field of social forces which are in our favor or against us, in varying ways at different times, and there's no escape from that.

A lot of my thinking about this has to do with being from the South Side of Chicago. That place was defined by inescapable social conflict. The people who did escape were in some fundamental way deluding themselves. The white suburban experience was based on the deep untruth that those who lived in the suburbs had managed to banish racism from their lives. I think that acting in response to social forces and conflicts that one lives among is a way of being and discovering at the same moment. My aesthetic is grounded in a commitment to continuing to move as time moves, and not trying to back out of that.

SR: So if there is this intense conflict happening, then to avoid that is to miss the boat. In "2 Pure Girls," Sally—who grew up in the suburbs—seems almost comically alienated from her newly adopted South Side surroundings.[3]

The narrator in "2 Pure Girls" says, "We hear a crash / stumble to the window. / Shots are fired. / A silky figure / walks away. Only / walking. / Whose dream am I in? / **Pow Pow BANG** / *Let's kill it,* / I tell June. / *Kill what?* She / wants to know."[4] You've been saying that if it doesn't kill you, it makes you more interesting. In the quoted passage, are you in any way valorizing these characters' internalization of the violence that surrounds them?

CR: I am not of the school that one ought to run around trying to have extreme experiences in order to become a more interesting person. I do think, though, that when things go really, really wrong, and people act out violently, it's in those moments that you see the playability of reality. Violence is often a performance based on a dream—merely interrupt the dream, or shift its premises, and the violence may stop. It's strange. I also think the world you live in is defined by what you know. You may know things that are very difficult. If you can live with that, then that has a lot of value. Some people can't live with all that difficulty.

I think one of the things some readers find disconcerting about my work is the possibility that some of my characters won't make it. I wrote a story called "J," as yet unpublished, in which the narrator says of the main character, "I didn't know if she would make it, but now she is an accountant and she lives in Los Gatos." What these characters have is a commitment to realizing the world that they know. And some of them are not going to make it. It is that difficult. When I was growing up in Chicago, there were people close to my family who didn't make it, mostly suicides related to drugs. The world is full of such people. The thing is, it is hard to see them as being like us, so we don't accept their relation to our community. But that is only because we don't know where they came from. Sometimes I walk down the street and I look at homeless people and think, Where did they go to high school? What did they look like when they were eleven?

Sometimes I think men can relate to what I'm doing more than women can. I think women, because they feel frightened, have a desire to live in a world which is safe. In fact, women end up in abusive relationships all the time, because they don't see the signs. They are caught in passivity and denial when the violence happens. Women often choose to stay sheltered out of delusion. It's the same syndrome as the white people who stay in their Polish neighborhood because they can't deal with racism. It's true that part of the feminine experience is to have stronger connections to family and other people, so living within that kind of shelter is not just delusion—but it is partly delusion. Men tend to be much less protected than women, which makes them better equipped to understand some of the emotions my characters have. Men more often can relate to being unprotected. They suffer because of that lack of protection. We don't tend to perceive that kind of suffering because we have a whole ideology of masculine identity that blocks us from that. So we can send eighteen-year-olds off to war and not really feel what we are doing.

SR: Some of your female characters who have experienced intense difficulty end up as ghosts, or as ghostlike figures. There is the ghost of Margery in the story "Perils," a brilliant physicist with a passive personality who gets screwed over by a series of men and abandoned by her professional community, and ends up killing herself.[5] In your play *Cheap Speech*, the character named grrl has a multiple personality. It's a funny play in many ways, but grrl doesn't come across as a playful venture into the dissolution of identity; she has suffered the kinds of horrifying things that clinically create that condition. She doesn't actually die, but she takes on a ghostlike presence at the end of the play.

CR: I was committed to doing an experimental representation of a real multiple personality. I didn't want it to be just a device. I think that she's a tragic character.

SR: Your play *Sometimes Dead Is Better* is often funny too, but there again, the Red Queen is a tragic character. She's the ghost of a bright, capable woman who got stuck at home with the baby while her husband was out having affairs. Perhaps by becoming ghosts, these women claim a kind of power: the power to haunt Camille as well as the reader, and to get their stories told, even though they are dead.

I was thinking about this ghost theme as tying into an aesthetic in your work having to do with "the cloud at the center of the story." In *Craquer* you write, "I've given up. That's my 'case.' I don't care what the truth is—not enough to pursue it, anyway. I'm registering something more vague—a sort of cloud at the center of the story, which is where I've spent most of my life." Later, you write, "I'm a seamstress of blur, performing nips and tucks on the empty center."[6]

CR: I feel that the stable referent "I" is another delusion, and that the truth of who we are is unknowable, although it can be felt. Lately I've been interested in the idea of imagining a large room that contains all your ancestors for the last 20,000 years. What would it be like to go back and wander around in that crowd, and look at everybody's faces, see how they talk, watch their body language? So much about our origins is lost to us because of the passage of time and the fact that people die. Where does a particular gesture or inflection come from? Where does a family history of abandonment come from? Where does the imagination come from? All of these things are mysteries. And if you were to start to follow them, it would be like a million trails in the forest.

SR: Is it more of a multi-determined "I" in that sense than an empty "I"?

CR: I think the emptiness has to be embraced in order to get to the next step, which is really paying attention to what is.

SR: In the online magazine you cofounded and co-edit, *Narrativity*, in a piece called "Quotes," you quote Gale Scott quoting Roland Barthes: "The text needs its shadow. This shadow is a *bit* of ideology, a *bit* of representation, a *bit* of subject: ghosts, pockets, traces, necessary clouds. Subversion must produce its own chiaroscuro."[7] Do you feel that in your writing there's the ghost of a more traditional narrative structure that remains, no matter how much you experiment?

CR: I feel that narrative is understood in a very unsatisfactory way. It's like those cases in scientific history where people look at a set of data and come up with some conclusion and then say, Ah look, the data makes the conclusion. Then others will say, No, your ideological bias determined how you interpreted the data. I think our theories of narrative are the same, in that we privilege the elements of narrative which subscribe to our dominant ideology, and then accuse narrative of upholding that ideology. For example, when people talk about narrative, they're basically talking about telling the story. Yet that is not a transparent description of what narrative does; such a description involves an ideological choice to focus on one aspect of narrative. As one thinks about it, a big part of what narrative does is to *not* tell the story, at least as much as it *tells* a story. It's the act of *not* telling that creates the suspense; it's the act of withholding that creates the reader's desire to find out what you are withholding. And all of those negative actions, negative in the sense of not seen, not foregrounded, get obscured by the way that we turn narration solely into a positive action.

I have a theory that I am testing out in a story that I am working on, which is that you do not need to answer the questions that you raise in a narrative; all you need to do is to replace them with other questions. That is a perfectly comprehensible experimental strategy; you can give a story with a structure like that to somebody who is not capable of reading experimental poetry, and they'll be interested. Playing with the structure in that way does not make it unavailable to a reader. People have said that narrative is "linear." Such terms are very unexamined, in terms of the diversity of narrative practices that exist. To bring this back to the ghost theme, the ghost is like the character who is present through absence, like when your grandparents are present in your life through their absence. And in some sense these aspects of narrative practice that I am talking about are the ghost-like aspects of narrative practice.

All these things relate to aspects of actual human experience. For example, certain emotions are more available in one kind of practice than they are in another. One of the things I talk about with my students is that it's good to have a tool kit. You want to know what your narrative devices are and how they work, so that if you have something happening in your writing, you know a diversity of approaches that you can use to work with it. A lot of the theorizing about writing has not addressed this. There is this big question: What happens when the narrative works? That question really interests me. So I write about characters who push me into having to examine my narrative practice just in order to represent them.

SR: You write in *Craquer*, "Families trail off like the ghosts to whom we are all connected. They don't have a bottom. And it's not only ancestors, but other ungraspable relations which shadow me—from my father's silence to mother's dreamy milk."[8] I see the speaker as trying to articulate her aesthetic in relation to her past and recognizing that this act of locating has to take into account all of the silences and unreliabilities of the past.

CR: One of the truths about the past is that one can't articulate reliable truths about it. That's a contradiction that we live in. Certain aspects of my family life made that contradiction more explicitly a part of my experience than may be the case for others, but I think it is a basic contradiction. Also, I think having an unreliable past is characteristically American. Young people here are always taking off and making up a new life for themselves. There's this idea of, My parents lived in Maine, but if I want to I will be a Texan. Though of course in reality there's a huge difference between Maine and Texas.

SR: I'm also interested in how that passage in *Craquer* sets up two poles of silence and fantasy and shows the speaker trying to locate herself between those poles. In the story, there's the dad who's really quiet and the mom who gets tipsy and tells flamboyant, not-quite-believable stories. It seems to me your writing is always operating between these poles and including both of them: on the one hand, silence, or what we could call the ghostly, untold story, and on the other hand, the vivid, unreliable story; the thrusting of language out in front of one to see what happens next. Your characters often seem to leap out into the unknown with their thoughts and speech.

CR: There's a quality of making oneself up in the moment.

SR: *Bye Bye Brunhilde* takes that to the hilt. That piece is for me the most challenging of your work. The reader has to be willing to let go of any expectations of what a play is and how characters behave. But when one does let go, it becomes an exhilarating experience, with language often carrying the show. We're still seeing the reality of human beings in an intimate relationship. But the language switches at a moment's notice from poetry to the logistics of daily living to relationship processing to storytelling to theory. The built-in conflict between the play's two characters generates language that spins itself out in arcs of possibility.

CR: It's like what I was saying earlier, that conflict is generative, not a mistake that needs to be resolved—you don't need to negotiate a peace settlement. Conflict actually generates language and experience. There may be a problem, but the existence of conflict is not in itself the problem. One of the possibilities that I hope comes through in my work is that the risk of taking on those conflicts is worth it.

SR: That play must have been thrilling to write, once you had the characters and got into that mode.

CR: It really was thrilling. There is a way, when you don't try to control whether or not your language is telling the truth, that you give language the freedom to be surprising. And even if it is not the truth, it exists in a truthful way. I am interested in the conflict around telling the truth. There's so much value associated with telling the truth. It's not that I am questioning if that has value, but I want people to pay attention to something else: the energy and the value of whatever happens, even if it's a performance that is not truthful. But if it happens enough, then it exists.

SR: There's a desire for bigness that comes up in your writing. In your piece "Quotes" in *Narrativity,* you quote a passage by Carla Harryman about the omniscient "I" in novels: "I am interested in uncovering the hidden, expansive 'I.' What happens when one concretizes it, making it evident in the writing, is carnivalesque."[9] Sometimes your characters suggest that they want to take up a lot of space in a colonizing or aggressive way. In *Bye Bye Brunhilde,* Technique says, "I want to be on stage, newly articulate and solid as a pebble."[10] In *Cheap Speech*, Sydney says, "Today, I want [my novel] to be so big, it'll have its own . . . climate" and "secretly I aspire to grow bigger & bigger."[11] At other times, the characters take up space in ways that seem expansive without being dominating. In "Missing," the narrator says, "These large sensations come and go. I want to be a star. I want to be adorable. Instead there are the larger sensations, so open there's a sense of leveling."[12] "I want to be a star" is the first level of realizing that one wants to expand somehow. But that's just a baby step compared to what happens in the rest of the quote, where the narrator lets go into a larger experience: a temporary dissolution of self.

CR: The Technique quote and the Sydney quote demonstrate varieties of craving. It's not even so important that they want this or that thing;

what I wanted to focus on was the experience of craving. Craving is part of the crust of the personality that sooner or later needs to get dissolved. When those two characters talk about their craving, they're talking about a secret desire to grow bigger and bigger. It's something they are seeking and at the same moment they are refusing access to what they seek to anybody else. When I write about their cravings, I'm actually mocking them, making fun of them, though hopefully not in a way that alienates the affections.

SR: What exactly do you mean by "refusing access"?

CR: "I'm going to secretly attend to my desire to be better than you. I'm going to secretly attend to my desire to completely eclipse you." Whereas in "Missing," I agree that the narrator's desire immediately gets taken over by a later stage of actually letting go. Craving and letting go are, in a way, opposites. One of the contradictions of the writing practice is that you're compulsively scribbling, and that it is a way of clinging to something.

SR: It's like constantly taking photographs when you're out in nature.

CR: Right, exactly.

SR: In *Craquer,* you write about rules: "Let's get to the basics. When we speak of rules we are referencing contested territory. . . . When [these rules are] violated, it's like invisible writing that appears when you hold the paper over a flame. There they are, the codes which describe intelligible experience. . . . As the rules become intelligible, finally specified and visible, the person who violated them becomes unintelligible, slides off the map towards *strange*."[13] The rules you describe are the ones that say, "Black girls play over here and white girls play over there." So they are rules to fight against. Yet in the language I just quoted, the rules sound like a pretty permanent, intractable feature of the landscape. What is your thinking about the continuum between learning to recognize these invisible rules and challenging them, changing them?

CR: The first step is to recognize that these rules are in some sense arbitrary; they are not permanent, although they do feel that way. I have been wanting to go back to Chicago now for a couple of years, just to drive around and see how things are different. There has been some development in areas where it seemed as if never again would anybody invest a penny. For example, I read recently about a new shopping center on 47th Street. The truth is, cities change; they go through cycles. After they die, they become resurrected. It's surprising how they can just keep on going. In fact, the rules do change, but people are reluctant to recognize that. What I wrote in the passage you just quoted was very true of my experience. I operate as a white woman in society, looking like a person who I am not. Most people who meet me don't understand my social history and my social knowledge. That's one of the things I meant by "sliding off the map towards strange." I don't occupy the understanding that is attributed to me, and I am misunderstood because of that. That is just something to be acknowledged. Social change is problematic, but it's important to have clarity about what's actually going on.

SR: In your piece "Monstrous" in *Narrativity*, you write about breaking invisible codes when you walk a block and a half from your house to go to your friend's birthday party in the projects. In that passage you also point out that in San Francisco, crossing those boundaries is actually more possible than in some cities. Yet I and many other whites do not cross those lines often.

CR: I think the inaction stems in part from a lack of curiosity. I went through a period, years ago, when I would spend hours flipping through the pages of *The New Yorker*. I didn't even know what was so compelling to me. Eventually I decoded the mystery. I realized that they had all these cartoons of urban life that showed no people of color. The understanding I couldn't occupy was what it was like for those cartoonists to live in New York City and not see any people of color. There is an intervention there—a rule about how you live in a city. Nothing keeps those cartoonists from walking out of their building, looking around, and seeing what's out there—except their ideology.

SR: So the rules are in our heads, and they're unexamined. In that case one can do a lot of social change by foregrounding one's assumptions, examining them, and deciding what to do about them.

CR: I also think that if people get clarity about their assumptions, their identifications and alliances change. And these changes enrich us—they multiply the pleasures that are available in our lives. My work is motivated by a powerful desire to be present. And I want that desire to be persuasive even when the work is difficult.

SR: Your interest in theater seems to tie into this desire for intense presence. Theater involves the living presence of people on a stage saying words in front of a live audience, or the potential for that in a script.

CR: I see drama as a concentration of the theatricality and performativity of daily life. We are always making up dramas; social life is a drama. Performativity and social life tend to be associated with people who are closer to the street, for one reason or another. And performative theatrical language is often street language. Innovations in American slang don't come from the educated middle class.

Most of the live shows I had gone to before writing *Bye Bye Brunhilde* were either drag shows or strip shows. My whole sense of theatrics and performativity came from the clubs and the sex industry. So it was sort of a private joke that I ended up writing this experimental play. While the language is experimental, the energy of the work really reflects those origins.

SR: You make direct use of the imagery and language of strip clubs to address issues of social identity. In "Baby or Whose Body Is Missing?" you write, "I was a bar dyke before all this gender-theory crap came along. I kissed and fucked like every other girl in my invisible world, and I stuck dollar bills in the g-strings of all the strippers in town. That world is still invisible, because I left my body there. . . . No one can see anything before I get dressed. After I get dressed, I am a sex toy."[14] That language seems to be talking about putting on your social/sexual identity—kind of a strip-tease in reverse.

CR: One of the curious aspects of the way our social life is organized, is that there are rules that split sexual life from other forms of life in rigid ways. So there's a lot of multiple identity and pursuing of secret identities and so on, and different sexual communities in any city. It's as if after I get dressed I have a sex choice; after I get dressed, "I" becomes my sexual self. Before I get dressed, I'm just one in the crowd. Growing up, I noticed that you had to be really careful about the kind of attention that you got. Sexually oriented attention was trouble.

SR: As a woman.

CR: Yeah. It overwhelmingly determined who you were, so that it was difficult to function economically as—in my case—an engineer. It affected, for example, the way I would dress going to work. It's not like

I wanted to wear anything sexy to work, but I just had a feeling that I needed to keep my sexuality out of it, or there would be trouble for me. For women particularly, there are pressures that affect our credibility. The idea of the "dumb cunt" is alive and well, and if you have a strong sexual presence, people categorize you as that, which affects your ability to make a living. The Margery character in "Perils" plays out that conflict between female sexuality and female intellect, and the challenge that poses to one's livelihood.

SR: A coming-of-age Camille appears in your writing, and she seems to be actively trying to sort out issues like these. In "Perils," Camille describes a conversation she has with Margery: "Some people are target practice for their era; it's important, I thought, to understand the wider causes and effects of personal disaster. 'Were you pretty?' I said."[15] She seems to be trying to understand how she's going to negotiate this terrain; how she's going to protect herself from negative attention. This question comes up in an extremely frightening way with the incident where the protagonist encounters Ted Bundy, which gets mentioned in a couple of different texts. In dealing with that incident, the protagonist seems to be inventing herself or somehow coming into herself in that moment, and that is what saves her life.

CR: If you're present, it might save your life, in that you're more available to take care of business. I think that in a way, my work is an argument for being present.

SR: What are you working on now in your writing?

CR: As always, I'm working on a novel. I am playing with different narrative devices, trying to understand what's at stake in a story, what is actually happening. Also, I've been returning to poetry. One of the things I'm working on is bringing speech and dialogue explicitly into poems—having voices in relation to one another without having characters, but using language in that way. I've also been working with nursery rhymes and fairy tales as tropes of female life. I rewrote "Red Riding Hood," "Cinderella," and *The Wizard of Oz*. I have a blog and a website, and I co-edited the web zine *Narrativity*, so I do a lot online.

SR: Early in our discussion you talked about having come of age within a Bay Area community of writers. Do you continue to experience the Bay Area writing scene as a support and a stimulus to your work?

CR: I absolutely do. I feel embedded in and attached to a community of writers that accepts me. Every experimental tool that I've ever learned from others—all the ones I haven't developed myself—I've learned here. I feel that we can develop a lot of clarity about what we are trying to do because we are immersed in a community in which these things are practiced with awareness and a sophisticated level of meta-criticism.

SR: And by meta-criticism you mean looking at one's own critical assumptions, asking, How do I bring theory into my writing? What assumptions do I continue to make about "experimental practice" that I need to challenge?

CR: Right.

SR: Do you have any fantasies about what you'd like to see more of, or less of, in the Bay Area experimental community?

CR: My fantasy is that people would continue to be theoretically serious and well-read, but become less intimidated by theory and more willing to take emotional risks, in terms of exposure and vulnerability and looking either trashy or ridiculous.

SR: Risks in their writing?

CR: And risks in the direction of becoming more performative. I think poets tend to get caught in their heads and that being on stage is a good place for poets to expand their brains. I think we want to be saved by theory. We want theory to be the lover that will change the world. But that desire is a mistake. There are things we can do to make our writing practice more present. If you start to reject theory, then you end up embracing anti-intellectualism, and I don't want that to happen. So what's the happy medium there? Is it possible to strike one?

I would also like it if our community fostered more deep thought and discussion about narrative. I think that we have more of a conversation happening about narrative than a lot of places do, and that it continues to develop. But I would like to have that be a little bit more present.

LESLIE SCALAPINO
Messing Up Linear Time

Sarah Rosenthal: I'd like to start with two quotes by other writers that appear in your work. One, the epigraph of *Way*, is from David Bohm's *Causality & Chance in Modern Physics*. The second, which appears in a passage in *R-hu* where you are discussing Philip Whalen's work, is from José Ignacio Cabezón's *Buddhism and Language: A Study of Indo-Tibetan Scholasticism*.[1] Both are about the nature of objects in the world; they get at the idea that all objects are interconnected in a giant web and that they're defined by each other. So there is no stability to any entity—to any person or thing.

Leslie Scalapino: Also, one thing that fascinated me about this thought was that behavior and emotions are also objects, they're things (events). They're all active at once, and nothing is the same thing as itself because it doesn't even have an instant in which it *is*, in a stable way.

SR: One of those quotes describes everything as being in a state of free fall. The other quote describes a constant flux, where there's no stability of any identity, even with itself, from one moment to the next.

LS: In the case of the second quote you mentioned, Charles Bernstein had made an observation which sparked my writing of that particular passage. There was a group reading of Philip Whalen's work in

New York, and many of the people reading had never heard him read. Some of them were young poets, and they were grappling with how to read it, because they wanted it to be almost as if there were one way to read it, which would be Philip's voice. But they had never heard his voice. So as they were speaking, they were trying to find out what this is. Bernstein remarked afterward how fascinating it was to watch people doing that, because Philip was doing something that was incredibly difficult to do, which was not even relying on resonance, or a sound pattern, or returning to anything, but it's just this free fall where there *could* possibly be inertia, or there could be anything. It would be whatever would occur, and you would be seeing what is. And that's really mind as phenomena, and sound as phenomena, and something very dangerous to do as writing. He didn't say that, but that's what I think. I realized that was something that I wanted to do—that you don't encapsulate or make endings to things, have ways to take care of it so that it can't allow that free fall.

SR: Your earlier works appear much more contained to me than your later works. For example, in your book *way* there are delineated topics as well as a clear movement between lineated poems and prose paragraphs. I experience your more recent work as enacting a more chaotic state. It feels faster, and seems to collapse boundaries more easily. There's a passage in *Defoe* where you write, "This gets so limpid that there's no reason to go on and then one can see really what occurs."[2] In *Defoe* I sense a radical giving up that's similar to what you're saying about Philip Whalen's work: a risk of not containing it in any way, of letting there be a kind of free fall.

LS: There are many interesting problems and thoughts in connection with this. For one thing, a question of prose or poetry. *way* has line breaks. I don't know whether you're saying it *looks* contained, or it *is* contained. The question would be, In what way? It was not at the time emotionally contained for me; that is, it was undertaking something that was very hard on me. Wrestling with such *might* constitute a change conceptually that's an invention, as much or more than a work derived from a cerebral approach. *way* is a sound pattern: Something occurs that is its sound and shape. The notion is that one would apprehend in the reading, whether it's read out loud or not, something that takes place as that sound and shape, which is an event. So it's not contained in terms of what the event is, perhaps. It may be an arduous event; it may even really hit the fan. But the point is, *way* is a potentially infinite space in which all events and relations, past and future even, can both be on a single space—conceptually, as text's abstraction—and at once be utterly changed there.

Defoe is a prose work. The quote that you are referring to is exactly what I was undergoing and engaging in that work, where there's free fall not only as writing but in terms of phenomena and how one's seeing the world. There aren't any boundaries in terms of a feeling of being safe knowing what it is that's happening, or imposing limits on one's seeing of something so that one can make sense out of it. I was dropping that, aware that I was trying to drop that. It was very enervating. Especially since some of the engagement was our being in the midst of war, the Gulf War, which was completely invasive. Context is where the inside and outside are completely imploded.

SR: So do you feel that that book was a visceral response to the violence of the Gulf War?

LS: It was partly that, but it didn't have that boundary either. The writing was taking in various events or strands at the same time. The Gulf War was one; I began *Defoe* during the buildup to the Gulf War. It was as if everything was being hurled into the same state and was appearing to be the same thing. A paragraph might read as the unfolding of rage, which when read appears identical to motionless calm. I referred in *Defoe* to the Oakland fire, for example, which came to within a block of our house. No one on this block left the area; they were watering down their roofs, cars exploding on the background, an inferno wind. It was as if the war had come to us. One drops any distinctions about things because one's trying to see what one thing is. When the boundaries are dropped, you begin to see the nature of phenomena, but also that the passage across the boundaries transforms those phenomena.

SR: It could make you wonder if you are crazy, I would think, or if you can handle it. If you can have the mental stamina to stay with all of that bleeding of phenomena so that you really are experiencing everything as one related morass.

LS: Well, the paragraphs in *Defoe* are paragraphs of attention, where a number of events, emotions, and sights will conflate in one paragraph. But I wanted to hold onto these, which were jumping ahead of themselves, not exclude anything and have attention at the same time. I wanted the writing to be itself attention, with all of the impinging of these events (historical, outside, not separate from any impression and emotion), so that the writer wouldn't forcibly exclude anything, and the reader would let it come in, but the writing would also be very clear and attentive so it wouldn't be crazy-making.

SR: Your work lets all this matter be seen as part of the same web. You get the ego out of the way, and pay really close attention. You let each thing emerge and have its place, and cycle back later but be different when it returns, as it is different. All of this goes against what in one of your books you call the capitalist-materialist system that we live in.

That system doesn't find it convenient for us to see this complexity. If we know that we're all really connected at some fundamental level, that insight is not good for producing widgets or selling them, or making wars, or keeping rich and poor divided, and so forth. In that sense I see your writing as an act of political resistance to the reduction of language, people, and things to little boxes of meaning. Yet at times I experience your writing not as activism but as something akin to a child's freeform, unselfconscious play, or a monk's meditation practice.

LS: I think people being actively aware are jumping out of a propagandized state of social conventions. Writing could be an active state outside social convention. Yet it is not to be alone, not to withdraw, or to fail to pay attention. In that case one couldn't write, because what would there be to write? My goal is to seek to change the perspective, and to try to perceive what is mind doing this or not doing this.

SR: In *The Front Matter, Dead Souls* you write, "Defoe doesn't know she is sauntering, her limbs flowing. She has to have new work each time she works so as not to know what she is doing. This is imagined as the utmost rigour, as having not to have formed anything, not to in the future. Yet to not form, or oneself to not be formed, can't be rigorous even, if it is to occur."[3] Elsewhere, in *Defoe*, you write, "To remove this from its former authority, what could be harder than that, this is very hard to do."[4] Put together, these passages suggest to me that on the one hand, it's extremely difficult to take oneself out of this clamp that we're in, to remove oneself from all the traditions of what writing should be and even how perception takes place. On the other hand, when you're actually doing it, it can't be hard or you couldn't do it. You have to somehow allow it to flow.

LS: I meant that living one's life, regardless of whether one's a writer, is a practice of observing. And you can't even have the sense of rigour because rigour is an authoritarian dictum in itself, which rules out other ways of approaching movement, for example perceiving something with gentleness. I think most of us were raised—I was!—with a masculine, tough-guy orientation that teaches you to be tough. There's a notion that that's rigourous and you can see things that way. So what I'm talking about is a kind of dictum, so to speak, that runs through U.S. custom, an embedded doctrine that things have to be hard, and that if you're a softie, then you're being cowardly or you're not doing something that's real. I didn't want to be having a mild and accepting attitude toward something observed because that wouldn't be uncovering what was accurate. But then it's a trap where you might become hard-edged and tight. And you can see friends doing that, where they absolutely would not be able to look at something in a different way, to change.

Another thing about that quote: I noticed that I kept returning to that thought in different works: The idea that you would have to change your work as mindset continually; you couldn't redo or stay on one track.

SR: "[S]o one has to be a nomad to / continually engage one's decomposing self / without 'meaning' and so in actual existence."[5]

LS: Right, you have to keep on going and not look back and assess a gesture because you will solidify it as an idea.

SR: That's interesting, because I find in your work a sense of being constantly on the frontal edge of consciousness. It's not exactly restless—there's focussed attention at each moment—but it's constantly in motion, with lots of different kinds of matter being brought in. Yet within a particular book, there are characters and scenarios that are noticeable or prominent. If you're not looking back, then why does the character of Akira appear all the way through *The Front Matter,* for example? Is it because you got attached to him? You write at the end of that book about clinging to Akira.[6] Or is it that the constants in a particular book provide some kind of baseline so that you can see how things are changing and how fast they're changing?

LS: One *is* very attached and writes *because* one's attached. Also, one is in a period of time when certain things are happening which focus one. In other words, I see nothing wrong with keeping on with the project of a particular piece, the world that exists for you then. It's not that you're just not going to allow anything to form; the writing would be nothing in that case. In the case of *The Front Matter* as well as *Defoe,* those were two prose works. They had characters because I wanted to write a work that would be like a detective novel. The character Defoe is supposedly a detective, but as soon as she appears in Part II of the novel, it's announced that she's given up being a detective, because the context of the world was all corrupt. So the book uses plot, but in a kind of humorous way, undoing it by deciding that it was too confining right at the start. The passage you referred to at the end of *The Front Matter* was a joke about being attached to Akira because I liked him, thought he was so wonderful.

Referring to our earlier discussion about poetry versus prose, making up characters is a difference between poetry and prose. Prose is much more amenable to longer passages about people's natures, personalities, and the things they say; their being personality and character, it's sort of the pleasure of life. Poems are inventions in their spatial shape and their syntax that may cause you to see something in a different way. Prose does that too, maybe—hopefully—but it transpires differently.

SR: What you're saying reminds me of Stein's *The Making of Americans* and *Malanctha*, which seem to enact the joy of studying individuals and interrelationships. But I suppose a lot of writers would say that that's what draws them to writing fiction.

LS: Also my work looks at people embedded in landscape as chunks of paragraphs, the relation of people to land and sky, in a way that seems Steinian. In *Defoe* I took great pleasure in rendering motorcycle scenes where people are being chased; the motorcycles are flying up into the air and are mirrored on the hoods of cars. I was in Italy when I was writing that, looking at all those Renaissance ceilings and paintings, thinking of Renaissance space, and trying to think about the difference between space then and space now. Can we see space that's also social and interior? Maybe we can't see it because we're in it. I had the notion of imposing a Renaissance space on all this mind stuff which I was doing and which seemed to be happening at the present time. I wondered if I could see something about present time and space by projecting the present time into the altered space of Renaissance ceilings, but changed as paragraphs of writing as if it were landscape, territory, and asking, What's the relationship of behavior and personality to that?

SR: You did that in *R-hu* too, by projecting Mongolian tanka paintings onto your travels and your writing.

LS: *R-hu* had been commissioned by Atelos Press, which is published by Lyn Hejinian and Travis Ortiz. I knew I was going to go on a trip to Mongolia, and I thought, This will be a really interesting way to do the commission. And I'll warm up by beginning it in Oakland, so that I'll have some steam up when I get to Mongolia and I won't have to begin to write something there. So that's what I did. I was writing in a notebook while I was traveling in a jeep across the Gobi Desert. We were driving all day long, and we'd see incredibly beautiful golden land and dark, indigo-blue sky at all times of the day, a few nomads here and there, camels, horses. Then we'd go into monasteries and look at tanka paintings. The tankas render the space of the land that you're actually seeing there; in the tankas it's rendered conceptually, in a way that has to do with Tantric Buddhism. I was trying to ask, What's the relation between one's conceptual, cultural, philosophical take on something—the space that one makes of that—and the space that one lives in? I wanted the writing to be that open, "free," Mongolian space, both landscape and tanka space, but also have the U.S. imposed on that, or impose that on the U.S. space, and see the difference between the two in the conceptual space of the writing.

SR: At the end of *R-hu* where you review Bernadette Mayer's *Studying Hunger* and *Midwinter Day*, you write, "Her writing enables one's perceiving something about outside and mind at once."[7] There's a common theme here about superimposing different realities onto each other to see what you learn in the course of that process.

LS: That was written as a talk and was given at the Page Mothers conference in San Diego, which celebrated Bernadette Mayer. I've taught her work in classes many times and been attracted to it precisely because I felt that some of her texts, particularly the two you mentioned, follow the mind in a time-based setting. *Midwinter Day* takes a single day and writes throughout that day and night. Mayer once gave a talk at Naropa describing how she did this, how she practiced in advance having interesting dreams since she could only have a few dreams on the night the book was written. It's such a heightened attention to the *act* of attention, that that then transforms what happens.

SR: So the writing and the life are two different things, but that difference is being challenged, and they're both being transformed by being brought into such close contact with each other.

LS: Exactly.

SR: And do you experience that also?

LS: Yes. I'm doing that too, but in a different way.

SR: Not, for example, in the context of a 24-hour experiment, where these conditions are set up in advance, but—

LS: —but what you mentioned earlier, traveling. It's like placing two tracks alongside each other, which would be almost like a comparison of waking and sleeping life, only in this case they're tracks of being here and being there. Conflating those two tracks so that they give total attention to and transform each other.

SR: You're imposing U.S. culture on, say, Mongolian culture and you're seeing both of them, and they're both interacting with each other.

LS: No. I'd say, you're aware that you do that imposing, of course, because you're unavoidably doing that. But it's as if you are eliminating that factor, supposedly, though you're aware that you're not. You eliminate it by trying to look at context simply as space, as if only physical. You make a series of paragraphs that *is* the space of one place—as if that were possible—and imposes it on the space of the other. You therefore remove the element of interpreting some other culture, though you may render things that happen there, events, and one moving seeing those events. But you're trying to make a physical seeing be the vehicle by which this happens. Yet it's only text that is taking place.

SR: I want to talk about dreams and waking in this context. There's a passage in *Defoe* where you record a dream and then you write, "What this [dream] is in real time doesn't matter. One has to see it up against any vision that is created in waking life to see that. Either of them without there being anything in between. I will have to remember and match them to waking life. . . . If they are two empty shining pans of reality which fit on each other in a certain way, one can see oneself before one is oneself."[8] This made me think about how, if I'm actually recalling my dream while I'm staring at a bookcase, then the two are conflating. I'm remembering images from my dream but my eyes are open; I'm awake. My dream is now an image that's being superimposed on waking. Dreaming and waking are facing and talking to each other, via images.

LS: This is something that is very hard to describe. It's as if the dreams that you have at night are in the day, and there's no difference between night and day, because the dreams are projected out in front of you and you can see them going on in the space that is the day. I couldn't say that in any other way. So you explode the social ordering of time capsules in which you exist and also the way in which you see things. It's a different way—gentler than the war context, and also interior and exterior at once—of working on the problem of not having any barriers or operating rules in which you gauge time or how you operate within that, or what time is, or what you are as a mind. You're not there, in a way. Also, as you become aware of dreaming and that you're creating fictions, that begins to change the fiction that you have already created. This is akin to what we were just saying about Bernadette Mayer and *Midwinter Day*.

SR: Her text works with dreams, and it experiments with the fiction-making that we all engage in all of the time. We become aware of fiction-making in a heightened way and see how we can actually have an impact on our fictions.

LS: Yes, all of those things. There are a lot of dreams that show up in *Defoe*; one of the dreams I suddenly remembered as you were speaking was during the Gulf War. At some point I dreamed that someone was pouring gasoline into a puddle to light it.[9] A child is beside the puddle and is going to catch on fire. And I realize in the dream that it is I who have done this, even though I'm watching somebody pour the gasoline. The gasoline is coming from me and toward me, as I am viewing the child and the puddle. In other words, a kind of unrest or rage has produced this effect in the outside world. It's not separate from myself or from text. You're completely swept up in a change of reality, and it's causal because of your engagement in it. One's dreams are this. Noticing this is as much a part of the present-time reality as anything else.

The book that I'm working on now is called *Dahlia's Iris: Secret Autobiography and Fiction*. I got the idea to do this based on a Tibetan written form, the secret autobiography, which is not one's outside chronological events, but has to do with seeing, that is, interior seeing. I traveled in Tibet. I then read a terrific Tibetan secret autobiography written in the eighteenth century, in a book called *Apparitions of the Self*. I thought that the Tibetan secret autobiography was much like some contemporary American poetry. The person who did the translation and wrote about the form of the Tibetan secret autobiography said that various Tibetans told her not to translate the text because Americans would not understand it. I thought, They're not familiar with contemporary American poetry, which uses similar non-narrative tactics.

SR: By which you mean, writing which operates outside a chronological sense?

LS: And also writing which puts into the text what the mind is envisioning. A highly trained lama sees things that would be accepted as visions and have a certain meaning in Tibetan culture, which they wouldn't have for Americans who didn't know about that. But a person considering the process of the mind's formation in seeing might recognize that process in a text, unrelated to Tibetan culture or beliefs.

In the course of writing my secret autobiography, it seemed that the Tibetan view of dreams was that they are references to exterior events, so they don't count as visions; they're just sleeping dreams. But I also thought it must be that some dreams which get at something that is real would qualify as seeing, as opposed to something that is simply a reference to events that are happening. This messes up linear time. Chronology is a false sense. It's not accurate to experience. So it's germane to any notion of how something is going to be narrated.

SR: When you write, do you feel that you're working against an ingrained sense of a chronological, linear mode?

LS: I don't have a sense that you're trying to work against writing in a linear mode or stop yourself from doing that. But rather, one persists in order to see something that has come up in the writing, it seems to be attached to other things, and those things may on the surface have nothing to do with each other. That is, an outsider might say, Well, what does that have to do with this? But it's not that you wish to explain the connections, or to break the connections. It's that you want to find out what they are. More and more things arise which bear on each other. But you're discovering something via an apparent union, not trying to escape linear thinking. Nor is the result linear thinking, which is just a convention. Though the result could be linear thinking as a convention.

SR: How do you know when you're done with a book?

LS: I go on for a while because I'm really connected to an investigation. There's some kind of interior unknown space or occurrence that finally materializes via one's putting things together, and I learn something.

SR: Is "putting things together" a good way to describe it, or could it just as easily be described as paying attention and seeing what arises?

LS: I wrote a poem recently where I was actually thinking about the quality that some people have of deciding to place things together. I was thinking how someone could, with a kind of humane rationalism, simply put one thing next to another thing and let it be there and see something about it, as opposed to my own tendency which is to have things really hit the fan, where you get really messed up by this, embroiled in it emotionally—or I do, as the writer or the person thinking about this. And I can't see the forest for the trees. Yet rationalism is a construct which is *also* illusion.

SR: Do you mean you let too many things in and you'd like to be a little more deliberate?

LS: No, I mean I'm not distanced from it and it may hurt or be just incredibly confusing and upsetting. So then, when that has become a morass that has a big effect on me, at some point I begin to see what it is. I was commenting humorously in this poem about the fact that some people could just simply place things together and let that be. But in parentheses I said, "'Simply' only if you *can* do it." So it's a different method than mine, and probably requires a different personality.

SR: One that can simplify a problem and distance oneself.

LS: Right, though it is that very distancing, I think, that enables you to put frames around events perceived so that you actually change them totally as linear thinking, convention. This goes back to what we were talking about earlier, how free fall involves letting go of the frames that one would put around perception which would supply or preserve artificial borders.

SR: So you're saying you can appreciate that approach but it's not your way because it's too simple.

LS: Or it would change reality. But on the other hand, by taking away those conventional frames you're changing reality also. So you're between these two views, and you have to see both views and ask if there's something outside the framing devices. The mind's framing being the text's phenomena.

SR: Given that we spend a lot of time framing things and having them framed for us, we're a little out of balance in that we don't spend as much time removing all those frames and finding a way to stay in the complexity of experience.

LS: Yes, that's true.

SR: In *Defoe* you write, "Out of the chrysalis of being children and some people remaining as that, one has the sense of a hardening that occurs in trying to leave that in oneself. There is actually no leaving that."[10]

LS: No leaving that: you can't get out of that. But also no leaving that: not letting that remain in oneself. So it's actually a contradiction.

SR: There's a sense in which we stop being children and there's another sense in which we never stop being children. In one way we harden but in another way we never do harden.

LS: Well, that's the fascinating question. It's the illusion of *How Phenomena Appear to Unfold*: whether somebody, when you see them later, is the same person that they were when you saw them earlier. And now later, they seem to be different because they're more clarified one way or another. You can see actions that you didn't know were in them that now seem significant. And that's probably true of yourself and you can't see that. So you don't want to harden in a way that is exclusive. But also, the childlike sense can be very destructive, something you should leave behind, because if you're not a child anymore and you're still doing it, *that* becomes the hardened thing which is destructive.

SR: I'd like to talk about your notion of the self. In *The Front Matter, Dead Souls* you write, "I'm taking the outer now current culture to be the inner self, drawing it in as one's core or manifestation, which it isn't. Then it is externalized as oneself and is projected outward again as one's sense of the real. That actually is one's inner self by acting upon its projection."[11] I found that sort of tricky, that you can't really say that current culture is the inner self but that maybe that's one way of trying to get at what the self is. That we take in current culture and then we project that back out and this circular process defines what we see. I'm trying to understand what you're saying the self is.

LS: That was the question. One takes the outside to be the inside; they are the same, opposite, and create each other at once.

SR: In *R-hu* you write, "I was looking at the mind in its relation to the real outside (*not* that the outside has created the mind . . . *or* that the mind has created the outside). That is, not discriminating as to the cause."[12]

LS: In that particular quote, I'm saying I do not start with a conclusion. We don't know how much the self is formed by the outside and imitating the outside somehow. One could not be formed only by the outside, because then how could the outside exist?

A major part of my *Dahlia's Iris: Secret Autobiography and Fiction* project deals exactly with that question: What would be the life seeing outside of constructed frames? Where would you ever make the distinction of what's an outside event and what is the life seeing? I use a discussion of film, primarily *Invasion of the Body Snatchers, Terminator II, Blade Runner*, and *The Sixth Sense. Invasion of the Body Snatchers* is about the destruction of the self by being completely consumed by an outside invasion, pod flowers, which duplicate people's appearances, everyone the same within, because they're all that pod flower. I think of that film, the second version with Donald Sutherland in it, as being an analogy to the notion of American democracy (which, when only propaganda, is empty); it's not taking place as something that's real. The interior of people is uniform when taken over by these pods. I see the film as grappling with the issue of whether one is socially formed, and also the need, the obsession with being socially formed—having to be that or one's an aberration. The film struck me as talking about that obsession in the form of this invasion, so there is no interior being except the people who hold out from that, and who are then finally destroyed.

One of the fascinating aspects of writing—and this goes back to our discussion of dreams as well—is that it can be jumping ahead of oneself and seeing where one is, what is self, and how it's creating the outside of you by dreaming and making changes in your way of perceiving things outside, so that you are also the outside. And that's a very intricate and involved consideration: You are the outside of yourself, and you're also the interior of that outside, and the interior is creating that outside. It's just something so fundamental to being that I don't know what the answer is or whether there would be any possibility of finding out the answer to that. But I think that writing, or at least my writing, investigates that. Stein does as well—the inside of the inside, the outside of the outside, the inside of the outside, etc.

Also, related to our discussion of dropping the barriers or the boundaries to the way you would approach events and perception, in the quote that you mentioned from *The Front Matter*,[13] I'm relating that to the point that if you hypothesized that there's an interior, like a soul or whatever, then that in itself would become a framework by which everything would be seen. And you would never be able to conjecture what is the self.

SR: Because you've already made a decision, in a way.

LS: Yes, you've already made a decision. The way I phrased that, in that particular quote, it sounds at first as if I'm already making the decision that there *is* no self because it's formed entirely by the outside, yet that cannot possibly be. The consideration calls into question whether there *is* an outside or whether there is an interior. You can't decide that either one does not exist.

SR: In *The Front Matter* you write, "'One''s only existence is in conflict *per se*, so that conflict is outside. It's only there moving. The union is the only 'self' when there's not one. Why is the being of 'one' conflict solely? . . . If one is without conflict it isn't the same thing (as one). If it is not oneself's orb (that which is only conflict) one is continually transgressing it in the conflict. This occurred in the past of my youth."[14] In *R-hu* you write, "A writing that is a center targeting one's mindscape sites and zapping them until fighting with oneself as being one's scrutiny per se. I'd like to do writing now that is inclusive of sites on the periphery and the spatial center at once. Transmogrification of space. I've tried that before but now there's a sense to work with of 'attention that's not a test.'"[15] I'm wondering if these reflections on conflict and test have to do with wanting to leave behind some sense of embattlement as a way of writing and of being in the world.

LS: The conflict had to do with leaping out of being "one" as a socially defined entity, because one is not that entity. I referred to that conflict as occurring at an earlier stage than I was at the time of writing that; I was recognizing that I wasn't doing that so much anymore. I thought maybe that conflict is a physiological stage of, say, your twenties and thirties, not a stage that persists, let us hope, because there's something about being in conflict that presumably arises from certain social sources defining what you're supposed to be, which you later drop, because you can simply understand those sources and interiorly get rid of them.

SR: And you're also getting closer to death and stripping away external definitions of what you should be doing.

LS: Yes, but you were already stripping away the definitions of what you should be at that earlier stage when you were being very rebellious. You were refusing to do these things that you knew were going to stop you, as conventional modes of how you should be, as a woman for example; this process seemed to require beating oneself up quite a bit. At least I experienced it that way. So then I want to get rid of that because that's destructive.

SR: Why did it involve beating oneself up?

LS: To leave "one." To see outside it, break its hold. The social definition of woman, and her in her behavior which is inside and outside of prescription, involves destruction of what she might be, as different from that social prescription.

SR: I think maybe just being in conflict is painful.

LS: Yes, but to increase the conflict was an idea. It was an ideology, which was also an unknown conflict, in the sense that at first one can't see entirely the ways in which we are prescribed: I felt I had to be in conflict with myself to dismantle myself from even whatever opinion I had of sense of myself at any instant. No gloss or explanation could be given in the text I was writing, only the action of being inside that combustion, deciphering as the reading of the text.

SR: You had to try to lift out by the roots these things that you felt controlled by, but they were in yourself, so it was almost like you were doing violence to yourself to try to eradicate these things?

LS: Partly, but also, whenever you would hold to something, even if that were "good" in one instant, one could not hold to any instant. Reactivity prolongs that which it opposes. This was a form of anarchism that was a plan. Whereas later on, one has the sense that you don't have to eradicate, because there's a peaceful way that is: being in any instant. As we were saying, even the plan of eradication—in other words rigour—is imposed. It changes what's happening and in that case begins to change it to be something that is more and more constrained in its own rigidity. The vocabulary to render being in a state of freedom is a language without allusion; language *itself is* allusion. This is the meaning of a passage from *Dahlia's Iris: Secret Autobiography and Fiction:*

> "Complete metamorphosis '*isn't*' the relation between things.
>
> '—one struggles in separation from something (as a butterfly from the chrysalis?)' The conflict 'doesn't make sense,' *and* is exactly what is expressed:
>
> Seeking this separation, as the *means* of not being translated 'back.'
>
> In one it is not even 'oppositional.' It is oppositional politically/socially. One thing is *not* transformed into another, ever. One is *already* outside."[16]

SR: You grew up in the Bay Area, and have spent your adult life here. How did your development as a poet intertwine with developments in the Bay Area poetry scene?

LS: I grew up in Berkeley, went to Reed College in Oregon as an undergraduate, and attended two years of graduate study in the UC Berkeley English department. After I left school, I began to write. I gave my first public reading at Intersection for the Arts in San Francisco in 1974. I was already attending readings, meeting and sometimes getting to know poets of all kinds. There were different elements occurring at once. There were the Beats—I had the opportunity to know Philip Whalen, then also over time to meet Allen Ginsberg and Michael McClure. Also Robert Duncan, whose lectures and readings I always attended. Also, poets in the New York School, whether meeting them in the Bay Area, in New York, or while I was teaching at Naropa in Boulder. In the late seventies someone told me I should check out the talk series going on in San Francisco held by a group called the Language poets. I went to some of these events, then attended many readings, plays, and talks in Language circles. The Language group was the dominant influence of my particular generation. For a long time, I would drive over from Berkeley or Oakland to San Francisco for readings. For years, I might attend as many as three readings a week.

SR: Are you still involved to the same extent you were then?

LS: No. I sustained two spine injuries which over a period of years involved two operations and much recovery time. Sometimes I couldn't go out. Also, I had to learn to conserve my energy and concentrate in order to do my work.

SR: What changes have you observed in the Bay Area writing scene since you first entered it?

LS: The changes are enormous. They are generational differences of tone and approach. The current work, of different types, is compatible with what was going on here in the last twenty years but takes it in a different way. There's a different feel to the language.

SR: Can you expand on that a bit?

LS: There are shifts in poetry syntax and view that are cumulative and that create a range, finally a broad spectrum, where current writing contains the past as well as the changes. One of the ideas put forth by many poets in the public talks and readings of the early eighties, for example, was that paratactic sentence structure in paragraphs rather than line breaks should be used by everyone, even uniformly. That is, the word "mechanistic" was used as a favorable designation to mean absence of individual self, a communal, social-political purpose. This is not an approach that is spoken of now. Yet in works like Renee Gladman's book *The Activist,* there's a subtle sense of a kind of new, "simple" as if one-dimensional, confessional/autobiographical tone that is used to get at a group sensibility and communal action, undercut in the sense of questioned by a kind of light humor that's as if all of the characters' thoughts at once. Judith Goldman's book *Vocoder* is very different from Gladman's writing; it includes conversations of many voices at once as both thoughts and speaking, incorporating levels that sound different, *are* different as a language pattern from past works, though perhaps similar in impulse and intention. The change in different sound-shapes of the syntax, a different language pattern in each period, is noticeable. For example, the Surrealists used group sessions exploring their unconscious and their dreams, etc. but they expressed this as a communal syntax which they developed together and which was different from what came before or after. So, those changes are indicative of a period and demonstrate the issues and concerns the poets have then.

SR: What are your current wishes, if any, for the Bay Area writing community? What would you like to see more or less of?

LS: On the evening of the day of the U.S. invasion of Iraq, I went to a reading hosted by Jen Scappettone where Kevin Davies and Judith Goldman were reading. The audience was composed of as many of the (mostly younger) poets as could get there in Berkeley since the bridge was blocked. I was very impressed by the discussion between the readers and the audience about their sense of language and the relation of poetry to this time and circumstance. I'd like to be more in touch with that impulse and intention amongst writers.

JULIANA SPAHR

How Does the Work Get Used

Sarah Rosenthal: I see your work as documenting both the beautiful, endangered details and the ugly, obliterating specifics of the world. There's detail that must be documented because it's precious and local and in danger of being lost, like the names of endangered plants in your "found sonnets" Nos. 1 and 2,[1] or because it testifies to facts that give hope, such as the list of all the cities where people protested the invasion of Iraq in *this connection of everyone with lungs*,[2] or because it's dangerous, such as the invasive plant species in "found sonnet" No. 3,[3] and the lists of weapons used in the Iraq war that appear in *this connection of everyone with lungs*. Often you juxtapose the endangered and the endangering details with each other.

Juliana Spahr: My first reaction when you say "detail" is to think of the tyranny of detail, the way that detail comes up in creative writing classes. As a teacher, I find myself saying these things to students that I don't really want to say, like "Add more detail to make it more like poetry." I'm a little resistant to detail in that it defines the worst sort of lyric poem, the poem that lists all the apparatuses of the middle class—the "I'm going to tell you all about my life and the special table that I have" poem. I want detail to do that other kind of work that you describe: the list of things that we need to hold onto, and the opposite, the list of things that we need to get rid of. I like to call that "information," though when it comes down to it, it's probably detail.

SR: In *this connection of everyone with lungs,* as well as in *The Transformation,* there's an ambivalent relationship to that project of documenting and marshalling information about political and environmental issues. At times the speaker widens the aperture to the point where she imagines herself in outer space looking back down at the earth, for example, "Once they let their bodies float up over what was happening now, they could see what was happening now as one small turn in the plot of history."[4] At other times she narrows her focus to the zone of intimacy: "An endless refueling and slipping out of port in the night. // We do not speak of it and instead press up against one anothers."[5] So in addition to documenting the facts, you're documenting the effects of that fact-finding work—the emotional overload that that can lead to, and the ways in which we seek respite from that sense of overload.

JS: The overload is a direct result of the access we now have to information. Thanks to the Internet, we have access to news from around the world in a way that we didn't have even ten years ago. We can read incredibly specific details about other parts of the planet, written by people in those other parts and not filtered through the U.S. media. It was during the war with Afghanistan that I suddenly realized I could read *Al Jazeera* and a million other news sources on the Internet. Suddenly, anyone anywhere could have access to information that previously was reserved for people who read Arabic or who frequented New York news kiosks. And then immediately that prompted the question, How do we sort through all this information, and how do we cope with it? What will all this information do to our brains? I don't really have an answer to the coping question other than that we have no choice but to embrace it, or at the least deal with it. It isn't going to go away.

When I wrote *this connection of everyone with lungs* I was thinking two contradictory things about media. One was what we've just been talking about—how I had access to all this information from outside the U.S. The other was how limited the U.S. media was at the time. I was thinking a lot about the argument that there are fewer and fewer independent news sources in the U.S. This really felt like a crisis because of the suspect reporting that the embedded journalists had done in Afghanistan—it was hard to take seriously the idea that war reporters are independent as long as they were going around with the permission of the U.S. military. It also felt like a crisis because of how major news sources were taking as truth the claim that Iraq had weapons of mass destruction. There were at the time a lot of suggestions to the contrary that were not getting represented.

In writing the poems for *this connection,* I made a deliberate decision not to rely much on U.S. media. Instead I used the Google news page—because it is so much more international (within obvious limits) than any other view we've really ever had of the news media, but also because I liked how it spans time zones and how stories appear and disappear on it all day long.

I find those two perspectives you mentioned—the very wide focus and the very small, tight focus—psychologically comforting. It's part of how the brain works. To be honest, I began playing with moving between these two perspectives because perspectival manipulation is one of the ways that trance states are induced. "Poem Written after September 11, 2001" in *this connection* was deliberately written so as to mimic the structure of a trance induction. I was taking a course in Ericksonian hypnosis at the time and I was interested in how much overlap there is between poetic devices and trance induction devices, how both are partial to metaphor and analogy. And then New York City was so unusually complicated after September 11. New York, like all places, has its own particular forms of myopia. The myopia got even more intense after September 11. That event was so large that it was hard to think about other places all that much. My thought was to write a poem that used the structure of a trance induction to suggest to its hearers, its readers, ways to take other places into themselves. I wrote the poem for a reading that I had at the Poetry Project, thinking very deliberately of the rooms and the neighborhood of the Project.

SR: Speaking of the small, tight focus, I'm interested in the role intimacy plays in your writing. It seems to be a double-edged sword, creating connection and community and yet at the same time becoming a form of escapism. In *this connection* you write, "Beloveds, my desire is to hunker down and lie low, lie with yous in beds and bowers, lie with yous in resistance to the alone, lie with yous night after night."[6] "Resistance to the alone" is an attempt to fight a sense of isolation, but "hunkering down" and "lying low" are isolating activities, and the phrase "beds and bowers" seems comically to point to a limited, head-in-the-sand version of the lyric. Shortly after that passage you point out the impossibility of escape: "I try to comfort myself with images of exile on this small piece of land in the middle of the large Pacific. . . . But I know there is no alone anymore here in the middle of the Pacific. // There is no uninhabited tropical island anywhere."[7] In the poem "switching" in *Fuck You-Aloha-I Love You* you're trying to get the sphere of the bedroom and the sphere of the roundtable discussion to cross-fertilize, enrich each other. Are you interested in showing intimacy as cutting both ways—toward community and toward alienation?

JS: When I sat down to write *this connection* I was thinking, What do we do with the lyric? I was thinking about that caricature of the lyric that shows up in early Barrett Watten and Ron Silliman essays where lyric subjectivity is called bourgeois. There is a certain absurdity to the argument that lyric subjectivity is necessarily or even mainly bourgeois when you look at the larger uses of lyric—though to be fair, Watten and Silliman were talking almost exclusively about New Critical U.S. poetry, let's say post-1950 and maybe even post-1960—a very small moment in the history of the lyric. But I was trying to ask, What's interesting about lyric? Or rather, is there anything interesting about it? I was thinking about that great line by Jennifer Moxley in *Imagination Verses*, "Even the love poem agitates the beloved to fall in love with the poet."[8] What Jennifer is getting at is that the lyric is a poem that desires to provoke. My question was, What kinds of action do people need to be provoked into, or can you use lyric intimacy as a way to provoke other sorts of activism, and to provoke people to become intimate with various political issues? Can lyric help us understand our connection, not only with our beloved, but also with the rest of the planet? Can contemporary lyric transcend that caricature of bourgeois lyric subjectivity? (It certainly does transcend it in early poetry—in Sappho's writing, of course, but also in a lot of seventeenth-century English poetry.) So that's what I was trying to work through in *this connection*. In the poem "switching," my specific thinking was, Here's the table at the university where I'm having a discussion with a number of colleagues that's defined by what we can and cannot say, a conversation that has a wonderful desire to impact the world, to change Hawai'i, to be anticolonial—but that is also incredibly restrained. And then on the other hand there are the endless hotel rooms of Waikiki, to which people are coming and where they are having an intimate relationship with Hawai'i. At the time, right after I moved to Hawai'i, people from Ohio would write to me and say, "I went snorkeling in Hawai'i and it changed my life." I felt that there were two possible reactions to that. One was dismissal, and the other was to wonder if that intimate experience could be activated into something ecological, into a desire to protect the ocean. In most cases it can't—tourism has never really been good at getting people to respect the environment. Waikiki is a prime example of that. There are thousands of high-rises right on the beach. But it was bothering me that at our table at the university we were completely dismissive of this other realm of tourists. I was asking, Is there any way we can acknowledge the tourist in ourselves? And, can we live our own tourist lives differently?

SR: In your interview with Joel Bettridge in *How2* you talked about bringing argument into poetry, and about a form of writing that builds structures.[9] I noticed structural elements in *this connection* that guided my focus, moving me through different vantage points and emotional experiences. For example, there's a gorgeous, moving section in *this connection* where you're playing off lines by Sappho, juxtaposing them with very flat, despairing material.[10] Many of the pieces in *Response* and in *Fuck You-Aloha-I Love You* appear to have a very deliberate structure, often ending with a more or less summarizing statement. When you think about bringing argument into poetry, are you thinking about crafting an experience that leads the reader through certain stages of awareness and/or toward certain actions?

JS: I wasn't aware of the placement of the Sappho piece in the way you've described. I always like Lyn Hejinian's notion that the use of a poem is that it helps you to think differently; it helps you to re-sort things. I think of that as a kind of argument. My drive in thinking about writing something is the question, How can I look at this information and re-sort it in a way that helps me to understand it? I'll think, Oh, gee, I'm really confused about colonialism and my role in it; I'm going to sit down and try to think about some ways that I can gain an understanding of it. Sometimes I will choose to write an essay about it; sometimes a poem. I'm often led to the structures that poetry offers when the subject feels too hard, or too embodied, to get at in an essay.

In *The Transformation*, I decided to spend a certain amount of space on writing about Hawaiʻi, and then to spend a certain amount of space on writing about New York, and to place a break in the middle. So, yes, I am thinking about structure, but I'm not thinking about guiding a reader through an experience. I love a lot of Beat poetry, but I have a huge distrust of all that Beat anti-Vietnam War work in which the poet-seer claims to be educating the general public. The work only makes sense to me as an attempt at dialog or as trying to think with other people.

SR: You often use that phrase: "think with other people." I take that as meaning that you want readers to interact with your work by formulating their own thinking. In that sense you're carrying forward the legacy of Language poetry—the desire to have an openness in the writing that other people can enter into and move around in.

JS: Yes, and I also take from Language poetry the idea that you're writing to enter into discussion with a group of poets. That's almost exclusively how I think of writing. I want to be having a discussion with these people, whoever they might be at any moment.

SR: You said a moment ago that you choose to write poetry instead of an essay when an issue is "too embodied." What does that phrase mean to you?

JS: It means too emotional, or something I'm too intimately connected with, or something that's too messy for the structured argumentation required in literary criticism. For example I think the ideas in "switching" would result in a really dorky article.

SR: I want to pick up on something else you said a moment ago, about adopting the Language writers' approach of writing to enter into discussion with other poets. *Response* seems "languagey" to me in its use of apposition and other techniques associated with the Language school. Yet your recent writing is noticeably much less disjunctive. I wonder if you see yourself as addressing a different or larger group of poets than experimental poets. I also wonder what you make of the fact that your work continues to be embraced by the experimental community in spite of your move toward clarity.

JS: I wrote *Response* when I was at SUNY Buffalo, at a time when I was reading Language poetry extensively. At Buffalo there was a lot of talk about "radical" or "experimental" poetries, which basically meant poetries that used modernist fragmentation. This work was juxtaposed with "lyric," "mainstream," or "MFA" poetries, terms that were used to describe short poems with quiet language. Then I went to Hawai'i and those categories of "experimental," "mainstream," "MFA," and so forth all flew out the window. The rules that dominate the discussion about poetry on the continent weren't visible from the distance of Hawai'i. Other questions came up, such as, How does the work get used? If it's so abstract that people come up with very different explanations about what it means, is that useful or not? Hawai'i's poetry is not by any means anti-experimental, but one would not call it "experimental" either. Parts of it are anticolonial and parts of it aren't, but the anticolonial part tends to use all the poetic tools available, both those called "experimental" and those called "conventional." This was eye opening for me.

I have no idea whether or how my readership is changing. I also don't know what it means to be teaching in an MFA program now that I'm at Mills. I tend to fit uneasily into academic institutions. I was at the University of Hawai'i based on my work as a literary critic, and there was a huge fight there for several years about whether I should even be allowed to teach creative writing. So I'm still trying to figure out what it means to be in the institutional machine in a different way.

SR: What conclusions are you reaching?

JS: I think there are differences, but ultimately it's very similar work. Mills is a smaller institution, and it doesn't have the same separation between the departments that exists at the University of Hawai'i.

SR: In *The Transformation*, you rake academia over the coals, talking about its instrumentality in the colonial project. You go further, critiquing yourself as an emblematic professor. You describe starting out idealistic and then realizing how implicated you are as part of a massive, powerful system. What keeps you in that system?

JS: I think if I were working in the computer science industry I'd be writing the same things. I'd be saying things like, Look, I'm developing all this technology that's destroying the world. I don't know if any U.S. citizen can escape being implicated. I'm constantly wondering about whether it helps if you leave the country. Most days, I don't think it does help.

SR: In spite of your critique of academia and your own earlier naiveté about changing the system, you seem to continue to approach teaching with a spirit of hope and idealism. For example, you noted on your blog that you had read an essay in the journal *Critical Inquiry* critiquing the way literature is taught in universities, and that you planned to assign it as classroom reading.[11] That tells me that you are actively thinking about how to help your students deconstruct the rules and roles of academia in order to achieve some measure of intellectual freedom.

JS: The fact that people spend four years in school reading books is an amazing thing. We could so easily not have that institution. It's almost anti-American for all these people to be taking the time to study humanities instead of working. When the Language poets finally began to enter the academy later in their lives—when Charles Bernstein and Bob Perelman and Barrett Watten and Susan Howe and Lyn Hejinian all started getting university jobs—many people criticized that. They argued that it was a hypocritical move because the Language poets were anti-academic. But I always felt strongly that you could enter the academy and start to change it. The people who are critiquing the academy are the very ones who *should* be in the academy, because they might be able to effect change from the inside. If they don't effect change, then that would be cause for complaint. But I think the work Charles Bernstein did with the Poetics Program at Buffalo demonstrates that real change is possible. Even at the University of Hawai'i—an institution in many ways even more riddled with colonial patterns than institutions on the continent—there are things like the Hawaiian Studies program, which basically trains students in activist, pro-sovereignty work and continuing cultural practices. But if the people who work in those institutions are not vigilant, nothing changes. The most frustrating thing about colleges and universities is that they are seedbeds for so many incredible utopian projects that are never realized—or that are at least very slow-growing.

SR: You said in your *How2* interview that the controversy surrounding Lois Ann Yamanaka's fiction contributed to your desire to be more clear in your writing. Yamanaka came under heavy criticism for featuring stereotypes of Filipino men as sexual predators in two of her books, *Saturday Night at the Pahala Theatre* and *Blu's Hanging*. Yamanaka responded that the writing was fiction and doesn't reflect her own views. The fact that the stereotype shows up in more than one text may work against that claim a bit. Still, I don't want to live in a world where "narrator" and "author" are treated as synonyms. In *Everybody's Autonomy* you note that Bruce Andrews's work includes racial and sexual slurs, and you describe it as something akin to the angry spewing of a 17-year-old boy.[12] What allows you to embrace Andrews's work while pushing away from Yamanaka's? Do you ever see a productive separation between the author and anything that we might call "voice"?

JS: I don't think I am pushing away Yamanaka's work. I am just trying to figure it out. The Yamanaka controversy left me mainly confused. I agree that a big part of the problem is that the figure of the bad Filipino shows up in more than one book. Candice Fujikane, who was instrumental in that discussion about Yamanaka's work, has studied what Yamanaka's characters say compared to what the omniscient narrator says. Yamanaka's first book, *Saturday Night at the Pahala Theater*, is clearly playing with the notion of the unreliable narrator. I love that book, and I think a lot of the complaint around it is unfair and undeserved. Still, if you placed *Blu's Hanging* in a continental context and wrote a story where the black guy next door raped the little white girl, that would be a novel whose intent people would have some questions about. It would be legitimate to ask how that novel engages racist stereotypes. In terms of Andrews's work, I keep thinking about the comedian Sarah Silverman's claim that she's not making racist jokes, but rather making jokes about racism. I see Andrews's work as attempting some of that same nuance—even as I think work about racism can risk being racist. Mainly, I think it's valuable to have work that takes on these really hard topics. Ideally, that's what literature does: It provokes hard discussions that you can't get at in other ways.

SR: Yet in your own writing, you've moved toward clarity. Is that from a desire to avoid confusing or hurting people?

JS: I'm not sure. I guess I would say that I'm worried about how the work can get used. I keep thinking of moments where someone wrote something that they thought said only one thing and then it got used in another way. There is a well-known instance in Hawai'i where an anthropologist wrote an article about how, in the name of resistance, indigenous communities were essentially claiming that places were "sacred" that had not been sacred in the past. Basically, there are certain limited ways that indigenous people can reclaim lands in the U.S. court system, and one way is to claim that the land has a sacred history. Her argument was that the activists were inventing cultural practices and claiming a history for them. She intended her article to be an "unbiased" study, a statement of fact. Or that is how the article is written. But of course the article got used in the courts to delegitimize the claims that Hawaiians were making to reclaim the island of Kaho'olawe. So that is one thing that I'm always thinking nervously about. But I also think this issue is really complicated, and I'm not sure I know what the proper conduct is. Lately I've been trying to think about some comments by a friend who had read a version of *The Transformation*. She told me she felt that I wasn't thinking about how some of the things I say in that book might play into people's preconceptions or skepticisms about small islands in the Pacific. So I guess I'm always trying to figure out what it is that I want to say, but I also don't want to say nothing or only say easy things. This is an issue, like all issues, which requires balance. But what it comes down to, finally, is that if I'm not at least somewhat clear, I feel like I can't figure out what I think. At the same time I would not want clarity to become a mandate, nor would I want a narrow definition of clarity. The work of someone like Bruce Andrews is to me very clear.

SR: Given your interest in taking clear stands in your writing, I'm curious how you read. Take someone like Paul Celan, who was completely impacted by Nazism, and who funneled that experience through his psyche and his speaking apparatus in an extremely interiorized way. The poetry that came out of that process is difficult to read, even impenetrable in certain ways. His work exemplifies the sort of text you describe in *Everybody's Autonomy:* "Rather than rewarding readers for well-deciphered meaning and allusion, the[se texts] reward readers for responsive involvement and for awareness of their limitations."[13] At this juncture, would you still be interested in such work?

JS: I would certainly still be interested in it. I keep wondering, now that I'm not in Hawai'i, whether I'm going to morph back to a stronger commitment to ambiguity. Coming out of Buffalo having read almost exclusively Language poetry, I felt I needed to spend some time with other poetries. Now that I've been immersed in some of those other poetries, I'm looking again at that poetry of ambiguity and thinking about what's worth keeping there. Celan still seems to me incredibly interesting and complicated. What's really great about his work is its refusal to tell an easy story about the Holocaust. I don't want to throw anything out, ever.

SR: *The Transformation* uses "they" as the predominant pronoun. I thought it would be interesting to discuss some of the associations spinning off your use of "they." One association that comes to mind is work such as Gertrude Stein's *Everybody's Autobiography* or Rigoberta

Menchú's autobiography *I, Rigoberta Menchú: An Indian Woman in Guatemala,* in which she writes, "My story is the story of all poor Guatemalans. My personal experience is the reality of a whole people."[14] These are works you refer to in *Everybody's Autonomy* as exemplifying the autobiography that explodes its own genre in a sense, using the self to go beyond the self. *The Transformation* seems to follow in those footsteps. The question arises, Why write something that resembles autobiography at all? Do you see it as a rhetorical device that pulls people in with the promise of feeding their desire to read about individual, solipsistic lives, and then draws their attention to larger communities? Or is there something else about the self telling his or her story that holds a fascination for you?

JS: I think the selfish answer is that I felt I had to think through my experience in order to understand it. But I also wanted to use the genre of individual exploration to think about how that shapes these cultural issues. So rather than using the pronoun "I," I used the pronoun *they*. In *Fuck You-Aloha-I Love You,* I had used "we." There are various "we's" in Hawai'i, and I was asking, Can I write myself into this "we" or not? I arrived at the answer that I'm always the "they." Then I had to ask, what do you do when you're a "they"? Again, I was interested in thinking about what I'm complicit with. At the same time I was thinking a lot about these wars that we'd already started having, and that were continuing. War always requires that there be a "they." In order to bomb someone, you have to make them into a "they"; they can't be part of "you" or "we." I was wondering, Can one think ethically from a position of "they"? Maybe the beginning of doing that work is to see yourself as part of that "they." I kept thinking of that moment in Barrett Watten's book *Bad History* where he talks about wearing a button that says "Iraqi" during the first Iraq war. There is something about that alliance that, in terms of current identity-politics models, is a bit uninvestigated—Barrett Watten's not Iraqi, and he's not being bombed. Nevertheless, the question that that button raises about how we act or interact with those that our country bombs is an interesting one. In the parts of that book that are about Hawai'i I wanted to take on the slur part of the term *haole*, to not avoid it, and I wanted to also take on the "they" in the way that it means "those others, those people who are not a part of us" and think about what happens when one starts by admitting that one is part of a problem.

SR: The predominant character in *The Transformation* is clearly you. What's interesting to you about telling your own story?

JS: I'm not sure that much about it interests me. The parts of the book that feel of interest to me now are the larger political/cultural issues. When I started writing this, and I think this is still true, it didn't feel like the writing I was doing was any more about me than any other thing I had written. Rather, I felt that I needed to think hard about issues around living with one's political convictions, about trying to figure out one's political life in the U.S. right now. What does one do with one's identity—all facets of it? What does one do with one's sexuality, race, class; what does one do with one's unavoidable consumption of unprecedented amounts of resources? I felt that I had to do this by writing something that explicitly addressed a number of issues that I saw being talked about in academic work, and instead of writing another essay in the passive voice, talk about how these ideas made me walk down the street differently. I felt there was no other way to talk about how hard it was to figure this stuff out except to use a somewhat true, somewhat false example of my life. I needed to write, not really to tell people that I knew the way out, but because I could not figure out the way out. My hope is that if I admit to that, someone might write something else that might help me find my way out. So I didn't want to write a memoir or an autobiography. It didn't end up as an autobiography because it isn't a life story really, but it might be a memoir of an attempt to come to a political consciousness.

SR: "They," because it's a distancing gesture, blurs the boundary between autobiography and fiction. Did you have any desire to blur that boundary?

JS: Yes. There are things in this book that are fiction. I started it under the influence of *Pamela: A Novel* by Pam Lu and also Renee Gladman's writing. Pam and Renee had come to Hawai'i to read, and so I was thinking a lot about what they were doing with sentences: how they weren't really writing the New Sentence, and how they seemed to be revising the sentence that's in Lyn Hejinian's *My Life*. I was also thinking about that movement in *My Life* between, on the one hand, confession and obvious autobiography, and on the other hand, something that's not the individual's life. So while autobiography was in my thoughts, I always thought of the book more as prose and less as memoir or autobiography.

SR: In *The Transformation* you write, "We was undeniably a contested word for them. They often felt too large in it, too large because there were three of them instead of two."[15] There I was thinking that "we" was unusable in this book in part because it's been co-opted by the institution of coupledom—the cozy little "we" of couples. It made me think about the limits of our language to describe people's efforts to create different kinds of communities and relationships. Was that part of your thinking too—that "we" has already been used up?

JS: Certainly. Elsewhere in that book I talk about getting out from under the normalcy of coupledom, and rejecting the term "queer" and yet feeling like a pervert all the time. Perverts are necessarily "they." It isn't only that "we" is all used up—because we can probably still squeeze ourselves into it—but that I wanted there to be more to the lyric than that discussion that we overhear between the lover and the beloved. That was one reason for making the "you" plural in *this connection*. That is also the reason I used "they" in *The Transformation*.

SR: The main character in *The Transformation* describes herself as feeling like a zombie. The use of "they" supports that state of psychic alienation.

JS: Yes, I wanted to get at that state of not being able to figure out even what actions to take, and feeling that any action is somewhat wrong, and that finding your way through it is hard and at times even impossible.

SR: Another feature of "they" is that it's not gendered. Your books tend to avoid gender, using options such as "he or she," "a person," or "gendered pronoun." Are you trying to move beyond gender?

JS: I feel like I don't know how to answer this question. I consider my work to be part of a larger feminist project, but I am also nervous about how gender shows up in poetry. There's the tradition of all those endless poems that men have written and continue to write about women's bodies, and there's the still-prevalent attitude that poems by women must be about women's issues. I seem to want to duck these problems by troubling the pronouns. Does it work? I don't know. I'm not sure I've thought about it enough. This troubling of the pronouns is something that I do more instinctually than intellectually. When I think about feminist art that I really respect, my mind goes first to all that body-conscious or body-aware art and writing, whatever the right term is for that work, that people like Carolee Schneeman, Marina Abramovic, Ana Mendieta, Kathy Acker, and Dodie Bellamy were doing and continue to do. I admire how these artists tested a number of limits on the artistic practice. I admire the work for its insistence on aggressively putting the gendered body forward and insisting on its importance, for how it takes the female body of the artwork and then reclaims it and messes with it, and for how it refuses to follow decorum. Yet I have to admit that I'm wondering right now if my instinctual ducking of gender might be the opposite of that work, and if this might be something that I might need to think about more in the future.

All that said, probably the main reason that I erase pronouns in my work is that I went to graduate school at the time of queer theory, where we were discussing the ways in which gender is merely a construction.

SR: I find your periodic admissions of uncertainty and confusion, both in your writing and in conversation, to be refreshing and unusual. That vulnerability contrasts with a position of certainty and self-confidence which I have to say I still associate more with men than with women, both within and outside the writing community. Your admission of uncertainty supports your stated desire to, as you say, "think with others," goes against the image of the confident author/teacher/critic, and admits of what is at times insoluble difficulty—the gray area we'd all rather shy away from. I wonder if you ever feel you pay a price for that kind of honesty.

JS: I ask all the time, Should I have answers? Because clearly there are things that are wrong, and what do you do with them? If you keep standing up and saying, I'm guilty, I'm complicit, then there's the response that guilt isn't any good, because it doesn't do anything. But there is a way in which you need to start with that. I think I'm kind of stuck getting to that next step. OK, I'm guilty—now what?

SR: Speaking of vulnerable admissions, a passage that really stopped me in *this connection* was, "Beloveds, weeks ago the doubleness of the news broke me down and I stopped writing and stopped loving all humans, mainly myself."[16] That's such an extreme statement: You feel so responsible for the events of the world that you actually stop loving yourself when you feel powerless to make things better.

JS: Right. You have these moments where you think, What we all need to do is come together and protest. But that clearly doesn't always work. We had a moment in which we had unprecedented global protests and it was amazing. And it might work in the future. Seattle worked somewhat, and there have been other anti-globalization protests that I would have to say worked to an extent. We're starting to see some change in that area. But that moment of trying to stop the war machine did not work. We need to go to the next level, but it's really hard to keep moving with people to that next level—and what can you do about it? I have no doubt that U.S. citizens could stop the war machine if we all got together and did it. But in the meantime, there's the despair about inaction, about the impossibility of moving things forward.

SR: You've been part of several writing communities at this point, in Buffalo, Hawai'i, and New York City. Now that you're here in the Bay Area, I wonder if you're noticing any distinct features of this writing community.

JS: Of course the Bay Area has a long literary tradition and I have not really been a part of it. Your question reminds me of a 1969 Robert Smithson and Nancy Holt film called *East Coast, West Coast*. Smithson plays the West Coast artist, who says, "Nature," and Holt plays the East Coast artist, who says something like, "You don't acknowledge the concrete." And then I keep thinking of that old argument that the West Coast Language poets are more lyrical and a little less aggressive than the New York poets, whose writing is a little more fractured.

SR: On the other hand, much New York School poetry employs the lyric mode in interesting ways.

JS: Yes, it's very close to that lyric subjectivity that we discussed earlier even though it isn't really talked about that way. I love New York School poetry.

Another distinguishing feature of the West Coast is that a lot of the ethnic and culturally specific literary traditions of the U.S. have come from here. That certainly has had a huge impact on U.S. literary scenes.

SR: When you think "Bay Area writing community," do you think more of experimental writers or are you discovering other aspects of Bay Area writing?

JS: Mostly I think of the mixture of experimental writers and writers who come out of specific identity communities such as the Chicano scene, which is really huge, and the Asian-American poetry scene, which is diverse and includes a significant Filipino-American presence. I think about all these different scenes coming into contact.

SR: Are they coming into contact as much as you might wish?

JS: I think they come into contact—probably not as much as one might wish, which is always true.

SR: Truong Tran comes to mind as someone crossing those lines.

JS: Yes, his writing is very explicitly working on that. Pamela Lu does that work too. The other striking aspect of the Bay Area is the queer writing scene, which is much more present here than anywhere else in the United States. And the Bay Area writing community is very decentralized, which I like. There are all these different thriving scenes, without the same mainstream power elite that exists on the East Coast, located for example at places like NYU and Harvard.

SR: Do you feel like part of things here yet?

JS: I still don't feel like a Bay Area poet. I'm not sure I ever will. I keep trying to figure out how to negotiate a question that Sean Labrador asked me recently: What's it like to move from Hawai'i—the thriving center of the military—to California, where the military is being cut but still plays a huge role, and where the tech industry is still so active? I'm always trying to think about California's environmental politics up against California's environmental destruction. I was just at a reading at U.C. Berkeley and someone was saying, "Berkeley's got a long liberal tradition" and I was thinking, Yes, combined with a long tradition of developing the atomic bomb. These issues are opportunities for Bay Area writers to delve into.

SR: You're saying we could pay more attention to the local—to the whole nexus of political and environmental issues that bump up against each other here in complex ways.

JS: Right. What does it mean that Silicon Valley has the most Superfund sites, given that technology was supposed to be a clean industry? How do you combine U.C. Berkeley's PR about the role it played in the free speech movement with the university's responsibility in developing the technology to kill millions at Nagasaki and Hiroshima? What does it mean that the technology economy of the Bay Area is seeded by military contracts, by Lockheed, Ford Aerospace, etc.? The Bay Area seems to be built on these contradictions.

SR: What do you want to work on next? What forms do you want to work in; what issues are drawing your attention?

JS: I've got to get back to critical writing. I've got about two thirds of a manuscript that looks at the connections between language politics and avant-garde practices. It starts with a discussion of how colonialism might have shaped the formalist experimentation of avant-garde modernism before World War I, and ends by looking at certain specific moments when language issues become political, and the literature that surrounds those moments. There is a chapter, for instance, that discusses the attention Pacific sovereignty movements place on language, and then turns to explore how a different concern with, or a reinterpretation of, the avant-garde cry for linguistic independence appears in Hawaiian and Maori work.

But what is really drawing my attention right now is that nagging question of how literature might make a difference. I've been obsessively reading the discussions that happened around the turn of the century between Brecht and Adorno and that intensified in the sixties in Central and South American resistance movements around literature's role in political education. I have this fantasy of doing an anthology that collects this work. When I taught at the University of Hawai'i it always struck me that, despite the fairly radical cultural politics of various Hawaiian activist organizations, in which writing is seen as an integral part of activist movements, creative writing was for the most part taught at the university as if it were a rarified aesthetic pursuit. The poetry that was produced by the Hawaiian community and valued by that community as political education was rarely seen as art or as something that should be discussed in the creative writing classroom. I can think of some key exceptions to this, some faculty members who really made an effort to include this work in their classrooms—but I can also think of a lot resistance to this sort of work. And this seems to be an even more urgent issue when teaching at a place like Mills, where this question doesn't even come up that much, because the college has even fewer ties to local activism of any sort. So I've been doing some slow work toward getting together an anthology that collects essays that discuss the importance of poetry to the political realm. My fantasy is that this anthology would be not just another collection of essays, but would be designed for use in creative writing workshops. But I have not yet figured out how to make that happen.

TRUONG TRAN

I Became the Other

Sarah Rosenthal: Your first book, *placing the accents*, has coherent themes but many formal experiments, including lineated and prose poems, and even a traditional form, the pantoum. All told, it reads more like a collection than a composition. There seems to be a big leap, after *placing the accents*, into a focus on the book as a unit of attention.

Truong Tran: I wrote *placing the accents* while I was in graduate school at San Francisco State. The book is really quite mapped out. It begins with succinct, self-contained poems, many of which are about my father. As it moves forward, those stories begin to break down, and by the end what you have are fragments. I began graduate school right after my father's death and I had a lot of very clear, shaped thoughts and memories about him, which took the form of poems. But as I moved through the three-year program, those memories became more fragmented.

SR: Why do you think that happened?

TT: I think we only have so many stories to tap into as writers. I had used up those stories. So then what I had were parts of stories—beginnings, middles, and endings. To force myself into a mode of creating a complete story out of such a fragment felt detrimental to me by that point. Myung Mi Kim, who taught at San Francisco State then, helped me see that fragments can exist on the page—they don't have to be relegated to a shelf where they sit and collect dust until a story comes out of them. In collecting these fragments on the page, I was able to create a collage narrative. The last poem in the book, "the crossing," was a series of fragments. That poem became a catalyst for my later work.

I also discovered a boxlike physical shape that helped me write the fragment poems. The shape symbolizes to me a certain controlled chaos. It's like being in a Catholic home: You have the structure of house and family, but within that structure there's chaos. I grew up in a household that had very specific parameters, and I tend to create parameters prior to the writing. For example, I'm now literally creating boxes, mounting them all over my apartment, and writing inside them. I'm trying to get myself out of the mode of thinking that a poem belongs in a book. Originally, my most recent book, *within the margin,* was supposed to be presented as a single line of text wrapping around the perimeter of a room. In the space of the room, I visualized artists and musicians and others brought together, symbolically representing the space of the margin. That didn't happen, but I still want to explore that idea.

SR: The boxlike prose form with no punctuation, which you discovered while writing the poems in *placing the accents,* became the form of your next two books, T*he Book of Perceptions* and *dust and conscience.* The latter uses mostly the same text as the former, and both have to do with a trip you took to Vietnam, but *The Book of Perceptions* more explicitly revolves around that trip, and around a collaboration with a photographer. Can you describe the nature of that collaboration?

TT: The grant I'd written for *The Book of Perceptions* proposed that two perceptions of Vietnam be documented, coming from two generations of Vietnamese Americans and two media (poetry and photography). The photographer and I didn't want to cloud each other's perceptions, so we each traveled to Vietnam separately, and then afterward got together to see how the poems and photos spoke to each other. But I should explain that there was a third collaborator, the book designer. He also traveled to Vietnam. Once we turned over the materials to him, he laid them out and put his own creative stamp on them. Part of my challenge in that project was to let go of control. I wanted someone who didn't read poetry on a regular basis to interpret the work and design the book based on his interpretation.

In the end, I didn't feel satisfied with *The Book of Perceptions*. There was something problematic about the whole project. I take full responsibility for the fact that I wrote the proposal and set the parameters. But when I visited Vietnam, I realized that I couldn't look at the people of Vietnam, my people, as the other. I couldn't write from that perspective. There was a *National Geographic* feel to the project as I'd conceived it. There are a lot of writers who approach writing in that way. But for me, with the subject of Vietnam, there was just no way I could do that. And thus we have *dust and conscience,* in which I tried to turn *The Book of Perceptions* into a collection of love poems, and in that way turn it back on myself.

SR: The title of *The Book of Perceptions* echoes Edmond Jabès's *The Book of Questions.* But Jabès's presence seems much more pervasive in *dust and conscience.* Every section is titled "the book of"—from "the book of beginnings" to "the book of endings." The language in the poems evokes him; for example, "his words were nomadic monks roaming the page" reminds me of the plethora of rabbis who appear fleetingly in Jabès's book.[1] The cast of characters in your book is also reminiscent of those rabbis.

TT: I appreciate the way Jabès uses the form of the book to frame the content. Thinking about that has helped me step away from the notion of writing "the poem." I've become more focused on the meta-existence of the text. I think everything we write ultimately comes together and connects. I assembled *dust and conscience* by printing out all the pieces, spreading them out on my living room floor, and playing with them to see how they spoke to one another.

SR: I assume you learned that approach from Myung Mi Kim, as I did.

TT: It's true. When Myung creates texts, she really thinks in terms of the book. I'm reading her book *Commons* again. When you open that book you find a very spare text on the left-hand side, and a voice that is allowed to speak on the right-hand side. If you read enough of it, you recognize that on one side is the voice of the self that is straining to speak, and on the other side is the voice that is allowed to speak. This duality is fascinating.

SR: *dust and conscience* is framed by the poet-speaker's relationship with the reader. The first poem, which starts "if only I were a dissident poet," talks about the poet's role and asks how the poems are going to be met by readers. One reading is that the poem describes a kind of survivor's guilt—a questioning of whether one's poetry can be taken seriously if one hasn't had the horrific experiences of, say, a prisoner of conscience. Another reading is that the poem is challenging the reader to shed any expectations about what the text will serve up.

TT: For me, it's the latter. I still encounter the expectation, thirty years into my existence in this country, that I'll deliver on the boat story. As a writer of color and also as a gay writer, I'm not supposed to have abstract thoughts. I'm supposed to tell the story and convey the experience. In that poem I wanted to say, There are going to be some abstract thoughts here—but they won't just be floating around; they're grounded. I believe we end up writing what we know—but I also believe that as writers, we shouldn't be limited by what we know. There's a world of possibility in what we don't know, and it's our right to explore that.

SR: *dust and conscience* is subtitled "the book of the familiar." One of the meanings of "familiar" is "closely acquainted." I thought about all the family intimacy in the book, with the notion of family extending outward to include both American and Vietnamese culture. "Familiar" also means "marked by informality," like the form of your writing: lower-case, and not much punctuation. As a noun, "familiar" means "intimate associate or companion." All of the humans and creatures in the book seem like the speaker's companions in some way. "Familiar" also denotes a spirit attendant or guard, often in the shape of an animal—I thought of the figure of the crab who appears a couple of times. I wonder what that subtitle means to you.

TT: It means everything you just described. Also, in the journey of this book I was concerned with how I looked at the other. By the end of the book, I became the other. In doing that, I felt that I was able to go beyond the sense of the self being divided from the other. The notion of the beloved, who is called k, was very much a catalyst for the book, but by the end it's not about that individual.

SR: You used a quote from Roland Barthes' *A Lover's Discourse* as an epigraph to *The Book of Perceptions*. What you're saying about k being a catalyst for *dust and conscience* reminds me of Barthes' book. In that text, he talks about his intense feelings in relation to the lover, but ultimately the relationship seems an opportunity for him to work out his ideas about language and philosophy.

TT: I see the lover in Barthes' book as a therapist who gives the writer the opportunity to contemplate life.

SR: Do you feel that similarly, k provided you with an opportunity to contemplate various issues?

TT: Yes. The figure of k is in part a way to speak about being gay. As a gay writer of color, I find that the process of coming out happens not once but again and again. You're constantly navigating between communities. For example, lately I've been in contact with a Vietnamese poet who's going to be visiting San Francisco State. He sent me an email saying, "I'm looking forward to meeting your family." I'm pretty sure he means "wife and kids," not "parents and siblings." In *dust and conscience,* I used the relationship with k to reveal the constant process of seeking ways to articulate my being to family members and to the world around me. But I'm not one to write about those issues in a direct way. I'm much more interested in the subtleties of language.

SR: Your most recent book, *within the margin,* explores various permutations of the word "margin." Trinh T. Min Ha, in her book *Woman Native Other,* argues that when we identify writers as marginalized, we thereby marginalize them, limiting the way their work will be encountered. But, she points out, even if one is aware of that, one also holds the knowledge that writing is, in her words, "a practice located at the intersection of subject and history," and that the writer is a historical subject who's writing within particular contexts.[2] One risks being reduced to a label, and yet one may still find it necessary to locate oneself by this label and try to examine it in the writing.

TT: That's exactly what I've tried to do in *within the margin*. My journey into that project was triggered by a highly problematic statement made by a well-known artist. He said, "In order for viable art to exist, there has to be some level of marginalization." "Marginalized" is not a word that I claim for myself. I'm a writer. Why make the added effort of trying to push myself out of the center?

SR: In *within the margin* you write, "is this silence self imposed he preferred to sit in the corners of the room away from the center away from where the words would gather."[3] I'm taking "is this silence self imposed" to be a very real, pressing question that you're trying to unpack for yourself.

TT: That's true. It's also a very personal exploration. When I embarked on the writing of *within the margin* and realized that the word "margin" would be central to the text, I was aware of the public nature of that word. But what I wanted to excavate from it were private stories and personal experiences. There's a section in the book where I use dictionary definitions of the term "margin." I juxtapose that with very private material. I didn't want to fall into the mode of writing in the language that has already been scripted. There is a type of poetry that would embrace the status of the marginalized writer. That is nothing more than rhetoric to me at this point.

SR: Desire and shame form an interesting duality in *within the margin*. You write, "within the margin the writer has no shame the page is in fact a platform for wants."[4] I'm reminded of the idea expressed by Jacques Lacan and some of the French feminists, that language operates like desire. Just as there's no end to desire except in death, there's no end to writing—writing leads to more writing.

TT: That's what I'm after there.

SR: But elsewhere in the book, the notion of being in the margin is associated not with desire but with shame: "and their heads hung low / naked and / ashamed / within the margin."[5]

TT: For me, the margin is the repository both of stories that are just too damned brazen to find themselves in the text—stories of sheer audacity that you can't find a way to share without feeling a little self-conscious—and of stories that you aren't able to articulate or that you think of as not worth telling. In writing *within the margin,* I came upon many stories that for one reason or another I'd relegated to the margin. I had to find another way to enter them to discover their worth.

SR: Did that come up in *dust and conscience* and *placing the accents* too?

TT: *placing the accents* was the beginning of my writing, so those were the stories that I wanted to tell. When I wrote *dust and conscience* there were still stories that I wanted to tell but they weren't complete—they didn't have the head or the tail or whatever—so I had to figure out a form to tell them. By the time I got to *within the margin,* all I had were the castoffs. I had to ask myself why these stories had been marginalized, and discover how to work with them.

SR: I'd like to take a look at some formal concerns and themes that are laced throughout your books, starting with your use of lower-case lettering. That gesture carries various connotations, including the rejection of rules and expectations, as well as the rejection of hierarchical systems, since the appearance—and therefore conceivably the importance—of each word is leveled in relation to the other words. In the case of your prose poems, for me the lowercase combines with the lack of punctuation to speed up the line and heighten the rushing, urgent tone. But at the same time, the lack of uppercase and punctuation also intensifies the quality of enjambment. So I'm racing forward but then I have to stop and absorb all the doublings-up of meaning.

TT: I removed the capitalization because I wanted, as you said, to alleviate that sense of hierarchy—especially in terms of my relationship to the world of the poem. I don't want to wield authority over that world. Removing uppercase and punctuation also added a layer of confusion. Part of the challenge I set for myself as a writer is to confuse myself or lose myself in the writing. I think that allows readers to enter into the work and find their own stories—not necessarily my story.

SR: I see you exerting pretty tight control over your writing. Where some authors leave the meanings of the text wide open, you seem to map out a fairly finite number of possible readings and deliberately fine-tune the writing to help the reader gain access to those readings.

TT: That's true—it isn't very accidental. But as I move forward, I am interested in accidental language. In *within the margin*, accidental language, as well as found language, crops up more.

SR: The use of lower-case lettering also contributes to the emotional tone your poetry carves: intimate, casual. Details about family life and banal daily events add to this feeling of casual intimacy. But, somehow at the same time, there's a constant feeling of tension, which I attribute to the tightrope your poetry walks between conflicting viewpoints. For example, there's the deep bond with the mother yet at the same time the need to deal with her homophobia. There's the presence of Catholicism, a force about which the speaker is ambivalent. There's the balancing between Vietnamese and American culture. And there's the balancing between an interest in experiment and an awareness of a more mainstream readership—some of the poems in *dust and conscience* are written in a voice that asks, "Why aren't you making sense? Why aren't you writing more easily digestible poems?" In all of these arenas I see a tension between an accommodation or acceptance of the other and the need to resist, to assert independence.

TT: I think the tension you're noticing comes about because no matter what I'm writing about, I'm interested in exploring the layers underneath what's perceived on the surface. Often in those explorations what I discover is that the issue I'm examining is unresolved. For example, I still feel that my experiments with language are not fully arrived. Rather than deny or shy away from that realization, I try to incorporate it into the writing.

I returned to the work of Jabès this summer. After reading him for so many years, I still feel that I don't understand his work fully—and that that is the beauty of his work. It's a continuous flow of language; you arrive at an insight only to realize he's just opened a whole new can of worms, posed a whole new question. It's almost as if his writing is a meditation. The more I write, the more I realize that writing is not about resolution, but about exploring that which we don't understand.

SR: Recipes and instructions appear throughout your work. The first section of *placing the accents* is called "watching over family recipes." I read that as a proposal that the poet is the guardian of his family's and his culture's traditions. Thinking of the poem itself as a recipe or set of instructions enacts both the promise of clarity and its ironic undercutting because poems point to the ineffable—that's part of their job. What are your thoughts about the recipes and instructions in your work?

TT: I believe writers work toward the development of authentic language. We want to find authentic ways of telling our stories. But I'm also very aware that there's a certain language that has been passed down—the language of recipes. I don't want to discard that language. It serves as the catalyst for authentic language. In some of those pieces, the language was passed down almost verbatim from someone in my life, and I wanted to capture those moments. For example, there is the poem in *dust and conscience* about the man telling me how the chair and the table fit together.[6] Or the poem "between thumb and index finger" in *placing the accents,* which enacts an interaction I had with a cousin. Those poems wrote themselves.

SR: So in those cases your job is to stay out of the way.

TT: Yes, to clear a path for the pieces to arrive.

SR: For the most part, in your writing, "I" is the poet is Truong, a particular individual with a particular past, particular habits and preferences. In your first book, other people are also clearly identified, through proper names or other labels—"cousin," for example. But in your more recent work there's a concerted effort to problematize identity, partly by leaning more heavily on pronouns than on more specific means of identification, and allowing the pronouns to become interchangeable.

TT: I'm also using more pronouns because they're more private than other labels. I believe that the more you write, the more writing becomes private. *within the margin* is a far more intimate text than *placing the accents,* and I think that the next text will be even more intimate. For me, it's the natural progression of writing. I used to think that you write for an audience. But the more I write, the more I realize I'm writing for myself. Besides, I think working in that more mutable territory is a lot more fun.

SR: The pronoun blurring is applied at times to the relationship between the mother and the son, confusing the boundaries between the individuals. For example, in *within the margin* you write, "i told her i was broke to which she replied that she says is the story of my life to control the spread of mint in her garden." After a story that seems clearly about the mother, you write, "i would do it again / surrendering all notions / of love and of language / its layers of meaning / its rhythms its rhymes // surrendering family / both the joy and the burden / it's just not worth it."[7] This passage starts out with an "I" who sounds like the mother, and slides into an "I" who sounds like the son. There's a poem in the "lost and found" section of *placing the accents* where a mother figure produces a son but also seems to claim to *be* this creation: "from fingers she springs this boy is who she in a way whispers it is i it is i."[8] These passages raise the question, When is it useful to see "I" and another entity as separate, and when is it important to recognize that there is no clear division there? In the quote I just read, where "I" creates something, the question becomes: Is that created object still "I" in a sense, or is it something separate from "I"?

TT: I'm interested in the constant tension between the effort to identify the boundaries of self and other and the impossibility of doing so. As you pointed out, in my writing, the figure of the mother is at times a reflection of the other and at times an exploration of self. Writing about place, in particular Vietnam, also brings up that self/other question: Am I separate from Vietnam or am I Vietnam? To what extent can I speak for the country and its people? I wrote the penultimate section of *dust and conscience,* "the book of ruptures," to try to complicate the picture of the poet self writing about, pinning down, the other—in that section, I allow the voices of others to speak as the self.

The self-other problem may never disappear for me. I thought I was very comfortable with who I am and my identity as a writer, but my trip to Vietnam really stirred that up, both as regards my teaching and my writing. I am constantly examining my role in academia—how I fit in and what I represent. I'm definitely the minority, the other, in that world. I am also constantly aware of how my writing can be perceived as fitting nicely into an identity-based curriculum in an ethnic studies department, rather than being received in a more complex way. For example, if Asian-American Studies professors teach my work, they almost exclusively teach *placing the accents,* because it's accessible. So then I have to ask myself, am I being rewarded for being a rigorous artist, or am I just the immigrant who fills the niche? This question is always in the back of my head.

SR: Another trope in your work, closely related to the self-other examination, is the awkward yet beautiful collage. In *dust and conscience* you write, "as if language like glue could piece together the gathered fragments resulting in a form mangled but cohesive" and "caliban and ariel are one and the same like a perfect teapot at once awkward yet graceful by design." There's the poem about the table and chair, which is also a metaphor for a lover relationship, "one slides right in to fit the other not always perfectly but they fit nonetheless and this is a lifestyle," and the one about the sand crab: "it feels nothing like a poem the language he says is awkward and crude you're a writer so write something beautiful write something fluid."[9] These passages reveal an awareness of things as jagged and not coming together in a perfect whole, and the need to both enact that in the form and point to it in the content.

TT: This goes back to what we were talking about earlier: My discovery that fragments can't necessarily become whole in and of themselves, but that they can be pieced together to create a mosaic. When I first started writing, I really believed that writing can achieve some kind of fluidity. Now I understand that all the gaps and silences that exist in between the fragments are very much a part of the story I'm trying to tell.

SR: The word "translation" appears in your work in a few places, and there are also some literal translations in your poems. What aspects of translation interest you?

TT: I've done a little Vietnamese-to-English translation in the poems. For example, in the poem "tongues," in *placing the accents,* there are words from three languages: English, French, and Vietnamese. In those cases, I'm after antipoetic language; I want it to sound guttural and jarring. But more than the translation of one language to another, I'm interested in translating thought. I attempt to translate the thoughts of the other into words that are fair representations of what they're trying to convey. It's very important, for example, that I translate my mother's thoughts in a way that is capable of capturing her complexities. I don't want to portray her as a one-dimensional character.

I'm also interested in the translation of silence. I believe that in the writing of the poem, another poem exists, a poem that sits right there on the page but never finds its way into words. People are always asking me, Why do you write in these blocks surrounded by so much space, and rarely allow your poems to bleed onto a second page? I want to try to bring in all that white space. I want people to realize that the act of turning a page is part of the silence. There's a subtext there, and that's where possibility exists.

SR: Choice—along with the necessity of taking responsibility for one's choices—emerges as a concern in your work, especially in *within the margin*. Often it's quite explicit: "because there is always room for such a word because he loves me because i choose to," or "he waits for the light what happens next will change his story he chooses to tell history in the i a voice a cop he is directing traffic."[10]

TT: The choices made in *within the margin* are perhaps the most personal choices I've made thus far in my writing. That book was very difficult to write at times. I don't think my family has read it yet, but it's about them. Every time I came to a fork in the road, I had to decide which way I was going to go: what to say, how much to reveal. In some cases I chose to present family stories in a very unflattering light.

In addition to choices about content and the revealing of self, I also have to make choices about how much I allow language to shape the writing of a piece.

SR: How does that play out in your process?

TT: It comes back to the notion of parameters. For example, recently, in the spirit of OULIPO, I've been looking for four-letter words to use. But when you look up "four-letter word" online, it's always associated with swear words. That's not what I was looking for. I was hoping to find lists of four-letter words.

SR: Have you turned to the dictionary and just started looking for four-letter words?

TT: Yes. But it would have been so much easier to do an online search!

SR: Some of the references to choice in your writing have to do with the reader's choices. For example, in *within the margin* you write, "you the reader   you know who you are // specifically you are asked // to decide   you must / also know it would come   to this / someday perhaps today."[11]

TT: I think that when approaching my writing, the reader has to make a series of choices, for example about how one image connects with another, and how one poem connects with another. Through making these choices the reader constructs his or her own stories. There are fewer opportunities for readers to make choices in *placing the accents*; the poems are more self-contained. But in the subsequent texts the reader has more choices to make.

SR: Your work makes reference not only to choice, but also to the diametrically opposed notion of fate. In *dust and conscience* you write, "that which happens happens for a reason."[12] In the "lost and found" series in *placing the accents* you write, "fated i was born the third of three brothers."[13]

TT: My thinking about fate stems from a statement my mother made. She said, If the war hadn't happened, you'd be in Vietnam, married, with two kids. When I went back to Vietnam I saw myself in that existence. There is no gay community in that world. But there are gay people, who are married with children.

SR: They're not trying to hide it?

TT: I didn't see them hiding it.

SR: Did they recognize you as gay?

TT: I made it a point to be very open in Vietnam. I felt that was the only way I could go through the experience. But in Vietnamese there's no word for "gay." There's an acronym, "BD." I was told that it's short for *bong duc,* which translates as "shadow of man." And that's the extent of it.

SR: Notions of choice and fate have everything to do with all the storytelling in your work. A lot of your storytelling seems to test out alternate realities, alternate possibilities—for example, what your life would have been like if you had stayed in Vietnam, or what would have happened if your father had been a scholar instead of a soldier.

TT: The idea of what-might-have-been is a concern in my writing because in a family of five kids, by the time it came down to me as the youngest, all the roles had been fulfilled. We had the doctor, the CPA—you name it, we had it. That left me free to be an artist. I often wonder if I would have had that freedom if I'd been a middle child. When the brother before me fulfilled my father's greatest desire, which was for one of us to become a doctor, the weight of the world was lifted off my shoulders. In the end my father was really thrilled with the idea of me being a poet—but that would never have been his first desire for his children.

SR: Storytelling is connected to truth and lies in your writing. In *within the margin* you write, "a boy a six year old boy concocts a scheme he learns to lie on this day the boy discovers he discovers the truth" and "as a child i liked telling stories stories that became lies and lies that became truths."[14] I thought about how when we're kids, "telling a story" means telling a lie. Robert Glück talks about fiction as a lie that knows itself. What are your thoughts about storytelling in relation to truth and lies?

TT: For me, there's always a line between "the truth" and personal truth. I detest the idea that I have to tell "the truth." Saying you have to tell the truth means that all you do is regurgitate. As an artist I want to be able to create. The truth has to transcend into personal truth. I believe everything we write about has some truth to it. That's the stance that I have to take. Otherwise it's really defeating.

SR: There's a lot of thinking in your work about the power of words, including the power of words to harm. In "Recipe 1" in *placing the accents* you write, "if words were bricks / bricks were words / would you break a window / would you build a house."[15] Many of the poems in *placing the accents* are about the power dynamic between the Americanized boy and the parents who are still located in Vietnamese culture and language. The boy separates from the parents by using English as a weapon.

TT: Yes, speaking English was the way that I separated myself from my parents at a young age. Becoming a writer was a way to further separate myself from my family, especially because in my writing I examine issues such as being gay and being raised Catholic. But the irony is that the more I've written, the more I've circled back to the connections and stories that originated in my family. This connects to the self-other issue we discussed earlier, in the sense that running from family is really running from yourself. For a while it really did work, because writing in English gave me a gap in which I could explore freely. But ultimately, you can't divorce yourself from the family connection.

The other part of your observation was that the boy learns that words can harm. I think that words are perhaps more powerful than any stick or stone. Take the word "fuck," which I explored in *within the margin*. It's just a little word, but depending on how you say it—playfully, or in a lewd way, or in a way that asserts your authority over someone, or with venom—you can really dismantle another person—or yourself. There were a couple of times in the writing of *within the margin* where my use of the word "fuck" shut me out from the world around me. By invoking that word I locate myself within the margin. That's such a powerful impact for a single word to have.

SR: It seems that in recent years the word has lost a lot of its punch. When we were children, it was more naughty. Yet now I hear it constantly—many people seem to use it in every sentence. Has that decreased its specialness for you?

TT: Yes, it has lost its potency. And by the end of the book, I relinquish it.

SR: Besides the violence that language can do, I noted other forms of violence in your writing. For example, the Vietnam War haunts all your books.

TT: I think it's always going to be present in my writing. I believe war shapes you. Look at Edmond Jabès and Myung Mi Kim; their writing is shaped in many ways by that experience. I never write "war poems"—it's never something that comes to me consciously—but it finds its way into the writing.

SR: Tell me about the loaded gun that keeps appearing in your books.

TT: That gun is bound up with one of the first difficult choices I had to make as a writer. I'd written a poem about a young man I knew who found a shotgun underneath the back seat of the family car, played with it, pulled the trigger, shot it right through the front seat—and killed his father. This boy had come to the U.S. with his father. The father worked as a janitor and raised enough money to bring the rest of the family over. The rumor was that when he brought the family over, the mother was having an affair with someone else, and the father had gotten the gun in order to do away with the lover. Anyway, the accidental murder was the beginning of my friend's demise. He eventually ended up in the prison system. When I wrote that piece, another childhood friend said, I strongly urge you not to publish it; if he ever read this he'd probably kill you. That was a moment of harsh reality. I didn't write it to judge him. It was a memory that I wanted to document.

SR: For me, the loaded gun in your books conjures a sense of danger always on the periphery.

TT: I also see it as a metaphor for the camera. There's that famous news photo of the man holding the gun to the other man's head in South Vietnam. The camera took the photo of the gun, but the camera itself was a gun, shooting an image into our heads that will never leave. Once the picture was shot, it became part of our consciousness and our history.

SR: We've mentioned Myung Mi Kim and Edmond Jabès as two sources of inspiration. Are there other teachers or writers to whom you feel deeply connected?

TT: I still consider myself a relatively new reader of poetry. It wasn't something I grew up with; it's something I sought out as an adult. But when I did discover poetry, I got excited by the writings of Jabès and also Paul Celan. I'm reading a lot of Berryman right now because his warped syntax gives a window into his psyche in a way that is very disturbing and intriguing. I learned recently that his writing is studied for what it reveals about people who commit suicide. I'm also really fascinated by writing that exists in the terrain between poetry and prose. Russell Edson is a surrealist writer who captures my imagination and whose language fascinates me because it's very ugly. Nicanor Parra also uses wonderfully ugly language at times.

SR: I wanted to end by asking you about the Bay Area poetry community. You grew up in San Jose and went to U.C. Santa Cruz and then to San Francisco State. You live and work in San Francisco. How do you view the Bay Area poetry community?

TT: San Francisco has a very sophisticated palate when it comes to poetry. When I give a reading or lecture outside of San Francisco, I find people's relationship to writing to be very identity-driven. All their questions for me revolve around how to connect the writing to the life. I think San Francisco is unique in that we are really interested in the process and the craft of writing. On the other hand, I think there are too many camps in the city.

SR: How do you relate to that? Do you step in and out of different camps?

TT: No, I tend to avoid them. But as much as I gripe about the camps, I'm happy that we have different schools of thought in the city. This multiplicity allows me to learn about a full range of possibilities, and within that diversity, create my own path. For example, I went to hear Carolyn Bergvall a couple of months ago. Her work is sound-driven—you have to surrender yourself to the sounds. At one point I closed my eyes and found that I could capture a narrative out of the sound. She redefined the boundaries of language for me.

SR: Who would be someone in a different camp whose work compels you?

TT: Lucille Clifton isn't from the Bay Area, but she can serve as an example. She writes very narrative poetry, but it too is sound-driven. There's a powerful rhythm to her language.

SR: Do you define yourself as an experimental writer, or is that a label that gets attached to you, like "marginal writer"?

TT: I don't think of myself as an experimental writer. I don't see myself as someone who's entrenched in any one writing community.

SR: Are there any changes you'd like to see in the Bay Area poetry community?

TT: I wonder if there's a way that we could connect these communities more. It seems a little disjointed. If you go to an experimental reading almost everyone in the audience is of that school and at times it seems there's no room for someone else to come in. It might be interesting to cross-pollinate between the more narrative writers and the more experimental writers and bring different audiences together.

SR: Is that your desire for your own writing—to cross-pollinate the more narrative-lyrical and the more experimental impulses?

TT: Ultimately, I write for myself. My desire is simply to write in a way that challenges me and yet is accessible to me.

Notes

INTRODUCTION

1. For an excellent discussion of "The Türler Losses" see Lundquist, " 'Two voices, one joking.' "

2. For San Francisco literary history up to and including the "New Americans" I draw heavily on Davidson's *San Francisco Renaissance.*

3. Dana, "San Francisco–Monterey."

4. Albert, "Ina Coolbrith."

5. Davidson, *San Francisco Renaissance,* 11.

6. Academy of American Poets, "Kenneth Rexroth."

7. For information about the history of the Berkeley Renaissance and in particular Duncan, Spicer, and Blaser, I draw heavily on Ellingham and Killian's *Poet Be Like God.*

8. Blaser, "The Practice of Outside," 275.

9. Spicer, "Workshop Questionnaire," 355.

10. Ellingham and Killian, *Poet Be Like God,* 356.

11. Ibid., 152.

12. Kyger, "Anne Waldman: The Early Years"; Loden, email to POETICS list.

13. Clay and Phillips, "A Little History."

14. Warsh, "Angel Hair feature: Introduction."

15. For information about the history of the Language movement I draw heavily on Eleana Kim's "Language Poetry" as well as Ron Silliman's blog. See also Perelman, *The Marginalization of Poetry*; Perelman et al., *The Grand Piano, Part 1*; and Watten et al., *The Grand Piano, Part 2.*

16. Shange, "An Interview with Ntozake Shange," 134.
17. Compomanes, "About Jessica Hagedorn."
18. For an engaging introduction to the Bolinas poetry community see Opstedal, "Dreaming as One."
19. Glück, "Long Note."
20. Many of the Language poets eventually became professors. On the one hand, this is highly ironic, given their ferocious critique of the cooptation of poetry by academia. Yet on the other hand, it is not surprising—the rigorous theoretical work these poets were accustomed to writing happened to make them ideally suited for academic work. Debate continues as to whether poets can effectively critique the status quo from within the institution. In her interview in this volume, Juliana Spahr argues that they can, citing Bernstein's exemplary work while at SUNY Buffalo.
21. Robinson, interview in this volume, 252.
22. Glück, interview in this volume, 98–99.
23. Scalapino, interview in this volume, 296.
24. Fraser, interview in this volume, 72.
25. Young, *Bay Poetics.* xi–xii.
26. Hillman, interview in this volume, 136.
27. Roy, interview in this volume, 272.
28. Spahr, interview in this volume, 312.
29. Tran, interview in this volume, 324.
30. Ibid., 333.
31. Palmer, interview in this volume, 170.
32. Robinson, interview in this volume, 227.
33. Glück, interview in this volume, 85.
34. Ibid., 74.
35. Mackey, interview in this volume, 156.
36. Ibid., 157.
37. Palmer, interview in this volume, 172.
38. Hillman, interview in this volume, 125.

39. Fraser, interview in this volume, 68.
40. Robinson, interview in this volume, 250.
41. Ratcliffe, interview in this volume, 200.
42. For further discussion by Ratcliffe of Stein's work, see Ratcliffe, "Memo/ Re: Reading Stein," 69–77.
43. Robinson, interview in this volume, 237.
44. Ibid., 239.
45. Palmer, interview in this volume, 178.
46. Ibid., 170.
47. Hillman, interview in this volume, 124.
48. Ibid., 132.
49. Guest, interview in this volume, 105.

KATHLEEN FRASER: PLACING SILENCE

1. Fraser, *Something (even human voices)*, 17.
2. Fraser, *Each Next*, 54.
3. Fraser, *Notes Preceding Trust*, 25–26.
4. Fraser, *il cuore*, 158–168.
5. Fraser, *Discrete Categories*, 57.
6. Ibid, 65.
7. McCorkle, "Topographies."
8. Fraser, *hi dde violeth*, 12; 16. When two or more quotations from the same source appear in succession within a single paragraph, they are combined into a single endnote with page numbers separated by semicolons.
9. Ibid., 23–31.
10. Fraser, *new time*, 71–76.
11. Fraser, *hi dde violeth*, 34.
12. Fraser, *20th Century*, 18. The pages of *20th Century* are unnumbered. Page numbers in the notes for this book were arrived at by counting the first title page as page 1. Page 9 begins, "entablature, missing elements."
13. Ibid., 19; 21.

Robert Glück: A Community Writing Itself

1. Glück, "My Community," 123.
2. Glück, "Truth's Mirror," 40.
3. Glück, "Fame," 220.
4. Glück, "My Community," 123.
5. This interview was conducted in late September of 2002.
6. Glück, "Caricature," 27.
7. Blake, "Marriage," 64.
8. Glück, *Margery Kempe*, 32.
9. Ibid., 49.
10. Clark, *Tulsa*, 55. The pages of *Tulsa* are unnumbered. The page number in this note was arrived at by counting the title page as page 1.

Barbara Guest: Clearing the Ordinary from the Room

1. Guest, *Forces of Imagination*, 100–101.
2. Guest, *The Confetti Trees*, 49.
3. Guest, *Miniatures*, vii.
4. Guest, *Forces of Imagination*, 106.
5. Guest, *Miniatures*, 41.
6. Ibid., 40.
7. Guest, *Rocks on a Platter*, 26.
8. Ibid., 33.
9. Ibid., 42; 23; 25.
10. Guest, *Miniatures*, 4; 11; 12.
11. Guest, *The Red Gaze*, 49.
12. Ibid., 11; 12.
13. Ibid., 17; 25; 34; 40.
14. Ibid., 18.
15. Ibid., 22.
16. Ibid., 36.
17. Ibid., 36.
18. Ibid., 28.

19. Ibid., 19; 22.
20. Ibid., 8; 23; 36.
21. Ibid., 48.
22. Friedel, *Hans Hoffman*, 88; 12; 91.
23. Guest, *The Red Gaze*, 26.

Brenda Hillman: Our Very Greatest Human Thing Is Wild

1. Hillman, *Cascadia*, 63; 69; 73.
2. Hillman, *Bright Existence*, 8.
3. Hillman, *Cascadia*, 55.
4. Ibid., 58; 59.
5. Ibid., 56; 1.
6. Hillman, *Bright Existence*, 11; 25; 26; 30.
7. Hillman, *Cascadia*, 42; 6.
8. Ibid., 43; 19.
9. Ibid., 18.
10. Ibid., 60.
11. Ibid., 5.
12. Hillman, "Brenda Hillman," 76.

Nathaniel Mackey: The Atmosphere Is Alive

1. Mackey, *Splay Anthem*, 26.
2. Mackey, *Eroding Witness*, 81–99.
3. Mackey, *Splay Anthem*, 18.
4. Ibid., 66.
5. Mackey, *Eroding Witness*, 60–61.
6. Olson, *Special View*, 20–23.
7. Mackey, *School of Udhra*, p. 21.
8. Olson, 20–21.
9. Mackey, *Splay Anthem*, 3.
10. Roberson, *Just in*, 12.
11. Naylor, "Some Ecstatic Elsewhere," 593.

12. Olson, *Special View*, 23.
13. Mackey, *Paracritical Hinge*, 260.
14. Mackey, *Splay Anthem*, 35; 28.
15. Mackey, *Paracritical Hinge*, 304.
16. Mackey, *Splay Anthem*, 102; 121; 31; 23.
17. Mackey, *Paracritical Hinge*, 275.
18. Ibid., 263.
19. Naylor, "Some Ecstatic Elsewhere," 602.
20. Mackey, *Splay Anthem*, 112.
21. Ibid., 17; 11; 61; 22; 32.
22. Baraka/Jones, *The Dead Lecturer*, 42.
23. Mackey, *Paracritical Hinge*, 293.

Michael Palmer: The Recovery of Language

1. International PEN Writers, "Three Journalists."
2. Palmer, *Company of Moths*, 7.
3. Ibid., 3.
4. Ibid.
5. Palmer, "Interview," 163–164.
6. Palmer, *Company of Moths*, 3.
7. Ibid., 33.
8. Ibid., 43.
9. Ibid.
10. Palmer, *The Promises of Glass*, 3.
11. Palmer, "Active Boundaries," 214–215.
12. Palmer, *At Passages*, 4.
13. Palmer, *Company of Moths*, 40.
14. Ibid., 15–16.
15. BBC, "Percy Bysshe Shelley."
16. Stevens, "Evening without Angels," 138.
17. Palmer, *The Promises of Glass*, 47–55.
18. Menand, "An American Prodigy."

19. Palmer, *Company of Moths*, 63.
20. Ibid., ix.
21. Ibid., 56.
22. Leland, "At Home."
23. Palmer, *Company of Moths*, 45.
24. Ibid., 15.
25. Palmer, *The Promises of Glass*, 4.

STEPHEN RATCLIFFE: ARTIFICE AND ACCIDENT

1. Merleau-Ponty, *Phenomenology of Perception*, vii.
2. Stein, *Writings and Lectures*, 115.
3. Ibid., 161–206.
4. Ratcliffe, *Listening to Reading*, 1–5.
5. Norris, *Deconstruction*, 51.
6. Ratcliffe, *Mallarmé*, 12.
7. Ratcliffe, *Listening to Reading*, 57.
8. Creeley, *Collected Essays*, 591.
9. Ratcliffe, *SOUND / (system)*, 15.
10. Creeley, *Collected Essays*, 490.
11. Ratcliffe, *Listening to Reading*, 63.
12. Ratcliffe, *SOUND / (system)*, 6–7.

ELIZABETH ROBINSON: FALLING IS THE SAFEST THING TO DO

1. Robinson, *Apprehend*, 66.
2. Ibid., 67.
3. Ibid., 19.
4. Ibid.
5. Ibid.
6. Ibid., 20.
7. Ibid., 20; 21; 22; 23.
8. Robinson, *Harrow*, 43.
9. Kenner, *The Pound Era*, 67.

10. Robinson, *House Made of Silver*, 31.
11. Robinson, *Apprehend*, 47.
12. Stevens, *The Necessary Angel*, 36.
13. Robinson, *Apprehend*, 37.
14. Ibid., 38; 39.
15. Ibid., 39.
16. Ibid., 80.
17. Ibid., 81.
18. Robinson, *Harrow*, 75.
19. Robinson, *in the sequence*, 33.
20. Robinson, *Pure Descent*, 55.
21. Ibid., 56.
22. Robinson, *in the sequence*, 77.
23. Robinson, *House Made of Silver*, 43.
24. O'Hara, "Autobiographia Literaria."

Camille Roy: Experience Is a Demanding Mistress

1. Roy, *Craquer*, 26.
2. Roy, "Notes on the Plays," ii.
3. Roy, *The Rosy Medallions*, 45–66.
4. Ibid., 52.
5. Roy, *Swarm*, 65–119.
6. Roy, *Craquer*, 12–13; 17.
7. Roy, "Quotes."
8. Roy, *Craquer*, 22.
9. Roy, "Quotes."
10. Roy, *Bye Bye Brunhilde*, 15.
11. Roy, *Cheap Speech*, 8, 57.
12. Roy, *The Rosy Medallions*, 39.
13. Roy, *Craquer*, 25–26.
14. Roy, *The Rosy Medallions*, 43.
15. Roy, *Swarm*, 90.

LESLIE SCALAPINO: MESSING UP LINEAR TIME

1. Scalapino, *R-hu*, 120.

2. Scalapino, *Defoe*, 293.

3. Scalapino, *The Front Matter*, 5. The character Defoe appears in both *Defoe* and *The Front Matter, Dead Souls.*

4. Scalapino, *Defoe*, 299.

5. Scalapino, *The Front Matter*, 73.

6. Ibid., 75.

7. Scalapino, *R-hu*, 118.

8. Scalapino, *Defoe*, 111.

9. Ibid., 155–156.

10. Ibid., 53.

11. Scalapino, *The Front Matter*, 5.

12. Scalapino, *R-hu*, 81.

13. Scalapino, *The Front Matter*, 5.

14. Ibid., 75.

15. Scalapino, *R-hu*, 94.

16. Scalapino, *Dahlia's Iris*, 184.

JULIANA SPAHR: HOW DOES THE WORK GET USED

1. Spahr, "Three Found Sonnets."

2. Spahr, *this connection*, 53–54.

3. Spahr, "Three Found Sonnets."

4. Spahr, *The Transformation*, 147.

5. Spahr, *this connection*, 44.

6. Ibid., 63.

7. Ibid.

8. Moxley, *Imagination Verses*, xi.

9. Spahr, "A Conversation."

10. Spahr, *this connection*, 45–52.

11. Spahr, "November 14, 2005."

12. Spahr, *Everybody's Autonomy*, 64.

13. Ibid., 6.
14. Menchú, *I Rigoberta Menchú*, 1.
15. Spahr, *The Transformation*, 40.
16. Spahr, *this connection*, 57.

Truong Tran: I Became the Other

1. Tran, *dust and conscience*, 79.
2. Trinh, *Woman Native Other*, 6.
3. Tran, *within the margin*, 50–51. The pages of *within the margin* are unnumbered. Page numbers in the notes for this book were arrived at by counting the first title page as page 1. Page 5 begins, "there are the words / margin."
4. Ibid., 20.
5. Ibid., 109.
6. Tran, *dust and conscience*, 43.
7. Tran, *within the margin*, 60–61; 170–171.
8. Tran, *placing the accents*, 55.
9. Tran, *dust and conscience*, 27; 32; 43; 65.
10. Tran, *within the margin*, 38–39; 35–36.
11. Ibid., 20–21.
12. Tran, *dust and conscience*, 53.
13. Tran, *placing the accents*, 54.
14. Tran, *within the margin*, 6–7; 71–72.
15. Tran, *placing the accents*, 12.

Works Cited

INTRODUCTION

Academy of American Poets. "Kenneth Rexroth: Poetry Wedded to Jazz." Academy of American Poets. http://www.poets.org/viewmedia.php/prmMID/5807

Albert, Janice. "Ina Coolbrith (1841–1928) and the California Frontier." California Association of Teachers of English. http://www.cateweb.org/CA_Authors/Coolbrith.html

Allen, Donald. *The New American Poetry, 1945–1960.* Berkeley: University of California Press, 1999.

Andrews, Bruce and Charles Bernstein. *The L=A=N=G=U=A=G=E Book.* Carbondale, IL: Southern Illinois University Press, 1984.

Blaser, Robin. "The Practice of Outside." In *The Collected Books of Jack Spicer.* Edited by Robin Blaser, 271–329. Santa Rosa, CA: Black Sparrow Press, 1989.

Clay, Steve, and Rodney Phillips. "A Little History of the Mimeograph Revolution." In *A Secret Location on the Lower East Side: Adventures in Writing, 1960–1980; A Sourcebook of Information.* Edited by Steve Clay and Rodney Phillips, 12–27. New York: Granary Books, 1998.

Campomanes, Oscar V. "About Jessica Hagedorn." *Modern American Poetry.* http://www.english.illinois.edu/maps/poets/g_l/hagedorn/about.htm

Dana, Richard Henry, Jr. "San Francisco–Monterey." Chap. 26 in *Two Years Before the Mast: A Personal Narrative of Life at Sea*. New York: Harper and Brothers, 1840.

Davidson, Michael. *The San Francisco Renaissance: Poetics and Community at Mid-century.* Cambridge: Cambridge University Press, 1991.

Ellingham, Lewis, and Kevin Killian. *Poet Be Like God: Jack Spicer and the San Francisco Renaissance.* Hanover, NH: University Press of New England / Wesleyan University Press, 1998.

Ginsberg, Allen. *Howl and Other Poems*. San Francisco: City Lights, 1956.

Glück, Robert. "Long Note on New Narrative." *Narrativity* no. 1. http://www.sfsu.edu/~poetry/narrativity/issue_one/gluck.html

Guest, Barbara. "The Türler Losses." In *Selected Poems*, 93–114. Los Angeles: Sun & Moon Press, 1995.

Kim, Eleana. "Language Poetry: Dissident Practices and the Makings of a Movement." *Readme* no. 4 (Spring/Summer 2001). http://home.jps.net/~nada/issuefour.htm

Kyger, Joanne. "Anne Waldman: The Early Years . . . 1965–1970." *Jacket* (April 2005). http://jacketmagazine.com/27/w-kyge.html

Loden, Rachel. Email to POETICS list, August 22, 1996. http://wings.buffalo.edu/epc/poetics/early_archive/logs/1996/9608

Lundquist, Sara. "'Two voices, one joking': the Metapoetic Comedy of Barbara Guest's Poetry." *Jacket* (February 2004). http://jacketmagazine.com/25/guest-lund.html

Opstedal, Kevin. "Dreaming as One: Poetry, Poets and Community in Bolinas, California, 1967–1980." *Big Bridge* 13, no. 1 (2008). http://www.bigbridge.org/bolinas.htm

Perelman, Bob. *The Marginalization of Poetry: Language Writing and Literary History.* Princeton: Princeton University Press, 1996.

Perelman, Bob, Barrett Watten, Steve Benson, Carla Harryman, Tom Mandel, Ron Silliman, Kit Robinson, Lyn Hejinian, Rae Armantrout, and Ted Pearson. *The Grand Piano, Part 1: An Experiment in Collective Autobiography; San Francisco, 1975–1980.* Detroit: Mode A, 2006.

Ratcliffe, Stephen. "Memo/ Re: Reading Stein." In *Listening to Reading*, 69–77. Albany, NY: State University of New York Press, 2000.

Shange, Ntozake. "An Interview with Ntozake Shange." *Black American Literature Forum* 13, no.4 (1979): 134–138.

Silliman, Ron. *In the American Tree: Language, Realism, Poetry.* Orono, ME: National Poetry Foundation, 1986.

—. *Silliman's Blog: A weblog focused on contemporary poetry and poetics.* http://ronsilliman.blogspot.com

Spicer, Jack. "'Poetry as Magic' Workshop Questionnaire." In *The Collected Books of Jack Spicer.* Edited by Robin Blaser, 354–360. Santa Rosa, CA: Black Sparrow Press, 1989.

Warsh, Lewis. "Angel Hair feature: Introduction." *Jacket*, March 2002. http://jacketmagazine.com/16/ah1-wars.html

Watten, Barrett, Ted Pearson, Rae Armantrout, Steve Benson, Kit Robinson, Tom Mandel, Ron Silliman, Carla Harryman, Lyn Hejinian, and Bob Perelman. *The Grand Piano, Part 2: An Experiment in Collective Autobiography; San Francisco, 1975–1980.* Detroit: Mode A, 2007.

Young, Stephanie, ed. Introduction to *Bay Poetics.* Newton, MA: Faux Press, 2006.

Kathleen Fraser: Placing Silence

Chester, Laura and Sharon Barba, eds. *Rising Tides: 20th Century American Women Poets.* New York: Washington Square Press, 1973.

Fraser, Kathleen. *20th Century.* Davis, CA: a+bend press, 2000. Unpaged.

—. *Discrete Categories Forced into Coupling.* Berkeley: Apogee Press, 2004.

—. *Each Next*. Great Barrington, MA: The Figures, 1980.

—. *hi dde violeth i dde violet*. Vancouver: Nomados Press, 2003.

—. *il cuore: the heart; Selected Poems 1970–1995*. Hanover, NY: University Press of New England / Wesleyan University Press, 1997.

—. *In Defiance of the Rains*. San Francisco: Kayak Press, 1969.

—. *Notes Preceding Trust*. Santa Monica: The Lapis Press, 1987.

—. "The Secret Life of a Convicted Lyric Poet." 53 min., 7 sec.; from Naropa Poetics Audio Archives. MP3. http://www.archive.org/details/naropa_kathleen_fraser_lecture_the

—. *Something (even human voices) in the foreground, a lake*. Berkeley: Kelsey St. Press, 1984.

—. *when new time folds up*. Minneapolis: Chax Press, 1993.

Fraser, Kathleen, and Sam Francis. *boundayr*. Santa Monica: The Lapis Press, 1988.

Guest, Barbara. *Herself Defined*. Garden City, NY: Doubleday and Company, 1984.

Heinrich, Bernd. *The Mind of the Raven: Investigations and Adventures with Wolf-Birds*. New York: HarperCollins Publishers, 2000.

McCorkle, James. "Topographies: The Play of Silence and Space in Kathleen Fraser's 'Etruscan Pages.'" Formerly published at http://www.studiocleo.com. Currently unavailable at this website.

Robert Glück: A Community Writing Itself

Blake, William. "The Marriage of Heaven and Hell." In *Selected Poems*. Edited by P.H. Butter, 51–65. Rutland, VT: Everyman's Library, 1991.

Clark, Larry. *Tulsa*. New York: Lustrum Press, 1971. Reprint, New York: Grove Press, 2000. Unpaged.

Glück, Robert. "Caricature." *Soup: New Critical Perspectives* 4 (1985): 18–28.

—. *Denny Smith*. Astoria, OR: Clear Cut Press, 2003.

—. *Elements of a Coffee Service*. San Francisco: Four Seasons Foundation, 1982.

—. "Fame." *Poetics Journal* 10 (1998): 218–222.

—. *Jack the Modernist*. New York: Gay Presses of New York, 1985.

—. "Long Note on New Narrative." *Narrativity* no. 1. http://www.sfsu.edu/~poetry/narrativity/issue_one/gluck.html

—. *Margery Kempe*. New York: Serpent's Tail, 1994.

—. "My Community." In *Discontents: New Queer Writers*. Edited by Dennis Cooper, 119–124. New York: Amethyst Press, 1992.

—. "Truth's Mirror Is No Mirror." *Poetics Journal* 7 (1987): 40–45.

Lukács, Georg. *Theory of the Novel*. Translated by Anna Bostock. Cambridge, MA: The MIT Press, 1974.

Barbara Guest: Clearing the Ordinary from the Room

Friedel, Helmut and Tina Dickey. *Hans Hoffman*. Manchester, VT: Hudson Hills Press, 1998.

Guest, Barbara. *The Confetti Trees*. Los Angeles: Sun & Moon Press, 1999.

—. *Forces of Imagination: Writing on Writing*. Berkeley: Kelsey St. Press, 2003.

—. *Miniatures*. Middletown, CT: Wesleyan University Press, 2002.

—. *The Red Gaze*. Middletown, CT: Wesleyan University Press, 2005.

—. *Rocks on a Platter*. Hanover, NY: University Press of New England / Wesleyan University Press, 1999.

Lehman, David. *The Last Avant-Garde: The Making of the New York School Poets*. Garden City, NY: Doubleday and Company, 1998.

Brenda Hillman: Our Very Greatest Human Thing Is Wild

Benjamin, Walter. "On Language as Such and the Language of Man." In *Walter Benjamin, Selected Writings, Volume 1, 1913–1926*. Edited by Marcus Bullock and Michael W. Jennings, 62–74. Cambridge, MA: Harvard University Press, 1996.

Dienstfrey, Patricia, and Brenda Hillman, eds. *The Grand Permission: New Writings on Poetics and Motherhood*. Foreword by Rachel Blau DuPlessis. Middletown, CT: Wesleyan University Press, 2003.

Herbert, George. "The Altar." In *The Essential Herbert*. Selected and with an introduction by Anthony Hecht, 13. New York: Ecco Press, 1987.

—. "Easter-wings." In *The Essential Herbert*. Selected and with an introduction by Anthony Hecht, 28. New York: Ecco Press, 1987.

Hillman, Brenda. "Brenda Hillman." In *Range of the Possible: Conversations With Contemporary Poets*. Edited by Tod Marshall. Spokane, WA: Eastern Washington University Press, 2002.

—. *Bright Existence*. Hanover, NH: University Press of New England / Wesleyan University Press, 1993.

—. *Cascadia*. Middletown, CT: Wesleyan University Press, 2001.

—. *Death Tractates*. Hanover, NH: University Press of New England / Wesleyan University Press, 1992.

—. *Fortress*. Hanover, NH: University Press of New England / Wesleyan University Press, 1989.

—. *Loose Sugar*. Hanover, NH: University Press of New England / Wesleyan University Press, 1997.

Hyde, Lewis. *The Gift: Creativity and the Artist in the Modern World*. New York: Vintage Books, 2007.

Mauss, Marcel. *The Gift*. Translated by Ian Cunnison. London: Cohn and West, 1954.

Palmer, Michael. "I Do Not." In *The Promises of Glass*, 97–99. New York: New Directions, 2000.

Stein, Gertrude. "Lifting Belly." In *Bee Time Vine and Other Pieces, 1913–1927*. Edited by Carl Van Vechten, 61–115. New Haven: Yale University Press, 1953.

NATHANIEL MACKEY: THE ATMOSPHERE IS ALIVE

Allen, Donald. *The New American Poetry: 1945–1960*. New York: Grove Press, 1960.

Baraka, Amiri/Leroi Jones, *The Dead Lecturer*. New York: Grove Press, 1964.

—. Liner notes for *Four for Trane: Archie Shepp*. Impulse A-71.

—. *Preface to a Twenty Volume Suicide Note*. New York: Totem Press, 1961.

Cherry, Don. *"mu" first part*. Affinity AFF 8.

—. *"mu" second part*. Affinity AFF 17.

Ellison, Ralph. "Richard Wright's Blues." In *The Collected Essays of Ralph Ellison*. Edited by John F. Callahan, 128–144. New York: Modern Library, 1995.

H.D. [Hilda Doolittle]. *Hermetic Definition*. New York: New Directions, 1972.

Harrison, Jane Ellen. *Themis: A Study of the Social Origins of Greek Religion*. Cambridge: Cambridge University Press, 1912.

Mackey, Nathaniel. *Eroding Witness*. Urbana, IL: University of Illinois Press, 1985.

—. *From a Broken Bottle Traces of Perfume Still Emanate*. Ongoing serial novel comprising, to date, *Bedouin Hornbook* (Lexington, KY: Callaloo Fiction, 1986), *Djbot Baghostus's Run* (Los Angeles: Sun & Moon Press, 1993), Atet A.D. (San Francisco: City Lights, 2001), and *Bass Cathedral* (New York: New Directions, 2008).

—. *Paracritical Hinge: Essays, Talks, Notes, Interviews*. Madison, WI: University of Wisconsin Press, 2005.

—. *School of Udhra*. San Francisco: City Lights, 1993.

—. "Sound and Sentiment, Sound and Symbol." In *The Politics of Poetic Form: Poetry and Public Policy*. Edited by Charles Bernstein, 87–118. New York: Roof Books, 1990.

—. *Splay Anthem*. New York: New Directions, 2006.

—. *Whatsaid Serif*. San Francisco: City Lights, 1998.

Naylor, Paul. "'Some Ecstatic Elsewhere': Nathaniel Mackey's *Whatsaid Serif.*" *Callaloo* 23, no. 2 (2000): 592–605.

Olson, Charles. *The Special View of History.* Edited by Ann Charters. Berkeley: Oyez Press, 1970.

Roberson, Ed. *Just in: Word of Navigational Challenges: New and Selected Work.* Jersey City, NJ: Talisman House Publishers, 1998.

Zuckerkandl, Victor: *Sound and Symbol: Music and the External World.* Princeton, NJ: Bollingen Foundation / Princeton University Press, 1956.

Michael Palmer: The Recovery of Language

BBC. "Percy Bysshe Shelley—The End Game." http://www.bbc.co.uk/dna/h2g2/A29265537

Benjamin, Walter. *The Arcades Project.* Edited by Roy Tiedemann. Translated by Howard Eiland and Kevin McLaughlin. Cambridge, MA: Harvard University Press, 1999.

Carruth, Hayden, ed. *The Voice That Is Great Within Us: American Poetry of the Twentieth Century.* Bantam Books, 1970.

International PEN Writers in Prison Committee. "Three Journalists Remain Imprisoned; Poet Describes Prison Conditions and Torture," press release. *International Freedom of Expression eXchange* April 2, 2001. http://www.ifex.org/en/content/view/full/13111

Jakobson, Roman. *My Futurist Years.* Edited by Bengt Nagfeldt. Translated by Stephen Rudy. New York: Marsilio Publishers, 1992.

Leland, John. "At Home with: Ved Mehta: In a Dark Harbor, a Bright House." *New York Times* (May 22, 2003): F1 and F8.

Menand, Louis. "An American Prodigy." Review of *Charles Sanders Peirce: A Life,* by Joseph Brent. *New York Review of Books* 40, no. 20 (December 2, 1993): 30–35.

Palmer, Michael. "Active Boundaries." In *Active Boundaries: Selected Essays and Talks,* 207–225. New York: New Directions, 2008.

—. *At Passages*. New York: New Directions, 1995.
—. *Company of Moths*. New York: New Directions, 2005.
—. *The Danish Notebook*. Penngrove, CA: Avec Books, 1999.
—. "Interview with Michael Palmer." By Peter Gizzi. *Exact Change Yearbook*. Edited by Peter Gizzi. Cambridge, MA: Exact Change, 1995.
—. *The Promises of Glass*. New York: New Directions, 2000.
Sebald, W.G. *Austerlitz*. Translated by Anthea Bell. New York: Random House, 2001.
Stevens, Wallace. "Evening without Angels." In *The Collected Poems of Wallace Stevens*, 136–138. New York: Vintage Books, 1990.
Zanzotto, Andrea. *La Beltà*. Milan: Mondadori, 1968.

STEPHEN RATCLIFFE: ARTIFICE AND ACCIDENT
Coolidge, Clark. *Research*. Berkeley: Tuumba Press, 1982.
Creeley, Robert. *The Collected Essays of Robert Creeley*. Berkeley: University of California Press, 1989.
—. "I Know a Man." In *Selected Poems: Robert Creeley*, 4. Berkeley: University of California Press, 1996.
James, Henry. *The Letters of Henry James, Volume III, 1883–1895*. Edited by Leon Edel. Cambridge, MA: Harvard University Press, 1980.
Mallarmé, Stéphane. *The Poems of Mallarmé*. Translated by Keith Bosley. London: Penguin, 1977.
Merleau-Ponty, Maurice. *Phenomenology of Perception*. Translated by Colin Smith. New York: Routledge and Kegan Paul, 1962.
Norris, Christopher. *Deconstruction: Theory and Practice*. Rev. ed. New York: Routledge, 1991.
Ratcliffe, Stephen. *CLOUD / RIDGE*. Unpublished manuscript.
—. *Distance*. Bolinas, CA: Avenue B, 1986.
—. *HUMAN / NATURE*. Unpublished manuscript.

—. *Idea's Mirror*. Elmwood, CT: Potes & Poets Press, 1999.
—. *Listening to Reading*. Albany: State University of New York Press, 2000.
—. *Mallarmé: poem in prose*. Santa Barbara: Santa Barbara Review Publications, 1998.
—. *MOBILE / MOBILE*. Los Angeles: Echo Park Press, 1987.
—. *Portraits & Repetition*. Sausalito, CA: Post Apollo Press, 2002.
—. *Present Tense*. Great Barrington, MA: The Figures, 1995.
—. *REAL*. Bolinas, CA: Avenue B, 2007.
—. *SOUND / (system)*. Los Angeles: Green Integer, 2002.
Silliman, Ron. "Tuesday, January 21, 2003." In *Silliman's Blog: A weblog focused on contemporary poetry and poetics*. http://ronsilliman.blogspot.com/2003/01/there-are-many-instances-of-poets-who.html
Stein, Gertrude. *Writings and Lectures, 1909–1945*. Edited by Patricia Meyerowitz. Baltimore: Penguin Books, 1971.
Woolf, Virginia. *To the Lighthouse*. London: Hogarth Press, 1927.

Elizabeth Robinson: Falling Is the Safest Thing to Do

Kenner, Hugh. *The Pound Era*. Berkeley: University of California Press, 1971.
McKuen, Rod. *Listen to the Warm*. New York: Random House, 1967.
O'Hara, Frank. "Autobiographia Literaria." In *The Selected Poems of Frank O'Hara*. Edited by Donald Allen, 3. New York: Vintage Books, 1974.
Pritchett, Patrick. "Patrick Pritchett Reviews *Apprehend*, by Elizabeth Robinson." *Jacket* (August 2003). http://jacketmagazine.com/23/prit-robin.html
Retallack, Joan. *The Poethical Wager*. Berkeley: University of California Press, 2004.
Robinson, Elizabeth. *Apprehend*. Berkeley: Apogee Press / Albany, NY: Fence Books / New York: Saturnalia Books, 2003.

—. *in the sequence of falling things*. Providence: paradigm press, 1990.

—. *Harrow*. Richmond, CA: Omnidawn Publishing, 2001.

—. *House Made of Silver*. Berkeley: Kelsey St. Press, 2000.

—. *Pure Descent*. Los Angeles: Sun & Moon Press, 2003.

Stevens, Wallace. *The Necessary Angel*. New York: Vintage Books, 1942.

Camille Roy: Experience Is a Demanding Mistress

Roy, Camille. *Bye Bye Brunhilde*. In *Cold Heaven*, 1–36. Oakland: O Books, 1993.

—. *Cheap Speech*. San Francisco: Leroy, 2002.

—. *Craquer*. Second Story Books, 2002.

—. "Monstrous." *Narrativity* no. 1. http://www.sfsu.edu/~poetry/narrativity/issue_one/roy.html

—. "Notes on the Plays." In *Cold Heaven*, i–v. Oakland: O Books, 1993.

—. "Quotes." *Narrativity* no. 2. http://www.sfsu.edu/~poetry/narrativity/issue_two/quotes_Camille.html

—. *The Rosy Medallions*. Berkeley: Kelsey St. Press, 1995.

—. *Sometimes Dead Is Better*. In *Cold Heaven*, 37–89. Oakland: O Books, 1993.

—. *Swarm*. San Francisco: Black Star Series, 1998.

Leslie Scalapino: Messing Up Linear Time

Bohm, David. *Causality and Chance in Modern Physics*. Philadelphia: University of Pennsylvania Press, 1971.

Cabezón, José. *Buddhism and Language: A Study of Indo-Tibetan Scholasticism*. Albany, NY: State University of New York Press, 1994.

Gladman, Renee. *The Activist*. San Francisco: Krupskaya, 2003.

Goldman, Judith. *Vocoder*. New York: Roof Books, 2001.

Gyatso, Janet. *Apparitions of the Self: The Secret Autobiographies of a Tibetan Visionary*. Princeton: Princeton University Press, 1999.

Mayer, Bernadette. *Midwinter Day*. Berkeley: Turtle Island Foundation, 1982.

—. *Studying Hunger*. New York: Adventures in Poetry / Bolinas, CA: Big Sky, 1975.

Scalapino, Leslie. *Dahlia's Iris: Secret Autobiography and Fiction*. Tuscaloosa: University of Alabama Press, 2003.

—. *Defoe*. Los Angeles: Sun & Moon Press, 1994.

—. *The Front Matter, Dead Souls*. Hanover, NH: University Press of New England / Wesleyan University Press, 1996.

—. *How Phenomena Appear to Unfold*. Elmwood, CT: Potes & Poets Press, 1989.

—. *R-hu*. Berkeley: Atelos, 2000.

—. *Way*. San Francisco: North Point Press, 1988.

Stein, Gertrude. *The Making of Americans*. New York: Harcourt, Brace and World, 1934.

—. "Melanctha." In *Three Lives*, 54–162. 1909. Reprint, New York: Mondial, 2007.

Juliana Spahr: How Does the Work Get Used

Goodyear, Dana. "Quiet Depravity: The Demure Outrages of a Standup Comic." *New Yorker* (October 24, 2005): 50–55.

Hejinian, Lyn. *My Life*. Rev. ed. Los Angeles: Green Integer, 2002.

Lu, Pamela. *Pamela: A Novel*. Berkeley: Atelos, 1999.

Moxley, Jennifer. *Imagination Verses*. New York: Tender Buttons, 1996.

Menchú, Rigoberta. *I, Rigoberta Menchú: An Indian Woman in Guatemala*. Brooklyn: Verso Books, 1984.

Smithson, Robert, and Nancy Holt. *East Coast, West Coast*. Video. 1969. http://222.robertsmithson.com/films/films.htm

Spahr, Juliana. "A Conversation with Juliana Spahr." By Joel Bettridge. *How2* 2, no. 3 (2005): http://www.asu.edu/pipercwcenter/how2journal/archive/online_archive/v2_3_2005/current/workbook/spa/spa.htm

—. *Everybody's Autonomy.* Tuscaloosa: University of Alabama Press, 2001.

—. *Fuck You-Aloha-I Love You.* Middletown, CT: Wesleyan University Press, 2001.

—. *Response.* Los Angeles: Sun & Moon Press, 1996.

—. "November 14, 2005." *swoonrocket*, http://www.swoonrocket.blogspot.com/2005/11/read-mark-mcgurls-program-era.html

—. *this connection of everyone with lungs.* Berkeley: University of California Press, 2005.

—. "Three Found Sonnets." *Mixed Blood* no. 1 (2004): 85–86.

—. *The Transformation.* Berkeley: Atelos, 2007.

Stein, Gertrude. *Everybody's Autobiography.* New York: Random House, 1937.

Watten, Barrett. *Bad History.* Berkeley: Atelos, 1998.

Yamanaka, Lois Ann. *Blu's Hanging.* New York: Harper Perennial, 1998.

—. *Saturday Night at the Pahala Theatre.* Honolulu: Bamboo Ridge Press, 1993.

TRUONG TRAN: I BECAME THE OTHER

Barthes, Roland. *A Lover's Discourse.* Translated by Richard Howard. New York: Hill and Wang, 1978.

Jabès, Edmond. *The Book of Questions.* Translated by Rosmarie Waldrop. Hanover, NH: University Press of New England / Wesleyan University Press, 1991.

Kim, Myung Mi. *Commons.* Berkeley: University of California Press, 2002.

Tran, Truong. *The Book of Perceptions*. San Francisco: Kearny Street Workshop, 1999.
—. *dust and conscience*. Berkeley: Apogee Press, 2002.
—. *placing the accents*. Berkeley: Apogee Press, 1999.
—. *within the margin*. Berkeley: Apogee Press, 2004. Unpaged.
Trinh, T. Minh-Ha. *Woman, Native, Other: Writing Postcoloniality and Feminism*. Bloomington, IN: Indiana University Press, 1989.

SARAH ROSENTHAL received a BA in Literature and Society from Brown University and an MFA in Creative Writing from San Francisco State University. She is the author of *Manhatten*, a cross-genre book combining poetry, fiction, and reviews (Spuyten Duyvil, 2009), and three chapbooks: *How I Wrote This Story* (Margin to Margin, 2001), *sitings* (a+bend, 2000), and *not-chicago* (Melodeon Poetry Systems, 1998). Her interviews, essays, reviews, poetry, and fiction have appeared in numerous journals. Her poetry has been anthologized in *Bay Poetics* (Faux, 2006) and *hinge* (Crack, 2002). She has taught creative writing at Santa Clara University and San Francisco State University. She is the recipient of the Leo Litwak Award for Fiction and grant-supported writing residencies at the Vermont Studio Center, Soul Mountain, and the Ragdale Foundation.

SELECTED DALKEY ARCHIVE PAPERBACKS

Petros Abatzoglou, *What Does Mrs. Freeman Want?*
Michal Ajvaz, *The Golden Age.*
The Other City.
Pierre Albert-Birot, *Grabinoulor.*
Yuz Aleshkovsky, *Kangaroo.*
Felipe Alfau, *Chromos.*
Locos.
Ivan Ângelo, *The Celebration.*
The Tower of Glass.
David Antin, *Talking.*
António Lobo Antunes, *Knowledge of Hell.*
Alain Arias-Misson, *Theatre of Incest.*
John Ashbery and James Schuyler, *A Nest of Ninnies.*
Heimrad Bäcker, *transcript.*
Djuna Barnes, *Ladies Almanack.*
Ryder.
John Barth, *LETTERS.*
Sabbatical.
Donald Barthelme, *The King.*
Paradise.
Svetislav Basara, *Chinese Letter.*
Mark Binelli, *Sacco and Vanzetti Must Die!*
Andrei Bitov, *Pushkin House.*
Louis Paul Boon, *Chapel Road.*
My Little War.
Summer in Termuren.
Roger Boylan, *Killoyle.*
Ignácio de Loyola Brandão, *Anonymous Celebrity.*
Teeth under the Sun.
Zero.
Bonnie Bremser, *Troia: Mexican Memoirs.*
Christine Brooke-Rose, *Amalgamemnon.*
Brigid Brophy, *In Transit.*
Meredith Brosnan, *Mr. Dynamite.*
Gerald L. Bruns, *Modern Poetry and the Idea of Language.*
Evgeny Bunimovich and J. Kates, eds., *Contemporary Russian Poetry: An Anthology.*
Gabrielle Burton, *Heartbreak Hotel.*
Michel Butor, *Degrees.*
Mobile.
Portrait of the Artist as a Young Ape.
G. Cabrera Infante, *Infante's Inferno.*
Three Trapped Tigers.
Julieta Campos, *The Fear of Losing Eurydice.*
Anne Carson, *Eros the Bittersweet.*
Camilo José Cela, *Christ versus Arizona.*
The Family of Pascual Duarte.
The Hive.
Louis-Ferdinand Céline, *Castle to Castle.*
Conversations with Professor Y.
London Bridge.
Normance.
North.
Rigadoon.
Hugo Charteris, *The Tide Is Right.*
Jerome Charyn, *The Tar Baby.*
Marc Cholodenko, *Mordechai Schamz.*
Joshua Cohen, *Witz.*
Emily Holmes Coleman, *The Shutter of Snow.*
Robert Coover, *A Night at the Movies.*
Stanley Crawford, *Log of the S.S. The Mrs Unguentine.*
Some Instructions to My Wife.
Robert Creeley, *Collected Prose.*
René Crevel, *Putting My Foot in It.*
Ralph Cusack, *Cadenza.*
Susan Daitch, *L.C.*
Storytown.
Nicholas Delbanco, *The Count of Concord.*
Nigel Dennis, *Cards of Identity.*
Peter Dimock, *A Short Rhetoric for Leaving the Family.*
Ariel Dorfman, *Konfidenz.*
Coleman Dowell, *The Houses of Children.*
Island People.
Too Much Flesh and Jabez.
Arkadii Dragomoshchenko, *Dust.*
Rikki Ducornet, *The Complete Butcher's Tales.*
The Fountains of Neptune.
The Jade Cabinet.
The One Marvelous Thing.
Phosphor in Dreamland.
The Stain.
The Word "Desire."
William Eastlake, *The Bamboo Bed.*
Castle Keep.
Lyric of the Circle Heart.
Jean Echenoz, *Chopin's Move.*
Stanley Elkin, *A Bad Man.*
Boswell: A Modern Comedy.
Criers and Kibitzers, Kibitzers and Criers.
The Dick Gibson Show.
The Franchiser.
George Mills.
The Living End.
The MacGuffin.
The Magic Kingdom.
Mrs. Ted Bliss.
The Rabbi of Lud.
Van Gogh's Room at Arles.
Annie Ernaux, *Cleaned Out.*
Lauren Fairbanks, *Muzzle Thyself.*
Sister Carrie.
Leslie A. Fiedler, *Love and Death in the American Novel.*
Juan Filloy, *Op Oloop.*
Gustave Flaubert, *Bouvard and Pécuchet.*
Kass Fleisher, *Talking out of School.*
Ford Madox Ford, *The March of Literature.*
Jon Fosse, *Melancholy.*
Max Frisch, *I'm Not Stiller.*
Man in the Holocene.
Carlos Fuentes, *Christopher Unborn.*
Distant Relations.
Terra Nostra.
Where the Air Is Clear.

SELECTED DALKEY ARCHIVE PAPERBACKS

JANICE GALLOWAY, *Foreign Parts.*
The Trick Is to Keep Breathing.
WILLIAM H. GASS, *Cartesian Sonata and Other Novellas.*
Finding a Form.
A Temple of Texts.
The Tunnel.
Willie Masters' Lonesome Wife.
GÉRARD GAVARRY, *Hoppla! 1 2 3.*
ETIENNE GILSON,
The Arts of the Beautiful.
Forms and Substances in the Arts.
C. S. GISCOMBE, *Giscome Road.*
Here.
Prairie Style.
DOUGLAS GLOVER, *Bad News of the Heart.*
The Enamoured Knight.
WITOLD GOMBROWICZ,
A Kind of Testament.
KAREN ELIZABETH GORDON, *The Red Shoes.*
GEORGI GOSPODINOV, *Natural Novel.*
JUAN GOYTISOLO, *Count Julian.*
Juan the Landless.
Makbara.
Marks of Identity.
PATRICK GRAINVILLE, *The Cave of Heaven.*
HENRY GREEN, *Back.*
Blindness.
Concluding.
Doting.
Nothing.
JIŘÍ GRUŠA, *The Questionnaire.*
GABRIEL GUDDING,
Rhode Island Notebook.
MELA HARTWIG, *Am I a Redundant Human Being?*
JOHN HAWKES, *The Passion Artist.*
Whistlejacket.
ALEKSANDAR HEMON, ED.,
Best European Fiction 2010.
AIDAN HIGGINS, *A Bestiary.*
Balcony of Europe.
Bornholm Night-Ferry.
Darkling Plain: Texts for the Air.
Flotsam and Jetsam.
Langrishe, Go Down.
Scenes from a Receding Past.
Windy Arbours.
ALDOUS HUXLEY, *Antic Hay.*
Crome Yellow.
Point Counter Point.
Those Barren Leaves.
Time Must Have a Stop.
MIKHAIL IOSSEL AND JEFF PARKER, EDS.,
Amerika: Russian Writers View the United States.
GERT JONKE, *The Distant Sound.*
Geometric Regional Novel.
Homage to Czerny.
The System of Vienna.
JACQUES JOUET, *Mountain R.*
Savage.
CHARLES JULIET, *Conversations with Samuel Beckett and Bram van Velde.*
MIEKO KANAI, *The Word Book.*
HUGH KENNER, *The Counterfeiters.*
Flaubert, Joyce and Beckett: The Stoic Comedians.
Joyce's Voices.
DANILO KIŠ, *Garden, Ashes.*
A Tomb for Boris Davidovich.
ANITA KONKKA, *A Fool's Paradise.*
GEORGE KONRÁD, *The City Builder.*
TADEUSZ KONWICKI, *A Minor Apocalypse.*
The Polish Complex.
MENIS KOUMANDAREAS, *Koula.*
ELAINE KRAF, *The Princess of 72nd Street.*
JIM KRUSOE, *Iceland.*
EWA KURYLUK, *Century 21.*
ERIC LAURRENT, *Do Not Touch.*
VIOLETTE LEDUC, *La Bâtarde.*
SUZANNE JILL LEVINE, *The Subversive Scribe: Translating Latin American Fiction.*
DEBORAH LEVY, *Billy and Girl.*
Pillow Talk in Europe and Other Places.
JOSÉ LEZAMA LIMA, *Paradiso.*
ROSA LIKSOM, *Dark Paradise.*
OSMAN LINS, *Avalovara.*
The Queen of the Prisons of Greece.
ALF MAC LOCHLAINN,
The Corpus in the Library.
Out of Focus.
RON LOEWINSOHN, *Magnetic Field(s).*
BRIAN LYNCH, *The Winner of Sorrow.*
D. KEITH MANO, *Take Five.*
MICHELINE AHARONIAN MARCOM,
The Mirror in the Well.
BEN MARCUS,
The Age of Wire and String.
WALLACE MARKFIELD,
Teitlebaum's Window.
To an Early Grave.
DAVID MARKSON, *Reader's Block.*
Springer's Progress.
Wittgenstein's Mistress.
CAROLE MASO, *AVA.*
LADISLAV MATEJKA AND KRYSTYNA POMORSKA, EDS.,
Readings in Russian Poetics: Formalist and Structuralist Views.
HARRY MATHEWS,
The Case of the Persevering Maltese: Collected Essays.
Cigarettes.
The Conversions.
The Human Country: New and Collected Stories.
The Journalist.
My Life in CIA.
Singular Pleasures.
The Sinking of the Odradek Stadium.
Tlooth.
20 Lines a Day.
ROBERT L. MCLAUGHLIN, ED.,
Innovations: An Anthology of Modern & Contemporary Fiction.
HERMAN MELVILLE, *The Confidence-Man.*
AMANDA MICHALOPOULOU, *I'd Like.*

SELECTED DALKEY ARCHIVE PAPERBACKS

SELECTED DALKEY ARCHIVE PAPERBACKS

Literature and Cinematography.
Theory of Prose.
Third Factory.
Zoo, or Letters Not about Love.
Claude Simon, *The Invitation.*
Pierre Siniac, *The Collaborators.*
Josef Škvorecký, *The Engineer of Human Souls.*
Gilbert Sorrentino,
Aberration of Starlight.
Blue Pastoral.
Crystal Vision.
Imaginative Qualities of Actual Things.
Mulligan Stew.
Pack of Lies.
Red the Fiend.
The Sky Changes.
Something Said.
Splendide-Hôtel.
Steelwork.
Under the Shadow.
W. M. Spackman,
The Complete Fiction.
Andrzej Stasiuk, *Fado.*
Gertrude Stein,
Lucy Church Amiably.
The Making of Americans.
A Novel of Thank You.
Lars Svendsen, *A Philosophy of Evil.*
Piotr Szewc, *Annihilation.*
Gonçalo M. Tavares, *Jerusalem.*
Lucian Dan Teodorovici,
Our Circus Presents . . .
Stefan Themerson, *Hobson's Island.*
The Mystery of the Sardine.
Tom Harris.
Jean-Philippe Toussaint,
The Bathroom.
Camera.
Monsieur.
Running Away.
Self-Portrait Abroad.
Television.
Dumitru Tsepeneag,
The Necessary Marriage.
Pigeon Post.
Vain Art of the Fugue.
Esther Tusquets, *Stranded.*
Dubravka Ugresic,
Lend Me Your Character.
Thank You for Not Reading.
Mati Unt, *Brecht at Night*
Diary of a Blood Donor.
Things in the Night.
Álvaro Uribe and Olivia Sears, eds.,
The Best of Contemporary Mexican Fiction.
Eloy Urroz, *The Obstacles.*
Luisa Valenzuela, *He Who Searches.*
Marja-Liisa Vartio,
The Parson's Widow.
Paul Verhaeghen, *Omega Minor.*
Boris Vian, *Heartsnatcher.*
Ornela Vorpsi, *The Country Where No One Ever Dies.*
Austryn Wainhouse, *Hedyphagetica.*
Paul West,
Words for a Deaf Daughter & Gala.
Curtis White,
America's Magic Mountain.
The Idea of Home.
Memories of My Father Watching TV.
Monstrous Possibility: An Invitation to Literary Politics.
Requiem.
Diane Williams, *Excitability: Selected Stories.*
Romancer Erector.
Douglas Woolf, *Wall to Wall.*
Ya! & John-Juan.
Jay Wright, *Polynomials and Pollen.*
The Presentable Art of Reading Absence.
Philip Wylie, *Generation of Vipers.*
Marguerite Young,
Angel in the Forest.
Miss MacIntosh, My Darling.
REYoung, *Unbabbling.*
Zoran Živković, *Hidden Camera.*
Louis Zukofsky, *Collected Fiction.*
Scott Zwiren, *God Head.*